African Women and the Shame and Pain of Infertility

"This book is a prophetic social critique of the negative characterization of infertility in African cultures and in some versions of traditional Christianity in Africa. It brings together a rich array of voices in Africa from different regions of the continent. These different theological traditions and bioethical positions are put into a healthy and creative conversation on these pages. I highly recommend this book to all as a unique contribution to African Christian studies, bioethics, womanist studies, and pastoral theology."

—STAN CHU ILO
Research Professor of World Christianity
and African Studies, Center for World Catholicism
and Intercultural Theology, DePaul University

"This fascinating work uses social-cultural tools to analyze and highlight the ethical issues around female infertility and the lifelong impact of this condition on their happiness, personal fulfillment, and sense of worth and dignity. The author, by incorporating the perspectives of prominent women theologians—Oduyoye and Uchem—psychologists, social workers, and pastors, challenges us to shun cultural and ethical practices that destroy life. Then to respect and promote socio-cultural practices, spiritual traditions, and interpretations (of Igbo moral principle of *onyeaghalanwanneya*), which foster human dignity, human rights, and well-being especially of African women. This book is invaluable to ethicists, theologians, healthcare professionals, pastors, and all who care about the plight of infertile people."

—PETER I. OSUJI
Assistant Professor, Health Care Ethics, Duquesne University

"In *African Women and the Shame and Pain of Infertility*, Damasus C. Okoro has made a case for taking seriously the plights of African women as they journey towards justice. This work showcases the fruits of elaborate research and dialogue with multiple interlocutors. In this work, Okoro shows clearly the intersectionality of social, cultural, theological, philosophical, and medical ethics. Scholars interested in women's studies cannot but embrace this work as their new vade mecum."

—SIMONMARY ASESE AIHIOKHAI
University of Portland, author of *Fostering Interreligious Encounters
in Pluralist Societies: Hospitality and Friendship*

"Dr. Damasus Okoro's book *African Women and the Shame and Pain of Infertility* embraces a problem which has plagued Igbo culture, the issue of childlessness. Utilizing multiple disciplines (science, African Traditional Religion, ethicists, theologians, and literature) and a comparative method, this book opens a conversation the author passionately thinks needs to be had within Igbo culture . . . This book is important in several ways. It opens conversation about how a Christian might approach the oppression of couples who are childless, especially African Igbo women who overwhelming bear the burden of childlessness. The book also, and more importantly, argues for scholars and practitioners to pay attention to ethical principles and practices already evident in a culture. Imposing ethical principles from outside a culture does nothing more than contribute to the oppression of the people. I highly recommended *African Women and the Shame and Pain of Infertility* as a valuable partner for theologians, ethicists, and practitioners interested in contributing to the liberation of God's people."

—**RICHARD PERRY**
Professor Emeritus,
Church and Society/Urban Ministry,
Lutheran School of Theology at Chicago

African Women and the Shame and Pain of Infertility

An Ethico-cultural Study of Christian Response to Childlessness among the Igbo People of West Africa

DAMASUS C. OKORO

Foreword by Stan Chu Ilo

WIPF & STOCK · Eugene, Oregon

AFRICAN WOMEN AND THE SHAME AND PAIN OF INFERTILITY
An Ethico-cultural Study of Christian Response to Childlessness among
the Igbo People of West Africa

Copyright © 2020 Damasus C. Okoro. All rights reserved. Except for brief quotations in critical publications or reviews, no part of this book may be reproduced in any manner without prior written permission from the publisher. Write: Permissions, Wipf and Stock Publishers, 199 W. 8th Ave., Suite 3, Eugene, OR 97401.

Wipf & Stock
An Imprint of Wipf and Stock Publishers
199 W. 8th Ave., Suite 3
Eugene, OR 97401

www.wipfandstock.com

PAPERBACK ISBN: 978-1-7252-6570-7
HARDCOVER ISBN: 978-1-7252-6569-1
EBOOK ISBN: 978-1-7252-6571-4

Manufactured in the U.S.A.   06/23/20

Copyright © 1973 1978 1984 2011 by Biblica, Inc. TM Used by permission. All rights reserved worldwide.

To all childless and barren couples in Africa, whose family situation continues to bring them endless pain.

Contents

Foreword by Stan Chu Ilo | ix
Preface | xv
Acknowledgements | xvii

Introduction | 1
1. A Historical and Socio-Context Analysis of Igbo World | 15
2. Infertility: A Problem among Igbo Couples | 45
3. Engaging African Female Theologies: The Thoughts of Mercy Oduyoye and Rose Uchem | 80
4. Engaging African Male Theology/Ethics: The Thoughts of Bénézet Bujo | 102
5. Onye Aghala Nwannc Ya: An Alternative | 133
6. Conclusion | 176

Appendix 1: Umuokpara Family Marriage List: Umuifa—Ubachima Awo-Omamma | 179
Appendix 2: Umuokpara Family Women Marriage List | 182
Bibliography | 183

Foreword

THIS BOOK IS A prophetic social critique of the negative characterization of infertility in African cultures and in some versions of traditional Christianity in Africa. It brings together a rich array of voices in Africa from different regions of the continent. These different theological traditions and bioethical positions are put into a healthy and creative conversation on these pages.

With the thoroughness and depth of a good scholar, Dr Damasus Okoro has harvested the stories and agonies of barren women among the Igbo people of West Africa. He analyses the painful cultural, religious and social consequences and stigma associated with infertility in Africa.

With the compassionate heart of a concerned priest, he tells the stories of the devastating impact of this situation on the African family—family break ups, marital infertility, and the agony and despair of African families who are incapable of begetting children. This book is filled with a moving analysis of the daily struggles of African families, who are trying to make sense of what in traditional society is often seen as the loss of one's womanhood and a curse to a family. It explores multiple narratives, and multiple identities, and challenges existing cultural stereotypes employed in the subjugation and oppression of barren women in an African ethnic group. The author employs a comparative methodology in writing this book, drawing from African literature, the works of African ethicists, theologians and psychologists, social workers, pastors, and healers.

This book pays detailed attention to the concrete everyday experiences of these barren women, their husbands, their families and their struggles. This book is built on a grounded theory through an appeal to the real stories of real people. The author employs the tools of socio-cultural analysis in unpacking the narrative identities of women who suffer infertility and the life-long impact of this condition on their happiness, personal fulfilment and sense of worth and dignity. He puts the cultural narratives of the people who maintain these cultural traditions in conversations with the teachings of the church, biblical practices, especially in the Old Testament, and the practices and canons proposed by the church on marriage and family life.

This book is a good representative model on how the contending narratives of modernity are playing out in Africa, particularly in the modern African family. Indeed, the modern African family today is a good case study of the devastating impact and failures of the modernization project in Africa. At the same time, many Africans who wish to reinforce what they perceive as the pristine traditional world of Africa with a presumed past characterized by social harmony, ethical and moral balance rooted in and sustained by traditional norms and institutions, fail to accept the limitations within that traditional system. In uncritically romanticizing the African past, some scholars fail to admit the limitations of a diffusionist account of history in Africa. The diffusionist approach defends the continuity of an essentialized notion of African culture or tradition without an internal differentiation and without disjuncture and discontinuities across the checkered path of African history.

What is evident to any discerning African historian is the reality of a struggle going on in Africa among African Christians. It is a struggle about fidelity and orthodoxy with regard to responding to the needs of African Christian families, communities and societies on one hand, while on the other hand maintaining the unity of beliefs, practices and morality which have a family trait within the canons of the worldwide Christian Communion. Being faithful to African cultures and traditions is, however, a critical function. It should proceed with a creative and discerning appropriation aimed at choosing what is good within African culture and rejecting what is opposed to the good of society. At the heart of African religio-cultural traditions, is the acceptance of the bond of life as a shared value, which everyone must participate in and draw from as from a well pool. The bond of life is the result of a state of harmony and life-giving relationships among humans, nature, spiritual realities, the living, the unborn and the living dead which promotes human and cosmic flourishing.

In this light, a critical function requires the clear-sightedness of the scholar in demonstrating through a depth analysis of culture, people's realities and the movement of the Spirit in history those cultural realities and ethical practices which destroy life. It also calls on people to reverence, respect, and advance those patterns of thoughts and cultural practices, spiritual traditions and interpretations which advance human dignity, human rights, holistic health and human wellbeing for everyone, particularly those who are on the margins like African women. This is why this book is very important because in engaging this challenging cultural practice and worldview about infertility and childlessness, Dr Okoro's prophetic work is helping us as Africans and people of the Igbo nation to discover and confront those aspects of our cultural traditions which needs to change in order for something new to be born in Africa. Dr Okoro's book is, in this light, a significant work in Christian humanism, theological anthropology, bioethics and theological and social ethics.

Like other parts of the world today, Africa is caught up in the contestations about modernity and history. She is caught in the throes of ideological, economic, cultural and political processes which are not for the most part of her own making. The greater convergence to the global community and integration into the world economy and into the global culture with its neo-liberal economic order, which Africa hoped for with modernity and globalization even in Christianity, is all but proven to be a nightmare. This is why the African continent and Africans continue to search for those values, practices and ethical choices which can resolve the African predicament by interrupting this current trajectory of history. Dr Okoro's book is another attempt at interrupting a movement of history in Africa beginning by the re-appropriation of authentic African and Christian values on womanhood, marriage, human life and family values.

The contestations about what being modern means for Africans has generated different forms of fragmentation in Africa and social tension, moral and ethical crisis and cultural unease. Many Africans are looking for 'a sacred canopy' where they can find some stability in a seashore of change and uncertainty. There are complexities facing many Africans today as they search for solutions to their problems and daily needs. Most religious people in Africa see the increasing number of churches, religious ministers, and the pentecostalisation of Christianity in Africa as part of the search in Africa for answers to the human problem through Christianity. It is obvious to many discerning Christians in Africa today that whereas Christianity is growing exponentially in number in Africa, it has not offered Africans a clear ethical framework, a strong praxis of reversal, and deep spiritual traditions which could help them deal courageously with the complex challenges of their daily lives.

Religious experience in Africa today through the pentecostalization of African Christianity at its best offers people some liberty and expansive space to express their religious faith and to vent their frustrations at the sorry state of things in the continent. Unfortunately, at its worst, it has turned some versions of African Christianity into sites for religious exploitation and enchantment with no enduring richness at the level of spirituality, ethics, praxis or prophetic performance. As a result, most of the problems which African Christians face like infertility are often spiritualized or drowned in the ritualistic proration which is built on a transactional notion of God and the abuse of miraculous cures. All these dramas of our times act as a fodder for an antiseptic Christianity which verges sometimes on fear, pseudo-spirituality and anti-scientific narratives which often exploit the vulnerability and worsen the pain of childless couples.

It is within this complex Christian faith and theological and ethical complexities that I see the significance of this work which you have in your hand. Dr Okoro uses scientific evidence, bioethical principles, innovations in reproductive science, and human genome science to interrogate the predominant cultural practices in African Traditional Religion and African Christianity on infertility and childlessness. He shows the continuity and discontinuity in the multiple narratives and explanations for infertility in traditional African understanding and in Christian understanding. He offers Africa and the world a third way. This third way is an attempt at a bioethical inculturation which embraces the fruits of science in understanding infertility, while deconstructing all the other negative characterizations in African culture and in Christian tradition about bareness and childlessness. He offers a way out of what in traditional African society is seen as the end of the road. This is achieved through his creative attempt at a bioethical inculturation and the transformation of unhealthy and unethical perspectives and traditions.

Infertility, our author shows, should not simply be projected as a Cross to be carried with faith, but rather should be understood in faith and scientifically as a human condition which can be embraced as part of the signs of human limitations and finitude. However, he offers a praxis of hope which can be realized not through healing homes, but with the help of science and a change in worldview about the goal of life on earth and family life. Infertility is not a curse from God for which people need to pray unceasingly for divine intervention and propitiate God through monetary donations from the lean purses of many poor African women to praying pastors who falsely claim that they have the ability to cure the curse of infertility.

This is a refreshing book which speaks to the pains of women, and offers a new hermeneutical and bioethical key for understanding infertility. It is very practical and concrete in both its analysis and its cultural hermeneutics of reversal. I am sure that this book will be a useful tool for pastors, theologians, and family therapists who are working with African families, healthcare workers and African families who find themselves facing this challenge. I highly recommend this book to all as a unique contribution to African Christian studies, bioethics, womanist studies, and pastoral theology.

Stan Chu Ilo
Research Professor of World Christianity and African Studies,
Center for World Catholicism and Intercultural Theology,
DePaul University, Chicago, USA;
Honorary Professor of Religion and Theology,
Durham University, Durham, UK.

Preface

THE HISTORY OF THE Igbo people of Eastern Nigeria, like that of many African ethnic groups in Africa, bears the mark of Africa's immersion into modern and post-modern currents. This complex history has significantly affected traditional Igbo culture. Some of these sad events include: colonialism, the slave trade, missionary incursion into Igbo land and their encounter with Igbo primal religions, immigration, and emigration. However, none of these agents of change much influenced the Igbo view of infertility and childlessness as being a nightmare. This is evident from oral tradition, fables, myths and stories on how barren couples were treated before the coming of the West into Igbo land. Some ethical theories have evolved, especially from African scholars, but none seem to adequately address the social malaise of infertility in marriage.

I have been personally very concerned about the disturbing treatment of childless couples. The Igbo indigenous ethical principle of *onye aghala nwanne* ya (no kith or kin should be left behind) highlights the need for its full application in dealing with infertility in marriage in Igbo land. As such, this book proposes this application as a constructive contribution toward affirming Igbo culture and liberating married couples from the social scourge associated with infertility in marriage.

This book refers to the period between when Igbo land was annexed by Britain and the coming of Christian missionaries in the 1850s to the present day Igbo life. This analysis of the historical cultural context sets the stage for understanding "traditional Igbo" and "modern-day Igbo."

This book aims at providing a unique and vital knowledge to existing scholarly works on infertility in marriage as well as a religious, theological and ethical analysis of the same. It suggests a sound indigenous ethical principle which will gear towards the emancipation of infertile couples in Igbo land and Africa as a whole.

Acknowledgements

THE CONNECTEDNESS OF OUR world and the connections in the different work we do, have made an accomplished task like this a joint project. In the light of that, I thank God Almighty for granting me the focus, strength, and all I needed to bring this project to completion.

The shape of this book and its scholarly "cleansing" would have been impossible if not for the meticulous reading of this work by many of my friends and scholars. I thank my doctoral dissertation supervisor, Dr. Richard Perry, whose expertise in Church and Society, cultural issues, ethics and sexuality gave this work the scholarly shape it has taken. I sincerely thank him for his patience and meticulous reading of my manuscript, and offering valuable suggestions. I owe him more than I can ever repay for his challenging but useful critical suggestions.

I deeply thank Dr. David Fletcher, one of my doctoral dissertation readers. His course in ethical theories at Trinity International University contributed immensely in the formulation of an indigenous ethical theory. I thank Dr. Mark Swanson, also one of my doctoral readers.

To you, my mother Ezinne Priscilla Okoro, and my late father Mr. Godfrey Okoro, I want to say thank you. Through you, I was launched into existence to pursue a goal that will positively impact our people, especially infertile couples in our community and on the continent of Africa. With your utmost love and support from the physical world and from the spirit world I have accomplished a task you will be very proud of. To you my siblings: Mrs. Bernadette Mbaegbu, Mr. Callistus Okoro,

Basil Okoro, Cyril Okoro, Divine Okoro, Ogechi and Nonso Okoro, I say thank you for your support. And to you my siblings on the other side of the bridge already resting, Patricia, Flora and Peter, I say thank you too for your interventions from the spirit world.

I thank my Provincial Superior Very Rev. Fr. Dr. Greg Olikenyi, CSSp for his fraternal support. I want to thank my friends whose love and support went a long way in "reformatting" my mind and brain when the going became tough in the process of this work. They allowed me to use them as resource materials when I was ready to process my thoughts. I thank Fr. Mike Okoro, CSSp, Fr Dr. Uju Okeahialam, CSSp, Fr. Dr. Ugochukwu Ikwuka, CSSp and Fr. Dr. Lawrence Okwuosa, SDV, who did a lot of proofreading of this work. I thank Prof.Stan Chu Ilo, for his constructive response to my postulations and equally for writing the Foreword. I thank Dr. Simon Aihiokhai, with whom I processed some of my thoughts. You all significantly contributed to the success of this project.

Some of my friends played significant and much appreciated roles during the process of writing this book. I thank Sisters Kosarachi Iweanya, Florence Tanwa, Dr. Maureen Akabogu, and Francesca Amanfo for their support. I thank Sir and Lady Hyginus/Chibuzor Okechukwu for their love and immense support. I thank members of St. Cecilia Church, Mt. Prospect, Illinois, where I lived in residence while my studies and this book project lasted. I must thank the late Fr Mike Olivero (Pastor Emeritus), who welcomed me to St Cecilia. May God continue to rest him. I thank Fr Oswaldo Guillen for his fraternal love. Members of staff of St Cecilia quickly absorbed me as a member of their ecclesial family; your love can never be forgotten. I thank the parishioners who showed me tremendous love while my scholarship lasted. I thank all the priests, sisters and members of the Igbo Catholic community in Chicago and environs for your support through my stay and ministering in your community as your chaplain. Your names have been written in the book of life and even in eternity, where we shall continue the fellowship.

I thank in a special way Mrs. Evelyn Vezzani and family, and Richard and Joan Saccone, your moral and financial support went a long way in easing the burden for me. I owe you more than I can ever repay. I thank all those who contributed one way or the other during my period of studies and during this book project; know that your names will remain indelible in my heart.

Introduction

WHAT THEOLOGICAL CONCEPTS AND ethical principles can be applied in addressing the problem of infertility among Igbo couples? This contextualizing question is necessary, as it helps us to understand a major problem in Igbo culture, infertility among Igbo couples. In considering the attendant problems of infertility, one can proffer adequate Christian, religious, theological and ethical responses. This is in line with a Yoruba proverb which says, "*Bi ina ko ba tan l'ori, eje ko le tan ni ekanna*" (the blood of the lice will be found on the finger-nails until all have been removed from the head)."[1] By extension, this means a problem will linger until a solution is found or until different approaches are proposed in solving it. Until we understand and engage with the superficial application of the ethic of *onye aghala nwanne ya*,[2] then, the oppression of infertile couples will continue in Igbo land. This is necessary because an 'Igbo heart' cannot become caring in some aspects of its life and community and become hardened in other aspects. This is where the paradox of Igbo culture lies. A culture which can defend one of its own at all costs but turns around to

---

1. Pachocinsk, *Proverbs of Africa*, 390.

2. This is an indigenous ethical principle among Igbo people of West Africa; this principle simply means that no one, male or female of the family should be left behind. All must be carried along and be salvaged especially during difficult times. This principle has different appellations in different parts of Africa. In southern Africa, especially among South Africans it is called *Ubuntu*, among those of East Africa especially among the Tanzanians it is called *Ujamaa*, and among the Kenyans it is called the spirit of *Harambe*.

humiliate or abandon another one of its own in utmost need repudiates its values. In other words, the Igbo spirit of compassion, love, hospitality needs to shine its light on those afflicted by infertility.

The novel *Efuru* written by Flora Nwapa puts the problem in perspective. In this novel, Efuru, a beautiful Igbo village woman, suffers greatly during her first and second marriages because of childlessness, thus placing a huge question mark on her femininity. Efuru is respectful and highly respected, not only because of her comeliness, but also because of her hard-working nature. She is respected also because of her kind-heartedness and how gracefully she conducts herself. However, despite her resourcefulness and beauty, and the bliss she enjoys within the first year of her second marriage, her inability to conceive nullifies everything, including the perception of her attractive features and good deeds.

Despite Efuru and Gilbert having a happy marriage, there is a huge set-back within the marriage. No children have been born, and the community considers the marriage to be unproductive. Efuru is blamed by the community for being childless. Even if the husband accepts their childlessness, the community mounts pressure by showing its aversion to an unproductive union. Though Efuru has been very good to her mother-in-law, her goodness and hard work vanishes with her childless situation. According to the community's tradition, ethos and practice, Efuru is guilty.

Four distinctive features in this novel bring out the problems of infertility in marriage which will be considered directly or indirectly in the course of this book. First is Efuru's childlessness and the disdain she suffers because of it. This sense of being uncomfortable with an unproductive wife is very much felt in Efuru's first marriage with Adizua. Adizua's family cannot fathom why he should not go for a second wife since Efuru was unproductive. For them, since Efuru cannot bear a child, she is considered to be a man and "two men do not live together."[3] In the second marriage, when Gilbert's family became tired of waiting for Efuru to conceive, as their patience reached its limit, they cynically said: "[i]t is expected that she should have a baby before the year is out. If no baby comes in the first year, it is our duty to probe her girlhood, and find out why."[4]

Second, because of her childlessness, spiritualists are consulted, and Efuru is chosen by *Uhamiri*, the goddess of the lake, to be her priestess.

---

3. Nwapa, *Efuru*, 24.
4. Nwapa, *Efuru*, 197.

"The goddess of the lake has chosen her to be one of her worshippers. It is a great honour."[5] In this regard, Efuru becomes one of *Uhamiri's* ". . . strict worshippers or ministers, whom she chooses and empowers."[6] Part of this empowerment bestowed on the worshipper is ". . . to make people especially women wealthy. She protects the town from invaders, diseases, and misfortunes."[7] This is important because Efuru as a worshipper of *Uhamiri* will make people find favor in the hands of the goddess through her intercession and ritual intervention. She will plead with the goddess to grant wealth, freedom from disease, and protection for her clients. Therefore, men and women will consult her for assistance in their daily problems. This point will be better considered in the argument of the ritual of breaking of the traditional Igbo kolanut, which is exclusively reserved for men.

Third, it is always the woman who is guilty of childlessness in Igbo land. Surely, this is because of the "belief that it is the woman that bears the pregnancy."[8] Unfortunately, there is typically no way of knowing who is fertile or infertile. In other words, the visible sign of fertility is portrayed through physical pregnancy, and it is the woman who has to display this when she becomes pregnant.

A fourth feature is the invisibility of the man in the marriage. In this scenario, the man has little or nothing to do with childlessness in marriage. No one thinks about him and whether he is virile or not, despite statistics to the contrary. For example, studies carried out by scholars at the University of Benin in Nigeria show that the "male factor infertility in Nigeria accounts for up to 50% of all cases."[9] The study elaborates:

> Hormonal profile of a group of azoospermic males was evaluated and it was observed that 40% of all azoospermic subjects had abnormal hormonal levels while 60% had normal hormonal values and 45% of the subjects had testicular pathology, it was concluded that endocrinopathies are common in azoospermia and their contribution to male infertility is great.[10]

---

5. Nwapa, *Efuru*, 153.
6. Okwuosa et al., "Disappearing Mammy Water Myth," 2.
7. Okwuosa et al., "Disappearing Mammy Water Myth," 2.
8. Ikechebelu et al., "High Prevalence of Male infertility," 657.
9. Uadia and Emokpae, "Male infertility in Nigeria," 51.
10. Uadia and Emokpae, "Male infertility in Nigeria," 49.

From the foregoing, one can see the enormity and complexity of this problem of discrimination and injustice against infertile marriages. It is particularly an unbearable burden on women who are childless and infertile. The social stigma has infested and permeated Igbo culture like an airborne deadly virus. The wanton injustice has humiliated and virtually brought childless couples to their knees.

To raise infertile married couples from their knees and for them to enjoy authentic freedom, there is a need for the whole community to go to work and collectively confront this problem. Like other social problems, this malaise "cannot be curbed unless all concerned—clergy and laity, civil leaders, and theologians, employers and employees, parents and children—are alerted to what is wrong and what needs to be done."[11] Traditional rulers and custodians of culture must not be left out in this crusade. This clear call to address this problem is urgent and serious, and it needs a collective scholarly appraisal and re-ordering of the Igbo sociocultural sphere toward establishing a healthy, moral and flourishing Igbo society in this regard.

Reviewing the history of the Igbo people, one can feel a sense of harmony and togetherness which can be taken to mean all is well. However, one can see that the application of the *onye aghala nwanne ya* ethical principle, which is a major source of succor, has been only partial. In this partiality, men exercise different draconian moral, religious, social and political authority. This multi-faceted exercise of authority by men includes control of women's sexuality, and punishing them when infertility occurs. I argue that a full application of the ethical principle of *onye aghala nwanne ya* will be feasible using the tools of theology, anthropology, women's studies, culture, African Traditional Religion (ATR), Christian ethics, liberation theology, the authority wielded by the church, and a deeper and critical understanding of Igbo cultural tenets. The engagement with all these will add vigor and intensity to our argument. When the deconstruction is done, there could be a new dawn for the Igbo community, and it would be "re-inserted into the situation of primeval anomie for renewal and regeneration."[12]

The full application of the ethical principle of *onye aghala nwanne ya* would solve the problem of subjugation of infertile couples, because a society is defined by the way it treats its vulnerable and defenseless ones.

---

11. Onwurah, "Marriage: Christian and Traditional," 43, as cited in Uchem, *Overcoming Women's Subordination*, 70.

12. Ekwuru, *Pangs of an African Culture*, 3.

Igbo society and its rich culture and traditions would not want to be seen negatively. However, with its modernizing civilization, including intermarriages, scholarship, interactions with other cultures, emigrations and immigrations, this negative aspect of Igbo culture has come under scrutiny. This scrutiny and the need for continuous evaluation have made the full embracing of the ancient indigenous ethical principle of *onye aghala nwanne ya* a timely and welcome idea.

METHOD OF RESEARCH

The research method used in this book is a comparative approach. I compared two or more worlds and works of African scholars (sometimes African and the Western world or African world and practices over time), weighing their strengths and shortcomings, and their similarities and dissimilarities. The comparative method, as a scientific methodology, followed the model espoused by Emefie Ikenga Metuh.

In underscoring the place of gods in Igbo spiritual space and other societies within the African continent, Metuh employs the Limited Comparative Method in his study of ATR. He acknowledges, but does not go in-depth, on the scholarly use of different research approaches saying that, ". . . different authors have adopted diverse and sometimes conflicting approaches to the study of African Religion."[13] He lists these approaches as elucidated by Aylward Shorter. "Shorter lists no less than eight different approaches adopted by different authors or group of authors—Particularist Approach, Enumerative Approach, Hypothesis of Unity Approach, Historical Approach, Limited Comparative Approach, Categorical Approach, Thematic Approach and Multi-dimensional Approach."[14]

Since ATR is not monolithic, Metuh finds the Limited Comparative Approach suitable for the study of these religions. With this approach, he is able "to draw and compare examples from West Africa (Negro), Central and East Africa (Bantu) and the Nilotic areas."[15] He further has the advantage of "selecting specific themes and studying them in depth, (sic) in the contexts of two or three societies, and comparing the findings

---

13. Metuh, *Comparative Studies*, xvi.

14. See Shorter, *African Christian Theology*, 38–58, as cited in Metuh, *Comparative Studies*, xvi.

15. Metuh, *Comparative Studies*, xxiv.

in order to identify the similar and dissimilar features."[16] The advantage of this method is that it "permits one to discuss each theme in depth (sic) and in its various dimensions, and at the same time draw examples from all over Africa."[17] Since ATR is strictly speaking diverse, this means that different themes will emerge as there are different societies within Africa. It thus behooves the author to select specific themes on which to concentrate. In the same way, religious persons, emblems and sacred spaces (such as shrines) play different roles or similar roles in different African societies. These differences make the Limited Comparative Approach a worthwhile method to be used in the study of ATR.

Since my work is largely descriptive in examining the Igbo worldview, belief system and moral ethos, the comparative method is suitable for this ethics project. With descriptive ethics, I was able to work with empirical or observational data of the Igbo moral landscape. Since the Igbo moral and religious sphere is vast, this method gave me the opportunity to choose pressing observational themes to respond to the Igbo question. Through this approach, I was able to compare what is the reality 'on the ground' and what ought to be. Thus, with an empirical analysis which is an embodiment of descriptive ethics I was able to unveil the paradox of the Igbo indigenous ethics of *onye aghala nwanne ya*.

Metuh's Limited Comparative Approach was adapted according to the themes of my work. The theological and ethical views of some scholars have been considered, such as Mercy Oduyoye, Rose Uchem and Bénézet Bujo on the themes of Christology, inculturation theology, the role of the *ecclesia*, *imago Dei* concept, sources and approaches, education, mutuality and 'voicing it out' (speaking out against forces of oppression). The strengths and shortcomings of their theologies have been discussed within the sections allotted to them within this book. From these, I argue that the Igbo indigenous ethical principle of *onye aghala nwanne ya*, which is deeply rooted in Igbo culture, can liberate couples suffering infertility. With this method, I contrasted different worldviews, the Igbo culture over time, and different theological and ethical theories. This book will be meaningful to readers not familiar with Igbo culture and worldview. As Metuh says, "[b]y comparing and contrasting . . . and

---

16. Metuh, *Comparative Studies*, xxiv.
17. Metuh, *Comparative Studies*, xxiv.

by pointing out their similarities and dissimilarities, the inherent meaning and structure of Igbo beliefs would be clear to any Western reader."[18]

Bujo calls his approach "African Theology in its social context."[19] A similar approach was adopted here as 'the indigenous ethical principle of *onye aghala nwanne ya* in the Igbo historical and social context.' The essence of this approach is liberation. Like Oduyoye and Uchem, Bujo is "convinced that African theology has a contribution to make to the liberation of all people towards life in its fullness."[20] So too, I am convinced that the Igbo indigenous ethical principle of *onye aghala nwanne ya* can contribute to the liberation of Igbo couples suffering infertility. Like Bujo, after social context analysis, we will "be in a position to turn our attention to the construction of an adequate model for a contemporary African synthesis."[21] To grasp this social context analysis, the perspective of inculturation theology is important since no scholar can satisfactorily talk about African theology and ethics without recourse to inculturation theology. This is important because it makes the final proposal "truly African and truly Christian."[22]

Inculturation theology, which is a proposition through which the Gospel message takes root within a culture, can answer questions on the connection between Igbo culture and the message of the Gospel. Inculturation theology has been defined to be:

> the incarnation of Christian life and of the Christian message in a particular cultural context, in such a way that this experience not only finds expression through elements proper to the culture in question, but becomes a principle that animates, directs and unifies the culture, transforming and remaking it as to bring about "a new creation."[23]

Transforming and bringing about "a new creation" is important as this is what this book is set to do in Igbo culture. Though inculturation theology is difficult, as Pope John Paul II acknowledges, it is useful in making Africans completely Christians and Africans in the finest sense of it. Instructing the Pontifical Council for Culture the John Paul writes:

18. Metuh, *African Religions*, xi.
19. Bujo, *African Theology*, 16.
20. Bujo, *African Theology*, 16.
21. Bujo, *African Theology*, 16.
22. Uzukwu, "Sacramentology."
23. Arrupe, "Letter to the Whole Society," 6.

> You are aware that inculturation commits the church to a path that is difficult, but necessary. Pastors and theologians and specialists in the human sciences must also collaborate closely, so that this vital process may come about in a way that benefits both the evangelized and the evangelizers, in order to avoid any simplification or undue haste that would lead in syncretism or secular reduction of the proclamation of the Gospel.[24]

In inculturation theology which is still evolving, Igbo Christians, especially those of the main-line churches, and particularly those of the Roman Catholic tradition, (though the process is slow), are now getting better disposed to the designs of inculturation. Inculturation theology is necessary because the way in which Christianity was transmitted to Igbo people make them "suffer religio-cultural nostalgia. They are in a system which has no regard for their roots. They belong to a religion imported just as their automobile, electronic or the whole of the country's technology has been imported."[25]

Inculturation theology has its short comings. A major one is that the large Nigerian Qua Iboe Church and other 'born again' churches do not embrace it. The Qua Iboe Church sees inculturation theology as unwarranted and an erroneous "effort to replace Christianity with idolatry in the name of cultural reawakening."[26] In the same line of thought, "the 'born again' or charismatic churches refuse to have any connection with 'traditional' African belief and ritual, and despise those denominations that, in their judgement, tolerate an unholy mixture of gospel purity with traditional precepts."[27] For them, this is a profane idea, almost an alliance of good and evil. For them, it is like going back to some of the 'pagan' practices they had abandoned to embrace Christianity. With this mindset, they reject this form of theology. However, one must not lose sight of inculturation theology still being a difficult area to navigate owing to some areas of African culture which need the light of the Gospel to challenge and purify.

Despite some seeming shortcomings of inculturation theology, these do not take away its numerous advantages in making the Christian

24. John Paul II, *A Fresh Approach*.

25. Nwabuisi, "Socialization," 10.

26. "Qua Iboe Church Revival," as quoted in Ilesanmi, "Inculturation and Liberation," 58–59.

27. "Qua Iboe Church Revival," as quoted in Ilesanmi, "Inculturation and Liberation," 58–59.

message more intelligible to Africans within their cultural background. Since the essence of inculturation theology is to appropriate the message of the Gospel in people's lives, one cannot wish it away because "[t]he argument holds that all religions including Christianity can be completely experienced, lived and celebrated through cultural embodiment."[28]

Inculturation theology becomes a significant perspective because it is a way to ensure that "Christianity becomes second nature to the Igbo, and deeprooted (sic) enough to withstand the anticipated twin attacks of secularization and prosperity."[29] This helps in the liberation mission of Jesus Christ, who says: "The Spirit of the Lord is on me, because he has anointed me to proclaim good news to the poor. He has sent me to proclaim freedom for the prisoners and recovery of sight for the blind, to set the oppressed free," (Luke 4:18). This liberation connection can surely heal the broken-hearted, including Igbo infertile couples who are not only captives of their culture but whose hearts are truly afflicted.

SOURCES

The sources for this book are diverse. The first source is personal and professional experience. This work is inspired by my experience growing up in an Igbo family in Nigeria, by my pastoral ministry in a parish in Nigeria, and by my scholarly enterprise in America. I grew up as a young man socialized into what I still see as a well-knit family system, where everyone cared for the other. Growing up, I was told that my father, being the only son, had to postpone getting married a number of times because he needed to save more money to take care of his four sisters, so as to give them some sense of stability, economic empowerment and protection. This was the sacrifice he had to make to give his sisters a brighter future and thus "not leaving them behind" or abandoned.

The second source is literature. Much is drawn from literature, especially from the fictional story of Efuru. Though this is a novel and the characters might be fictional, the setting and story in *Efuru* is a meaningful documentation of the life of the people of Oguta in Imo state, as it relates to their connection and worship of Mammy water.[30]

28. Appiah. "Challenge of a Theologically Fruitful Method," 257.

29. Ebelebe, *Africa and the New Face of Mission*, 216.

30. 'Mammy water,' which some authors spell in broken/Pidgin English as 'Mami Wata,' is a powerful aquatic spirit believed to be benevolent and malignant, as it can

Oral tradition, through which the Igbo ethos and traditions are transmitted, is another source for this project. Since the Igbo community is a relational one, oral sharing of stories and things of moral concern remain important ways through which elders and witnesses of events transmit to listeners their experiences and the life of the community. Listeners to such stories and the ethos of the land are in turn expected to transmit the same to future generations.

Other disciplines used as major sources include aspects of theology, and history, particularly the history of the Igbo people and Christian ethics. This is important because Igbo history is critical for contextual analysis and understanding the nature of infertility. Christian ethics make it possible to identify and position the ethical principles and values which emerge from the history of the Igbo people. Other reference disciplines include those pertaining to anthropology, culture, and ATR.

Papal documents and teachings of the Roman Catholic Church such as the encyclicals *Caritas in Veritate* of Benedict XVI and *Populorum Progressio* of Paul VI are also rich sources that have been explored. These two encyclicals are important because of their emphasis on love in which the ethic of *onye aghala nwanne ya* is encapsulated, it further places emphasis on ". . . the elimination of social ills; broadening the horizons of knowledge; acquiring refinement and culture."[31] These are sources which provide insight for religious, spiritual, theological, ethical and pastoral guidance, especially to those disadvantaged and those suffering emotionally. The perspectives of these sources enrich the argument of the book.

Numerous social genres offer a rich reservoir to tell the Igbo and African stories. Song notes used in various forms, Igbo poetry, and many cultural symbols and arts like carved images are referred to as useful sources too.

The illustrative materials in this book are gathered from the Igbo ethnic group of southeast Nigeria. From time to time, I have interchangeably referred to Igbo or African cultural anthropology as the same, since some of the practices in Igbo culture have a wider application in other

---

give wealth and power as well as illness and misfortune. It is "typically represented with a woman's body and a fish's tail . . . these water spirits harass fishermen and those who dwell near rivers and seas." Ndiokwere, *Search for Security*, 42. This source is important because it narrates a concrete life experience relevant to our topic of discussion. See also Okwuosa et al., "Disappearing Mammy Water Myth."

31. Paul VI, Pope. *Populorium Progressio*.

African societies. This project dwelt on the traditional understanding of marriage among Igbo people as a covenant between a male and a female or a man and a woman.³²

INTERDISCIPLINARY

This work is inter-disciplinary in nature. It entails considering the similarities and dissimilarities between points of view, be it a Western point of view, the Christian (or Roman Catholic) tradition, or ATR. Comparing assists in identifying religious, theological and ethical principles that can liberate couples who experience infertility in marriage.

There are different ways to discuss infertility in marriage, such as its shaming effect on Igbo couples, and its relation to Christian ethics. I maintain that no one discipline provides all the knowledge needed for Igbo couples to gain liberation. The tradition of Christian theology and ethics, especially with its moral code, its criteria of moral judgement, action and methods of moral decision-making, will resonate with Igbo people as a way for liberation of infertile couples. ATR as an indigenous religion and its role in community building and cohesion will be a vital component in this book.

All of these are essential components, which collectively find expression within the indigenous Igbo ethic of *onye aghala nwanneya* which can liberate Igbo couples who suffer infertility.

SIGNIFICANCE AND CONTRIBUTION

In a 2015 article reviewing the issue of male infertility in Nigeria, Uadia and Emokae write, "[w]hereas the field of gynecology has been growing, there was little or no growth recorded in the field of andrology. It is only recently that andrology was established as a medical specialty devoted to the study of male fertility."³³ Researching this crucial but neglected reproductive and social issue is my contribution to scholarship.

---

32. The Nigerian Constitution and the Same Sex Marriage Prohibition Act of 2013 and the United States Supreme Court ruling of June, 26, 2015 spell out their respective understanding of marriage, accessed. See National Assembly of Nigeria, "Same-Sex Marriage (Prohibition) Act, 2013"; Obergefell v. Hodges. 135 S. Ct. 2584, 2015.

33. Uadia and Emokpae, "Male infertility in Nigeria," 46.

Identifying the Igbo indigenous ethic of *onye aghala nwanne ya* as an ethical principle which can liberate infertile couples, is pioneering and original. One distinctive feature of my approach is its constructive scholarly ethical dimension, such as, using existing Igbo religious paradigms like the *Chi* and *Ani* to argue the case for married couples who are childless and suffer infertility.

SUMMARY OF CHAPTERS

Chapter 1 is an analysis of the social context of the Igbo people and their culture. Attention is given to the origin, geography and language of the Igbo people. This gives a holistic picture of a people and culture that were once extremely conservative, but have evolved, chiefly through encounter with Christianity, colonialism and other bearers of Western modernity. The analysis of Igbo culture unveils a highly patriarchal society, which to some extent contributes to the oppression of infertile Igbo women and men in Nigeria. This type of social analysis establishes a methodology for ethics on the continent of Africa in general, and in the country of Nigeria in particular. It is within this context that we can recapture the tenets of the indigenous Igbo ethical principle of *onye aghala nwanne ya*, with its potential to liberate infertile married couples. The Igbo cultural hemisphere is broad, so, in trying to understand the Igbo social context, I have concentrated on key factors that shape Igbo culture, and which will significantly contribute to what this book is arguing and proposing.

Chapter 2 explores and analyzes the social weight of infertility in general. It later focuses on the negative effects on Igbo couples in the context of marriage, and examines the theology and ethics of infertility. Since infertility and by extension child-bearing can be understood only in the context of marriage in Igbo land, this chapter examines how marriage is conducted in Igbo land. Special attention is paid to the idea that "marriage is not simply a union or an affair between a man and a woman but between families and sometimes the whole community."[34]

Chapter 3 explores the work of two female African theologians and ethicists. Their thinking, from their different cultural contexts and religious and church experiences, in Ghana and Nigeria, raises important questions about appropriate ethical principles. Mercy Amba Oduyoye is a Methodist theologian who is from Ghana and married to a Nigerian.

---

34. Okoro, "Christian Marriage and Divorce," 22.

Her passion for the liberation of women is manifested through the numerous women she has empowered and mentored. Her deep knowledge of her Akan culture reveals her as an expert in the African cultural terrain. Rose Uchem is a Roman Catholic nun and a theologian of Nigerian heritage. She shows great passion in the course of women's liberation and so confronts two goliaths: the patriarchal Igbo culture, and the ultra-conservative Roman Catholic Church. The latter is especially so on the sensitive issue of the ordination of women to the priesthood.

Chapter 4 is an engagement with the thought of Bénézet Bujo who is a Roman Catholic priest from the Congo, and a moral theologian and ethicist. Bujo is one of the pioneering African scholars who laid the foundation of African theology. He pursued this with a keen interest in re-expressing Christianity through African cultural identity such as ancestorship and communitarianism. These three theologians and ethicists offer principles worth investigating for their contribution to the liberation of Igbo couples suffering infertility.

Their different perspectives enriched the identification of a sound Igbo ethical principle that can liberate Igbo couples from the opprobrium of infertility. I argue that the indigenous Igbo ethical principle of *onye aghala nwanne ya,* because of its numerous advantages, is a viable ethical principle for this liberation. Igbo people are more likely to honor the ethical principle of *onye aghala nwanne ya* because it embodies core Igbo values, consciousness, and culture and Igbo people are known for their lasting and deep attachment to their cultural heritage.

Chapter 5, argues for the indigenous ethic of *Onye aghala nwanne ya* as a constructive extension of Oduyoye, Uchem and Bujo's theological and ethical principles. From a traditional African religious point of view, this chapter evaluates Igbo cultural and religious tenets, such as the veneration of the earth goddess, and the ironic vilification of her human counterpart, the female, especially in the area of infertility. It draws comparisons and, in the process, puts Igbo culture into a spotlight along with some of its inherent contradictions. The religio-socio-cultural construct is my challenge to Igbo socio-religious and cultural rules, stereotypes and ideas, using exponents of inculturation theology to argue for the liberation of infertile couples. I further propose a review of the ritual of breaking kola nuts although this will definitely threaten the culture of the day.

This is followed by chapter 6 which is the general conclusion, this summarizes the arguments. I have underscored some phases of culture as a human product, and as something that is dynamic, and therefore subject to change. Through the process of change, new elements can be added to the culture. In that same process, some elements can be lost; while some can be substituted or even fused, and others challenged. Such changes can lead to further conversation on the subject of this book.

1

A Historical and Socio-Context Analysis of Igbo World

INTRODUCTION

THE CULTURE AND HISTORY of a people define who they are explaining what makes them laugh, cry, shout, express happiness and behave the way they do. Seen from a more encompassing anthropological perspective:

> Culture is a people's total way of living, the totality of what a person learns from the elders, peers, and teachers. It includes toolmaking and behavior, customs and tradition, ideas of the deity and supernatural, beliefs of what is noble and good, technology which is the people's major way of coping with environment, economy and social organization (kinship, common territory and special interest groups).[1]

Culture unveils a people's strength, challenges and how they formulate solutions to human problems, and thus providing them with a sense of purpose and identity. In other words, culture is the "ideas, beliefs, values and judgement of good and evil that shape communal behavior."[2]

To understand a people, one needs to engage in a contextual analysis of the people and their culture. In this case, it will entail paying special attention to their origin, geography, power structure, language, and connection to the supernatural. It will further entail how they process issues

---

1. Akukwe, *Towards a New Society*, 18.
2. Appiah, "Challenge of a Theologically Fruitful Method," 266.

about life, how they engage with all the intricacies surrounding their being, including the gender of human persons, the ethical principles employed for making ethical decisions, and the values that guide them in life.³

Toward understanding a people and their world, analyzing the tools they use in navigating their world can help to make their world intelligible and meaningful, even to an outsider. In the anthropocentric understanding of the Igbo cosmos, humans are viewed from different perspectives—from the light of their origin, and of their final destiny. The social analysis of the Igbo socio-cultural context here will cover religious, cultural, and social connections. It is an analysis of the Igbo world, which includes: the ". . .—material, spiritual, and sociocultural—(and) is made intelligible to Igbo by their cosmology, which explains how everything came into being."⁴

Victor Uchendu's (veteran Igbo sociologist and anthropologist) analysis and knowledge of the socio-cultural context plays a major role in understanding an Igbo perspective on Christian ethics, ". . . which defines what the Igbo ought to do and what they ought to avoid . . ."⁵ This becomes their moral code, which could be either oral or written, and people are—de facto—called to religiously adhere to it. An Igbo moral code will be "the totality of the lore of the land, customs and tradition, a complex of beliefs and practices which every Igbo person inculcates as a guiding philosophy and code of behavior."⁶ Examples from these Igbo moral codes include: "patricide, incest, killing of sacred animals, murder, women climbing palm trees, abuse of elders, improper sexual relations, stealing, lying, secretive life, poisoning, and witchcraft."⁷

Generally speaking, Igbo people "are a distinguished group of people who live in Southeastern Nigeria. In numbers alone, the Igbo are one of the three dominant ethnic groups of Nigeria, with the Hausa and the Yoruba."⁸ Igbo culture has come in contact with numerous other cultures and civilizations, which have changed other aspects of Igbo culture significantly, although other aspects have remained almost unchanged. Some of these catalysts of change include migration (immigration and

---

3. Uchendu, *The Igbo of Southeast Nigeria*, 11.
4. Uchendu, *The Igbo of Southeast Nigeria*, 11.
5. Uchendu, *The Igbo of Southeast Nigeria*, 11.
6. Nwala, *Igbo Philosophy*, 76.
7. Nwala, *Igbo Philosophy*, 205.
8. Ogbaa, *Igbo*, 9.

emigration), meaning the movements of people in and out of Igbo land, and the movements of Igbo people in and out of different cultural spaces. Other factors include the devastating and excruciating experience of the trans-Atlantic slave trade, colonialism, the Igbo war of secession known as the Biafran war,[9] and the arrival of Christianity and its effects of change on Igbo culture, theologies, ethical principles and morality.

George Ekwuru is one of the many Igbo scholars who hold the strong opinion that colonialism was another disastrous form of slavery. He sees it as one of the major forces that depleted and eroded the values of Igbo culture:

> [w]ith the coming of the white man as a strange form of cultural encounter, and its full-blown revolutionary impact on this society, the central pillars of the traditional Igbo cultural world started to disintegrate.[10]

Like colonialism, another major agent of change for much of Igbo culture was Christianity. The evangelizers came with an indoctrination style that changed the cultural, religious and ethical horizon of Igbo land. No one disputes that Christianity brought many good things to Igbo land. It educated the people in almost all aspects of human life, which improved the lives of Igbo people. The messengers of the Gospel brought western education, too, which to a great extent dispelled the darkness of ignorance.

However, Chinua Achebe is among many Igbo historians, ethnographers and cultural anthropologists whose research has concluded that Christianity punctured the pristine social network that celebrated and revered Igbo culture. In the novel *Things Fall Apart,* Achebe sets out to tell the story of Okonkwo, a somewhat dominating figure in his family. In a conversation about the church and Christianity and what it has done to the community, Obierika, Okonkwo's friend, says it is because "'[t]he white man is very clever. He came quietly and peaceably with his religion. We were amused at his foolishness and allowed him to stay. Now he has won our brothers, and our clan can no longer act like one. He has put a knife on the things that held us together and we have fallen apart.'"[11] From this perspective, one can argue that because of the White man's lack

---

9. The Nigerian civil war, also known as war of secession was a war fought between the state of Biafra (comprising mostly of Igbo people of southeastern Nigeria) and the government of Nigeria. The war took place from July 6th 1967 to January 15th 1970.

10. Ekwuru, *Pangs of an African Culture*, 4.

11. Achebe, *Things Fall Apart*, 176.

of knowledge of Igbo culture in the course of introducing Christianity, some Igbo cultural values became submerged. Josephine Akah shares this same view with Achebe: "With the introduction of Christianity, western culture advanced unabated. Westernization resulted in the destruction of Igbo culture and imposition of alien 'ways of life.' Westernization equally furthered the incipient destruction of Igbo values."[12]

However, it is good to note that before the advent of Christianity in Africa, many African cultures like that of the Igbo had their own challenges. All human societies are imperfect. The intention here is not to present Igbo socio-cultural sanctity, as if the Christian faith was by itself evil. However, we want to acknowledge that:

> The arrival of the Whiteman changed the traditional pattern in Umuopara society. The Okonko society was condemned, polygamy was said to be an uncivilized practice, *ojam umuopara*, which united all of us in the past, was destroyed, the religion we used to know—all our *Njoku, ofo, iyi, afo*—were discarded with the advent of Christian churches and schools.[13]

This discarding of Igbo sacred institutions devastated Igbo culture. This connection is important, because the arrival of Christianity and the method by which the message was spread came with the good, the bad, and certainly the ugly. The method of evangelization and the message itself will remain a land mark through which Igbo culture is seen in this book.

Kalu Ogbu writes in his book, *The Embattled Gods,* that, "Christianity has served as a change-agent in Igbo land."[14] He argues that the unconquered spirit of Igbo deities and culture refused to retreat: "In spite of virtual over-evangelization, the Christian message left only a superficial imprint."[15] In terms of Igbo cultural heritage, little really changed, as the core tenets of Igbo culture—community life, being one's brother/sister's keeper, respect for elders and reverence for ancestors—resisted the 'onslaught' of Christianity. This socio-cultural contextual analysis is important, because to understand Christian ethics and Igbo ethical principles, the origin of the Igbo people is paramount.

---

12. Akah, "Resilience of Igbo Culture," 138.
13. Isichei, *Igbo Worlds*, 93.
14. Kalu, *Embattled Gods*, 307.
15. Kalu, *Embattled Gods*, 307.

ORIGIN OF THE IGBO PEOPLE

A statement of the origin of the Igbo people is complicated by how Igbo people are identified. There are two alternative spellings of 'Igbo,' which here designates a people and their language. The spellings include 'Igbo,' which is commonly used by the indigenes themselves, and 'Ibo.' The second is a colonial appellation arising because of the colonial masters' inability to pronounce 'gb' in a word. During the colonial days:

> 'Ibo' was in almost universal use, both among the Igbo themselves and internationally. Although a handful of linguists and anthropologists used the technically more correct 'Igbo,' an overwhelming majority of the Igbo now prefer 'Igbo,' which they regard as indigenous, in contradistinction to the inaccurate 'Ibo' of colonial days.[16]

The origins of the term and the people have remained a matter of intrigue and controversy. We shall look at two of these hypotheses of Igbo origin: the Igbo-Jewish connection, and the Nri foundational myth. These two hypotheses are important because they reveal so much about Igbo philosophy, life, and value systems.

The Igbo-Jewish Ancestry Connection

In recent years and in contemporary discourse, the Igbo scholar Dozie Ikedife has been trying to trace Igbo roots for a possible connection to those of the Jewish nation. He sees some marked semblance between Igbo culture and Jewish culture. In trying to verify this connection, an association known as the Israeli-Yahweh group[17] was invited to Igbo land to take a random sampling of cells from some Igbo people of southeast Nigeria, for a DNA analysis and comparison in Houston, Texas.[18] Ikedife, the former President-General of *Ohanaeze Ndigbo* (a pan-Igbo

---

16. Isichei, *History of the Igbo People*, xv. Professor Elizabeth Isichei is from New Zealand but married an Igbo man, Dr. Peter Uche Isichei. She developed an extraordinary love for Igbo history and so wrote many books on Igbo and African history. She taught history at the University of Jos, Nigeria, and at the University of Nigeria in Nsukka. The thorough research she did in her work has made her books widely quoted as an authentic chronology and analysis of Igbo history.

17. This is a Jewish group investigating the claim to Jewish ancestry of groups and people outside of Israel.

18. As quoted in Nwafor, "Jewish/Igbo Relationship."

socio-cultural group), initiated this scientific verification. He and his group wanted to ascertain whether there was a shared Igbo heritage with the Jews. He notes that there have been stories of Jewish-Igbo relations, based on mythology and archaeological discoveries, and he wanted to facilitate Jewish scholars coming to prove or disprove the claim.[19]

Daniel Lis, a Swiss-Israeli anthropologist and scholar at the Institute for Jewish Studies at the University of Basel, corroborates the Igbo-Jewish connection. Considered one of the foremost authorities on this subject, Lis argues that there is a connection which is the result of a long history of identity. He argues that this connection is "not just something that happened yesterday, but which has a long history of identity."[20] This connection and identity relate directly to the origin of the Igbo people.

This intercultural comparison captured the research interest of one of the pioneer missionaries in Igbo land, George Thomas Basden (1873–1944).[21] Basden was a distinguished Anglican missionary of the "Church Missionary Society, Niger Mission; Archdeacon of the Niger and nominated unofficial member of the Legislative Council of Nigeria."[22] He was an ethnographer, and as such his research in the cross-cultural comparisons between Igbo people and Jewish people revealed that "the word 'Igbo' evolved as a corruption of the word 'Hebrew.'"[23] Basden, continued this link with his advice to prospective missionaries to Igboland, when he admonished: ". . . I would recommend a careful study of Levitical law. In many ways the affinity between Native Law and the Mosaic system is remarkable."[24] This affinity or link to the Jewish heritage includes a number of Igbo ritual practices. For example, naming ceremonies and some shared traditional practices, including "circumcising male children eight days after birth, refraining from eating 'unclean' or tabooed foods, mourning the dead for seven days, celebrating the New Moon and conducting wedding ceremonies under a canopy."[25]

---

19. As quoted in Nwafor, "Jewish/Igbo Relationship."
20. As quoted in Oduah, "Nigeria's Igbo Jews."
21. George Basden's work is considered one of "the most comprehensible, genuine, and reliable earliest reports and best source materials on western Igbo." Ibewuike, *African Women*, 24.
22. "Supplement to the London Gazette," 13.
23. As quoted in Oduah, "Nigeria's Igbo Jews."
24. Basden, *Among the Ibos of Nigeria*, vi.2017
25. Oduah, "Nigeria's Igbo Jews."

In all these, Igbo people have remained at a cultural and religious stage of development comparable to that of Hebrews before the Christian era.²⁶ Some Igbo practices, like naming ceremonies and circumcision, predate the advent of Christianity in Igbo land, and these rituals are still being practiced. "To this day, the naming ceremony of an Igbo child is regarded as a significant event for the child's immediate family and the wider unit. In most cases this event takes place after the child's circumcision would have healed."²⁷ The similarities in Jewish-Igbo ritual practices make the Jewish-Igbo ancestry connection tenable. Apart from ritual, the semblance can be found in trade, industry and commerce. Igbo people are always depicted by other ethnic groups in Nigeria as the 'Jews of Africa,' because of their prowess in commerce and trade.²⁸ Their migrant nature is another factor that has made the Igbo-Jewish connection plausible. Igbo people are found in almost every part of the world, and are known, like their Jewish counterparts, to survive difficult situations:

> Even though 'ala' Igbo is the only territory the Igbo call a home, there is however, no part of the earth the Igbo do not find abode—ranging from their homeland to the New World, the Arctic and the Alps, they are seen in all walks of life—from ghettos of the dirty world to the Hollywood villages, from the streets and toilet cleaning jobs of the world, to the National Aeronautics and Space Administration Offices of Americas.²⁹

While this investigation of an Igbo link to Jewish ancestry is ongoing, historians and archeologists have traced the period of human habitation in Igbo land to five thousand years ago. Elizabeth Isichei, a foremost Igbo historian, says that "the first human inhabitants of Igboland must have come from areas further north, possibly from the Niger confluence. But men have been living in Igboland for at least five thousand years, since the dawn of history."³⁰ This historical finding has some semblance with what is adjudged as "one of the standard versions of Igbo myths of origin"³¹ (as there are many versions of Igbo myths of origin³²). The *Nri*

---

26. Falola and Njoku, *Igbo in the Atlantic World*, 193.
27. Agbasiere, *Women in Igbo Life*, 135.
28. Nzewuba, *Sights and Sounds*, 334.
29. Nzewuba, *Sights and Sounds*, 334.
30. Isichei, *History of the Igbo People*, 3.
31. Ekwuru, *Pangs of an African Culture*, 1.
32. The multiple versions of the foundational story are a result of the problems

myth has it that the origin of Igbo people traces to the ancient kingdom of *Nri* in present-day Anambra state.[33] This is so because "the traditions of the Umueri clan—which includes the ancient kingdom of *Nri*—state that 'both they and the Igala descended from a still more ancient community in the Anambra valley.'"[34] The *Nri* myth traces Igbo origin to have been around this Anambra valley.

The '*Nri* myth' Igbo Foundational Story

An Igbo creation story, popularly known as the *Nri* myth, has it that the Igbo people have "*Nri* in Awka and Amaigbo in Orlu as their spiritual and ideological headquarters, the centers from which their different branches spread out to occupy their present locations."[35] This myth, which is believed to be the cradle of Igbo cultural civilization, reveals that:

> . . . [a] certain superhuman being, *Eri*, and his wife were sent down from the sky by *Chukwu*, God almighty . . .
> When *Eri* came down from the sky, he had to stand on a termite mound, because all the earth was then marshy. *Eri* complained to *Chukwu* who sent a metal worker, Awka, with bellows, charcoal and fire to dry up the land.[36]

Accordingly, *Eri*, and later his sons, became the father of Igbo people. In this narrative, *Eri*, is seen as an Igbo proto-ancestor, the first king of the Nri ancient kingdom, and de facto the first man in the Igbo cosmos. The origin of the Igbo people has remained an ongoing research topic as some of the myths and historical analyses look plausible to adherents of any of the given positions of the myth.

---

associated with myth. "Myth is not usually dated nor has it any given author or number of authors . . . myth is not narrated in logical or coherent terms. Therefore, its meaning can be ambiguous." Abanuka, *Myth and the African Universe*, 2. These characteristic features of myth make it possible to have different interpretations of the same myth or to have multiple myths narrating a foundational story.

33. Ekwuru, *Pangs of an African Culture*, 1.
34. Isichei, *History of the Igbo People*, 4.
35. Awolalu, *West African Traditional Religion*, 3.
36. Abanuka, *Myth and the African Universe*, 77.

THE GEOGRAPHY OF THE IGBO LAND

Igbo land is located within the eastern part of Nigeria. It comprises five states within southeast region. These states include Imo, Ebonyi, Anambra, Enugu and Abia. However, there are other Igbo people who live at the peripheries of what may largely be considered non-Igbo states. Emmanuel Okonkwo, who is interested in marriage in Nigeria and inculturation, writes, "Igboland is also divided into zones. The Northern Igbo is comprised of communities located around Onitsha, Akwa, Udi, Agwu districts and parts of the Nsukka and Okigwe areas. The North-Eastern Igbo subculture area embraces Abakaliki and Afikpo, while the Cross River or Eastern Igbo consist of Afikpo, Bende and the whole of Arochukwu."[37] In terms of vegetation and land mass, "Igboland is located in the north of the Delta swamplands, east of the Niger River and West of the Cross River. It covers an area of 15,800 square miles."[38] As for the climate, it is tropical and it has two distinct seasons, rainy season and dry season:

> with average annual temperature of about 80F and annual range between 5 and 10 degrees. There are two principal and distinct seasonal variations the rainy and dry season, *udu mmiri* and *okochi*. April is the beginning of the former and lasts till October when dry season begins and lasts till March. The average rainfall is 70 inches yearly with fewer further from the south.[39]

THE IGBO LANGUAGE

The word 'Igbo' refers both to the indigenes of that geographical designation in Nigeria, and the language spoken by the same people. As a language of the people, some Igbo historians and cultural anthropologists like Kalu Ogbaa and Catherine Acholonu agree that Igbo people belong to the Sudanic linguistic group of the *Kwa* division. Ogbaa writes that the Igbo language ". . . is a member of the kwa language subfamily of West Africa, which was developed as a separate language about 4,500 years ago."[40] The uniqueness of the language accounts for why, apart from the

---

37. Okonkwo, *Marriage*, 7.

38. Ifemesia, *Traditional Humane Living*, 15, as cited in Ibewuike, *African Women*, 35.

39. Okwu, *Igbo Culture*, 1.

40. Ogbaa, *Igbo*, 9.

Igbo people of Nigeria, "there are no other Igbo-speaking peoples elsewhere in the world."[41] In the same line of thought, Acholonu argues that:

> Based on our Ethno-semantic analysis of the relationship between European, Asian and languages of the Niger-Congo family of African languages, using the Igbo example, we can comfortably assert that Proto-Indo-European was a language of the Niger-Congo family, not unrelated to the Kwa family of languages.[42]

Belonging to the '*Kwa* family of languages,' an outstanding characteristic of the Igbo language is that it is 'tonal': both grammar and speech tones play an essential role. "The tone of a word, whether high, intermediate or low, determines the meaning."[43] Being a 'tonal language,' one word could mean different things in terms of the ". . . pitch, voice inflections, and context for meaning. For example, the word *akwa* could mean four different things, depending on the context and which syllable is stressed: 'clothes' (ákwá), 'bed' (ákwà), 'egg' (àkwà), or 'to cry' (àkwá)."[44] The variation in connation makes it "a rich and musical language."[45] Despite some dialectical differences in the Igbo language, the language is generally compatible among Igbo-speaking people. However, because of "dialectical variations, that is a source of difficulty to Westerners, and a tendency to vowel elision which makes it difficult to express a few of the spoken words in writing."[46]

Proverbs in the Igbo Language

As a genre of formulaic language, proverbs and idiomatic expressions are synonymous with the Igbo language. Proverbs are important components of the Igbo language, as they are seen as "the palm-oil with which words are eaten."[47] In that case, "[a]ny speaker who does not know how to apply idioms, proverbs, and myths is said to be a novice or learner, of the language."[48] To totally grasp Igbo values and ways of doing things,

41. Ogbaa, *Igbo*, 11.
42. Acholonu et al., *They Lived Before Adam*, 6.
43. Edeh, *Towards an Igbo Metaphysics*, 45.
44. Nnoromele, *The Way People Live*, 15.
45. Bleeker, *Ibos of Biafra*, as cited in Nnoromele, *The Way People Live*
46. Obiego, *African Image*, 34.
47. Achebe, *Things Fall Apart*, 6.
48. Nnoromele, *The Way People Live*, 15–16.

A Historical and Socio-Context Analysis of Igbo World 25

one must be in touch with proverbs and idiomatic expressions, "because they were used to express and transmit community values, beliefs, and attitudes towards life."[49] Living among Igbo people more than a century ago, Basden observed that "[p]roverbs, fables stories enter very largely into the ordinary conversation of the people, and some acquaintance with them is absolutely necessary in order to take an intelligent interest in any subject of discussion."[50] We are going to examine some of these linguistic tools, because they form the basis of Igbo indigenous ethics.

Proverbs not only emerge from a people's worldview, they express the basics of what they consider to be eternal truths. Proverbs unveil how a people see reality, and how they interpret their moral ethos. Proverbs, though concise, add meaning and a special flair to words and conversations. Francis Nwonwu puts it well when he says, "*Ilu bu nnu eji eri okwu,*" which means Igbo people regard proverbs "as the salt that flavours Igbo literature and oral communications."[51] Since oral tradition is the basic platform of Igbo tradition, proverbs play an important role in preserving, transmitting and enriching it. We can analyze some of these proverbs, paying greater attention to the proverbs that deal with our topic of discussion. These include proverbs concerning human destiny, Igbo relationality, and the Igbo indigenous ethic of *onye aghala nwanne ya*. It is worth attempting an explanation of the phenomenon of *chi* which will pervade subsequent proverbs. It is believed among Igbo people that "[t]he moment Chukwu creates a human spirit he gives him a 'Chi.' Chi determines and dispenses a person's destiny, and protects and guards him/her much like a guardian angel."[52]

On human destiny, Igbo people have these proverbs: "*Onye chi ya kwelu—ofufu obagodu na mbubo be ya, ma ya fue* meaning: One whose Chi (a kind of guardian spirit) has decreed that he would be lost, would even get lost in his own garden."[53] This implies that one does not have control over one's destiny. The *chi* has the overriding say in what one can become or what one does in life. "Numerous examples among the Igbo buttress this belief: a lucky fellow is called, *onye chi oma*, (meaning) someone who has a good *chi*, and on the other hand, the unfortunate

---

49. Nnoromele, *The Way People Live*, 16.
50. Basden, *Among the Ibos of Nigeria*, 257.
51. Nwonwu, *Philosophy of Proverbs*, xiii.
52. Nwonwu, *Philosophy of Proverbs*. 28.
53. Nwonwu, *Philosophy of Proverbs*, 28.

person is called '*onye chi ojoo*,' (meaning) someone who has a bad *chi*."[54] *Chi* therefore plays a dominant role in the life and destiny of every individual. There is another side of the understanding of *chi*, in which some Igbo proverbs show that an individual can have control and fully participate in his/her destiny.

Igbo people believe in the determinant principle of *onye kwe chi ya ekwe*, which literally means "if a person says yes, his *chi* also says yes, (i.e, a god helps those who help themselves)."[55] With this understanding, the *chi* is not seen as a determinant of one's destiny but a collaborator, a supporter of what one decides to do. This gives room for individuals to take their destinies into their hands. The role of *chi* as the guardian spirit and as a collaborator is brought out by the Igbo proverb, "*nwata n'amu iri enu, chi ya achiri uche n'aka*' (which means) when a child is learning how to climb a tree, his *chi* is breathless with anxiety."[56] This implies that the *chi* can be a passive observer, and sometimes can be a major determinant in the life of an individual. In other words, *chi* can be paradoxical and ambivalent.

Despite this dual or ambivalent belief about the *chi*, the stronger feeling in a traditional Igbo application is that the *chi* determines the total destiny of a person. My argument here is: why should someone be blamed and vilified in Igbo land if their *chi* is the determinant agent of their destiny, and if it had kept childlessness as a package for them? Their *chi* should be blamed or pacified, and not the infertile person. The family should take the traditional responsibility of pouring libation to pacify the ancestors or the person's *chi*.

Understanding the dominant factor of *chi* further, one can see that the resilient Igbo spirit of conquering sustains the Igbo person in taking his/her destiny into his/her hands. However, there is a popular surrender to the *chi* who determines one's destiny. That is why Igbo people still have a proverb which says: "*agbataghi ajo chi na uzo oru* meaning, even with 'determination you cannot escape bad fortune by resourcefulness.'"[57] This belief, where the *chi* has an upper hand in one's destiny, is further expressed in this proverb, which acknowledges that resourcefulness may not always be rewarded: "*omelu ma chi ekweghi, onye-uta atakwana ya*" (which means) one who has tried his or her best, but (his/her) *chi* did not

---

54. Nwonwu, *Philosophy of Proverbs*, 111.
55. Nwonwu, *Philosophy of Proverbs*, 27.
56. Nwonwu, *Philosophy of Proverbs*, 27.
57. Nwonwu, *Philosophy of Proverbs*, 28.

consent should not be blamed."⁵⁸ In this case, we see that the *chi* remains a determinant factor in influencing the destiny of an Igbo person.

On Igbo morality, such as encouraging the treatment of others and their children and handling of their property the way one would like to be treated, this Igbo proverb which asks a rhetorical question confers a foundation for an Igbo ethic: "*Omegbu nwa ogbenye okpo nke ya ana muo*? Will the oppressor of an orphan take his own child with him to the land of the dead when he dies?"⁵⁹ This means that what goes around will definitely come around, and the best way to avoid misfortune is to treat others well. The best way to avoid one's children being mistreated by others is to treat other children with utmost respect and love. This proverb invites Igbo people to love and treat the other with respect and dignity. In trying to avoid misfortune, respect and dignity become two ethical values which emerge from Igbo people's moral sense of looking out and caring for the other.

Igbo people have another proverb which highlights relationality and interconnectedness. It goes, "*Anya bewe imi ebewe,* which literally means 'when the eye cries, the nose will also cry.'"⁶⁰ This shows that what affects one member of the community affects every member of the community. This defines the core value of the ethical principle of *onye aghala nwanne ya*.⁶¹ In the same line of thinking, anyone who harms his/her *nwanne* (brother or sister) harms himself or herself. Thus the saying, "*Oji nwanna ya anu mai ji onwe ya na-anu*, meaning one who drinks against his brother drinks against himself,"⁶² could be the finest proverb depicting Igbo connectedness.

Igbo Names as Means of Communication

Like their proverbs, Igbo people bear names that depict the omniscience and omnipotence of *chi*. Common Igbo names, like: Chibugomma, meaning "*chi* is golden or beautiful," is used to placate *chi* by describing it glowingly. In the long run, the expectation is that one gains some favors

---

58. Udeani, *Inculturation as Dialogue*, 37.
59. Pachocinsk, *Proverbs of Africa*, 70.
60. Pachocinsk, *Proverbs of Africa*, 41.
61. The core principles of *onye aghala nwanne ya* will be examined in a later part of this work.
62. Pachocinsk, *Proverbs of Africa*, 41.

for praise-singing one's *chi*. Sochima, meaning "*chi* is all-knowing," and Chimdi, which means "my *chi* lives or my *chi* is powerful," become a vehicle of communication. These names and their meanings are significant in understanding the moral foundation and the destiny of Igbo people. Above all, African names, and by implication Igbo names, "designate the personality, status, occupation or destiny of the bearer."[63] The names that people bear narrate the history of an event of the family, or the circumstance in which the child bearing the name came into existence:

> Igbo names are not mere tags to distinguish one thing or person from another, but are expressions of the nature of that which they stand for; they contain memories of a human experience, every shade of human sentiments and emotions in the struggle for existence . . . an everlasting and imperishable record of their life and death struggles and their attempts to live in harmony with other men.[64]

These *chi*-oriented names not only suggest the powers inherent in *chi*, but go a long way toward showing how the Igbo cultural hemisphere is ruled by *chi* and, by extension, God. They suggest that Igbo space is religiously charged.

A popular name among Igbo people is Nwagborogu which means "the child that ends the feud." This kind of name is given to a child when a couple has been childless after many years of marriage. The birth of the child brings an end to the feud that came as a result of childlessness. A child who is given this kind of name by the parents becomes an "opportunity for parents to tell the world around them what is most important to them."[65] This is similar to Efuru's situation. When Efuru gave birth to a baby girl in her first marriage after a protracted period of childlessness, her husband, Adizua, filled with great joy, immediately reacted, "Welcome, my daughter. Your name is Ogonim."[66] Ogonim is a short form of the name Chinagorom or Chinagonim in Oguta dialect, a popular Igbo name meaning "*chi* is my defender." In their case, *chi* is defending the couple, their families, and probably all those who were humiliated from the nasty comments and persecution they must have suffered during the period of childlessness.

---

63. Ehusani, *An Afro-Christian Vision*, 127.
64. Obiego, *African Image*, 78.
65. Ekeocha, *Target Africa*, 97.
66. Nwapa, *Efuru*, 32.

A name can also be used to teach a moral lesson, or designate a major event that happened with the birth of the new child. There are names like Obidike which means "my heart is very strong."[67] This name is given to a child in a circumstance where the parents may have already lost many children through death. This name is given to indicate that despite the multiple deaths that have occurred, the parents are courageous and hopeful that this particular child will survive, and that through his/her survival, more children will come to stay.

In all, to give a name is to confer a personality. Parents and families take a long time before they come out with a child's name, because that name becomes the child's identity and destiny. "A newborn child is not a person until the naming ceremony has been performed. Before then it is a nonentity."[68] Like all African societies, Igbo society adheres to oral tradition; names in this context become the identity of the bearer, which "tells some story about the family of the bearer, carries the parents' aspirations for the future of the bearer, and points to the values of the society into which the bearer is born."[69] This indicates that families sometimes try to retell the story of the community from the kind of names they give to a child. Sometimes they would want to influence the destiny of a child by giving a name wherein they try to map out a path that the name-bearer is to walk.

IGBO POLITICAL STRUCTURE

Igbo political arrangements are like a loose federation, though with different positions of honor and rank. In other words, the loose federation and devolution of political structure is "based on decentralization of power and delegation of authority exercised by the holder of the staff of authority, *ofo*."[70] This decentralized structure creates a balance and a sense of equality:

> The Igbo world is based on an equalitarian principle. Equality or near equality ensures that no one person or group of persons acquires too much control over the life of others. This is

---

67. Pachocinsk, *Proverbs of Africa*, 424.
68. Oduyoye, "Man's self."
69. Ehusani, *An Afro-Christian Vision*, 124.
70. Obiego, *African Image*, 39.

an ideological obstacle to the development of a strong central authority.[71]

This decentralized structure does not mean a case of lawlessness or of no one being in charge. Despite being decentralized, there are holders of *ofo* (an Igbo ritual symbol of authority) who are titled men with some sense of authority. These men are "made up of chiefs and titled men,"[72] and are charged with the administration of different units. "Each village has its own assembly or council, whose members are family heads or holders of *ofo*. This council of old men, *okpara*, has a great influence in the village."[73] Part of their influence is that they are custodians of authority, and, to a great extent, of morality. Since they hand down cultural tenets to younger people, it is little wonder that the Igbo have this proverb: "*onwu egbule ndi okenye ka umuazi ghara iri udele*," which can be translated to mean, "May the elders never die so that children will not take to devouring the carcass of the vulture."[74] This simply means that elders have the responsibility to maintain social harmony by guiding the young ones, "against contravening the laws of the land."[75] To maintain some kind of harmony in community living, it should be noted that "Each village or ward has its own chief who enjoys the dignity and rights of a patriarch. He takes the lead in all public affairs, religious, social and political. Disputes are settled by him, and he presides at the trials of criminal offenders."[76] Within this village arrangement, the entire group of the lineage, and even the extended family members and dependents living out of the geographical location, recognizes the authority of the compound head, and will not make any political decision without consulting him.[77]

In these modern times, this political arrangement has slightly changed. Without undermining the power of the *okpara* (the first male child), associations are formed wherein different units divided on gender lines exercise powerful authority. This authority is visible among the

---

71. Uchendu, *Igbo of Southeast Nigeria*, 19.
72. Okoro, "Christian Marriage and Divorce," 18.
73. Ibewuike, *African Women*, 57.
74. Ekwuru, *Pangs of an African Culture*, 3.
75. Ekwuru, *Pangs of an African Culture*, 3.
76. Basden, *Among the Ibos of Nigeria*, 31.
77. Uchendu, *Igbo of Southeast Nigeria*, 39–40.

kin-based units called patrilineage of *Umunna*.[78] This organ, which some people call the extended family, "is the central or basic social unit of Ibo society. It is made up of the descendants, in the male line, of a founder ancestor by whose name a lineage is sometimes called."[79] The patriarchal flame is much more visible in this political structure, as it is all about how life is dominated and influenced by males. The association which exercises this power in a group administrative style is called the *Umunna*.

However, in the same way and to maintain some kind of balance, there is also a powerful female unit called *Umuada*. About these two groups, the noted authority on Igbo women's life Salome Nnoromele writes:

> They created two different powerful political and autonomous political systems that handled the affairs of men and women separately. Consequently, men have their own political institutions where they managed and discussed issues affecting them and women had their own separate and equally powerful political institutions through which they manage their affairs.[80]

Like the *Umunna* political group, the *Umuada* political group has its own role to play in the sphere and affairs of community living. Their existence creates balance in the community, as we will see in a later part of this section.

The *Umunna* Political Unit

The *Umunna* political unit formulates ethical policies and enforces them among the kindred unit. They are considered to be "the highest ruling and decision-making body in the Igbo socio-political structure, constituted by certain democratic principles."[81] It is always dangerous to contravene the decisions of the *Umunna*. When a decision is flouted, it may lead to one being ostracized, although it takes a long time and thorough deliberation before decisions of ostracizing any person are made. On the other hand, despite the seemingly stern outlook of *Umunna*, they are the protectors and

---

78. Umunna is a lineage of a people with probably generations of forebears. They could descend "from one father . . . (in this case) both men and women born in a patrilineage were regarded as sharing the same blood and were equally subject to the rules and taboos associated with patrileanage spirits." See Amadiume, *Male Daughters, Female Husbands*, 57.

79. Ilogu, *Christianity and Ibo Culture*, 11.

80. Nnoromele, *The Way People Live*, 26.

81. Ekwuru, *Pangs of an African Culture*, 135.

custodians of community moral values. Through oral tradition, they teach upcoming generations the sacred sanctions of the land. They are the 'watch tower' of the community, on guard against outside invaders or aggressors. Amongst their overall function, and as an association of "lineage men," they are "duty bound to help members so also are members individually bound by certain codes of conduct in order to remain members of the group."[82] These dual and seemingly contradictory roles of *Umunna* will be our major focus when we discuss the paradox of the ethical principle of *onye aghala nwanne ya* in subsequent chapters.

Umuada—the Igbo Brand of Feminism

To maintain equilibrium in Igbo culture, we have the *Otu Umuada*. They are considered to be ". . . the most powerful women's group in a lineage, consisting of all married daughters of the lineage. Even though traditional Ibo society was patrilocal (all daughters were expected to marry and move to their husband's community), women still retained rights and responsibilities in their birth communities."[83] This implies that their power and sphere of influence are expansive. *Umuada* women are aware of the inherent powers bestowed on their group, and one can refer to them as trailblazers. This power and influence are seen in marriage situations in "their birth communities." For example, "[a] brother was not permitted to get married without first informing and receiving the approval of the *Umuada*."[84]

They are given much respect as they are experts in reconciliation and conflict resolution. They ". . . were also called upon to settle disputes within the family, especially those between brothers or between a brother and his wife."[85] In the wider community they wield enormous influence. Their powers are as "extensive as they are ambivalent. They include the right of arbitration within their natal lineage, settling of quarrels concerning political, economic and ritual matters which are beyond their male relatives' power to settle."[86] Most often, they have the final word on marriage disputes in their natal homes. These power structures exist to maintain some

---

82. Amadiume, *Male Daughters, Female Husbands*, 58.
83. Nnoromele, *The Way People Live*, 33.
84. Nnoromele, *The Way People Live*, 33.
85. Nnoromele, *The Way People Live*, 33–34.
86. Agbasiere, *Women in Igbo Life*, 40.

kind of balance within Igbo political space. With this kind of balance, there is an understanding that no one group completely dominates.

IGBO RELIGIOUS WORLDVIEW

To better understand a people, it is worth looking at what drives the people to do what they do. The religiosity of the Igbo people has a lot to say about the general demeanor of an average Igbo person. Victor Uchendu, Igbo foremost sociologist and anthropologist writes, "[t]o know how a people view the world around them is to understand how they evaluate life, and a people's evaluation of life, both temporal and non-temporal, provides them with a 'charter' of action, a guide to behavior."[87] To adequately understand the Igbo moral landscape and ethical beliefs, one needs to understand the Igbo religious worldview and religious connections, because like African ethics in general, Igbo ethics are "very religious. God, the spirits of the departed (the ancestors), and good and evil spirits have a pervasive influence on the morality of the people."[88]

The Igbo world is not just the physical world; it includes those who are living, and those in the spirit world. Fellowship in Igbo land does not end when one departs from the physical world but continues even when one transits into the realm of the dead. It is of little wonder that in Igbo land the deceased members of the family are buried within the family compound or ancestral land—a public cemetery is hard to find. This communion among the living and the 'living-dead' continues because the Igbo universe is conceived as a unit. In this worldview, ". . . the dead are not considered as very far removed from the living, and those who are still living are conscious of their journey to join those who have gone before them to the land of the dead."[89] This means that whether a member is living or dead, the Igbo family is a continuum. No one is forgotten or left behind, even if one exits from the physical world.

This sense of religiosity may account for why when comparing a Euro-American style of worship and most African styles of worship the difference is always clear. Compared to Euro-American (Greco-Roman) style of worship with stillness of the body and recitation of creeds, John Mbiti, recounting how Africans worship God, writes, "[t]hey have no

87. Uchendu, *Igbo of Southeast Nigeria*, 11.
88. Kunhiyop, *African Christian Ethics*, xv.
89. Abanuka, *A New Essay*, 36.

creeds to recite: their creeds are within them, in their blood and in their hearts."[90] Igbo people and Africans in general worship with the consciousness of all the realities in their visible world and the invisible world. Worship for Igbo people is holistic.

Furthermore, in these two simultaneous and inter-penetrating worlds, the visible and the invisible, there is always an unhindered intervention from the spirit world into the physical world. There is a thin line between the spirit world, *ala muo,* and the physical world, *ala mmadu.* There is no obstacle to the spirit or the spirit world influencing or directly intervening in the affairs of those in the physical world. Metuh describes this religious world view succinctly:

> All beings known to the Igbo belong to either of the two worlds—the visible world (Uwa), and the invisible world (Ala Nmuo). The visible world is peopled by men and contains material surroundings familiar to man. The invisible world is the spirit world. Here is the abode of the Creator, *Chukwu*, the deities, *Mmuo*, the spirit forces, *Alusi*, and the ancestors, *Ndichie*. There are besides, disembodied and malignant spirits such as witches, *Amusu*, and evil spirits of the dead, *Ogbonuke*. These categorizations notwithstanding, the Igbo world-view presents itself as one fluid coherent unit in which spirits, men and other material beings engage in continuous interaction.[91]

From this perspective, one can say that an individual is not just a body of protoplasm, isolated from the spirit world. As an individual, he/she can make decisions about different options in his/her life; however, this ability could be moderated or influenced by entities from the spirit world. While a person is free to make some decisions in life, there are forces in the world outside him/her which are capable of enhancing or impeding his/her efforts. These forces from *ala muo* can come in the guise of a spirit. They directly influence life in the spirit and physical worlds. To better understand the powers that are inherent in the spirit world, it is worth itemizing the hierarchy of beings in the spirit world.

---

90. Mbiti, *African Religions and Philosophy*, 67.
91. Metuh, *African Religions*, 24.

The Supreme Being and Other Beings in Igbo Cosmology

In the Igbo spiritual realm, it is believed that there is a Supreme Being who can be equated to the Judeo-Christian God of creation. This Being holds the world in His palm. This Being is called *Chineke,* Edmund Ilogu explains thus: "The principal God of the Igbo is called *Chineke* or *Chukwu.* Chi-ne-ke literally means 'the Creator God' whilst Chukwu (Chi-ukwu) means 'the Great God.'"[92] As in the Christian tradition, where we have God the creator and the saints as heavenly beings, we have God the creator in the Igbo worldview, and a collection of other gods who could be seen as messengers of *Chineke.* Ilogu further identifies these messengers: "*Anyanwu* (the sun god), *Igwe* (the sky god), *Amadioha* (the god of thunder and lightning) and *Ala*[93] (the earth goddess)."[94] The creative effect of *Chineke* is the significant role the *chi* played at the dawn of human creation. However, in all these spiritual structures and hierarchy the power of *Chineke* cannot be overemphasized:

> The great God (*Chi-ukwu*) is believed to be the author of heaven and earth who makes animal and plant life grow. As source of human life, he gives to each man at the time of his birth that man's particular portion of the divine being called *Chi*. It is this idea which also leads to *Chi-ukwu* which, as the name for the great God, explains that the individual *Chi* which each human being possesses derives from the great *Chi*—the over Soul who is the creator of all that has life and being.[95]

Among the pantheon of other gods, *Ala* is known as the earth goddess. *Ala* is regarded as the mother of plants, animals, and numerous other terrestrial creatures.[96] She remains the point of entry and point of departure in the life of Igbo people:

> *Ala,* the earth goddess, is the most important deity in Ibo social life. She is the guardian of morality, the controller of the minor gods of fortune and economic life . . . it is she who works in conjunction with the spirits of the dead ancestors to order the

---

92. Ilogu, *Christianity and Ibo Culture,* 34.

93. We shall pay more attention to *Ala* the earth goddess which Igbo people deeply venerate, in the later part of this chapter. *Ala* is appeased when it does not yield a harvest, and it is never vilified or abandoned.

94. Ilogu, *Christianity and Ibo Culture,* 34.

95. Ilogu, *Christianity and Ibo Culture,* 34.

96. Ekwuru, *Pangs of an African Culture,* 2.

> prohibitions and the ritual avoidances . . . Because of her importance in ensuring health, agricultural fortune and hunting successes, she is well known all over Iboland.[97]

Comparatively, this hierarchy of spiritual powers in the Igbo worldview could be likened to the Roman Catholic Church's honor and veneration given to supernatural forces. In Roman Catholic theology, the hierarchical structure is known as *dulia, hyperdulia* and *latria*. *Dulia* is "a theological term signifying the honour paid to the saints."[98] Then, ". . . *latria* means worship given to God alone, and *hyperdulia* the veneration offered to the Blessed Virgin Mary."[99] This hierarchical structure seems to suggest a God who lives in relationship with other roles divided according to their hierarchical placement. This structure can be seen as analogous to life in the spirit world of the Igbo people. The Igbo belief system:

> consisted of three hierarchical layers of the supernatural world. At the head of the hierarchy was the ultimate supernatural being, known as *Chukwu* (the Great God), or *Chineke* (God the Creator). Underneath *Chukwu* were the lesser but powerful gods, *Umuagbara*. Below the gods were the spirits of dead ancestors, Ndi Ichie, and the personal gods, Chi.[100]

This structure introduces us to the Igbo spirit world, the world of the ancestors popularly known as the "living dead." We will dwell more on the ancestors in chapter 4 of this book.

The Place of the Dead in the Igbo Cosmos

From a general perspective, death has remained humanity's last enemy to be destroyed.[101] Comparatively, in the Christian tradition, the perception of death suggests an eschatological understanding. In this religious tradition, death is understood not as an end but as a means of enjoying the beatific vision. Death is seen as a life which is changed, and not a life ended. With the hope of resurrection, "the sadness of death gives way to

---

97. Ilogu, *Christianity and Ibo Culture*, 35.
98. Pace, "Dulia."
99. Pace, "Dulia."
100. Nnoromele, *The Way People Live*, 21.
101. See 1 Cor 15:26.

the bright promise of immortality,"[102] which the Christian enjoys when he/she sees God face-to-face. This is the basis of Christian faith and its attitude towards death.

For Africans in general and Igbo people in particular, death is understood as a continuum in a cyclic process:

> Death is not the final end of man in Igbo thought. All men continue to live in some form or the other after their death. Those who lived a good life and died a good death (Onwu Chi = natural death at ripe old age), and received funeral rites appropriate to their status, go to the Spirit land, '*Ala mmuo*,' where they continue a life similar to their earthly life and are eventually allowed to reincarnate '*ino uwa*.' While those who lived bad lives, or died evil deaths '*Onwu Ojoo*,' (e.g. violent deaths, or deaths by horrible diseases) are banished to 'Ama nri mmuo na mmadu,' an intermediate state between the spirit-land and the land of the living. This latter place is the Igbo concept of hell. Its occupants are visualized as frustrated, wandering and restless evil spirits.[103]

With the understanding of death in this worldview, the belief in evil spirits and the doctrine of reincarnation come to the fore. Therefore, among Igbo people there is a belief in the survival of the human person after death, with ancestors as "living dead," and in reincarnation. With reincarnation, especially, if one dies at an old age, death becomes a channel to re-initiate this cyclic process of death, rebirth and death again.

In this worldview, it is a common belief that when one dies and becomes a spirit, his/her intention is to commune with those already in the spirit world. Within this space, "although the primary concern of every spirit is to reach the spirit-land, and to be installed and reverenced as an ancestor, yet they all aspire to be reincarnated in their offspring or relatives. There is no idea of 'heaven' or 'hell' in the Christian sense as a place of reward or punishment; it is rather seen as a transit camp for those who are awaiting reincarnation to continue life's cycle."[104] In this world view, one can adduce three possibilities about infertility as it pertains to reincarnation. There is a possibility that those who reincarnate and become childless may not have had children in their previous existence and so when they reincarnate they continue the cyclic life of childlessness.

102. *Sunday Missal*, 87.
103. Metuh, *African Religions*, 116.
104. Metuh, *Comparative Studies*, 260.

Another possibility is about those who had abused children in their previous existence, when they reincarnate they are punished with childlessness. The last option will be those who were childless in their previous existence when they reincarnate they are compensated with multiple fruits of the womb.

VENERATION OF THE EARTH GODDESS

The veneration of the earth goddess is a powerful cult among the Igbo people. This goddess (called *Ani, Ala* or *Ana*—in various dialects)[105] is considered the most important deity in Igbo public and private cults, and in the universe.[106] *Ani* is highly revered and honored in Igbo religious space. The earth goddess *Ani* and the sky deity *Igwe* are creatures of *Chukwu* the Supreme Being (God). According to this tradition, *Ani* was first "created by *Chukwu* as contrasted with the sky (*Igwe*)[107] who is said to be her husband."[108] P.A. Talbot's research among the Southern Igbo people of the Delta State of Nigeria showed that they view *Chi* or *Chineke* as the creatrix (feminine gender), while *Ani* the earth goddess is known to be "the sole daughter of *Chineke*. She *(Ani)* is believed to have made the ground and the vegetable kingdom."[109] Having made the vegetable kingdom, she is venerated as the goddess of fertility. Again, *Ani* is venerated as the goddess of fertility because she is present:

> at the beginning of the cycle of life, making children grow in their mother's womb, and she is there at the end of the cycle, to receive the souls of the dead into her own womb . . . *Ani* is also responsible for many aspects of Igbo society, and guardianship of women and children in general.[110]

---

105. I will be using *Ani*, which is used by a majority of Igbo people.

106. Meek, *Law and Authority*, 21.

107. *Igwe* is the male deity also referred to as *Amadioha*. As the deity of thunder and rain he is highly revered among Igbo people. "*Amadioha*, the deity of thunder, is the lord of the sky, and male deity." Metuh, *African Religions*, 10. Symbolically represented, *Amadioha* also " falls into the class of gods known as war divinities often depicted in the Mbari house by a statue of man holding a gun" Ibeabuchi, "Amadioha."

108. Horton, "God, man, and the Land," 18.

109. Talbot, *Tribes of the Niger Delta*, 25.

110. Jaide, "Ani the Mother of the Igbos."

With this powerful role, *Ani* has a significant position among the pantheon of all deities, since she is considered the source of all fertility and the mother of all things.

In the light of the above reverence and honor accorded to *Ani*, one can argue that if Igbo women were honored even half as much as *Ani* is honored—spiritually as the priestess and symbolically as the earth goddess—then there would be no need to engage in this research project. Put in another way, if Igbo women are honored as the nurturers of the Igbo people the way *Ani* is honored, this would yield the dividend of harmony, and create a flourishing Igbo community where women would live in dignity and without abuse even if they are infertile. This connection is important because of the affinity and semblance of the earth goddess *Ani* to the female human being. This direct prayer of personification and appeal to *Ani* the earth goddess as if she is a human person puts this point in a better perspective:

Ala idi nso,	Mother—Earth you are sacred
buru mma gi	maintain you sacredness.
Ala ihe mbiara bu ncho	Mother-Earth, why I have come
afo mula umuazi	here is to safeguard my children going hungry.
Okpa njiribia kam ga	With the same healthy feet I have come,
ejikwa la.	the same will take me home.
Makala eje ana bu isi ije	Because travelling safely and returning safely is the essence of travelling.
Ihe okuko bu mmiri achu bu afo ya	why the fowl works under rain is not to go hungry.
Obiara bonye obigbula ya onajee, mkpukpu apula ya	Let a visitor not be an omen of death to his host, so that he may not get hunch-back when going.
Isee—Ihia	Amen—So be it.[111]

This semblance of the picture of *Ani* as a true picture of a woman is described well by Dorcas Olubanke Akintunde, who comes from a Yoruba background. She writes, "Women within traditional Nigerian Yoruba society, as in other cultures, play the role of caregivers. They not only bear life, but they nurse, they cherish, they give warmth, and they care for

---

111. Ifesieh, "Prayer in Igbo Traditional Religion," 90.

life because all humanity passes through their bodies."[112] In architectural designs, *Ani* "is often depicted as a mother with a child sitting on her lap."[113] We can see that the earth goddess has full functionality with her human counterpart. Why then is *Ani* revered while her human counterpart, the woman is vilified in the same culture, especially when there is unproductivity? This becomes an inherent paradox in Igbo religious and cultural ethics.

For Igbo people who practice deep veneration of *Ani*, any form of defilement of *Ani* is met with grave consequences. This is because *Ani* is in charge of fertility and human morality. The earth goddess is duly pacified when the earth does not produce a rich harvest, as could happen when the land has been defiled. "Most heinous crimes are called *Nso-Ani*, or *Alu* (land taboos). Of a person who commits such a crime, it is said, '*Omeru nso Ala*' or '*omerula Ala*' (he defiled the land)."[114] Or better still, *aru* puts the community in a state of "cosmogonic chaos and disorder."[115] In the Igbo orthodox ethical norm, to maintain balance and harmony, "Ala deprives evil men of their lives and her priests are the guardians of public morality."[116]

The deep veneration of *Ani* by the Igbo people made Hafiz Ahmed presume and erroneously argue and advocate for the power of women in Igboland. Ahmed focused on Chinua Achebe's novel *Things Fall Apart*, arguing that the depiction of the most powerful deity *(Ani)* in Igbo land as a woman is a logical conclusion of Igbo people equating their reverence for *Ani* to that of the woman. This is indicative of the actual deep-rooted power and overwhelming clout of women in Igbo land. In his review of *Thing Fall Apart*, Ahmed notes why Okonkwo was reprimanded and eventually sent to exile when he violated the rules of *Ani*: "When Okonkwo breaks the Peace of Ani, Ezeani proclaims, 'The evil you have done can ruin the whole clan. The earth goddess whom you have insulted may refuse to give us her increase, and we shall all perish.'"[117] Because of this, he has to be punished because he desecrated the land (*Ani*).

---

112. Dorcas, "Women as Healers," 157.

113. Jaide, "Ani the Mother of the Igbos."

114. Meek, *Law and Authority in a Nigerian Tribe*, 102 as cited in Metuh, *African Religions in Western Conceptual Schemes*, 49.

115. Ekwuru, *Pangs of an African Culture*, 3.

116. Meek, *Law and Authority*, 102, as cited in Metuh, *African Religions*, 49.

117. Hiatt, "Role of Women."

Furthermore, after killing his clansman Ezeudu's son, Okonkwo became a refugee as he "returns to his mother's clan after being exiled"[118] To further strengthen his argument on the significant role of women/motherhood in Igboland, Ahmed went on to argue using the moving words of acceptance of Okonkwo into his mother's clan by Uchendu, premised on the connection of Igbo people to motherhood: "*It's true that a child belongs to its father. But when a father beats his child, it seeks sympathy in its mother's hut. A man belongs to his fatherland when things are good and life is sweet. But when there is sorrow and bitterness he finds refuge in his motherland. Your mother is there to protect you. She is buried there. And that is why we say that mother is supreme.*"[119]

To further strengthen his argument, Ahmed goes on in his review to say, "*Ani* is described as playing a greater part in the life of the people than any other deity. She was the ultimate judge of morality and conduct. And what more, she was in close communion with the departed fathers of the clan whose bodies had been committed to earth."[120] He concludes that "[i]t seems logical that a society that views its female members as inferior beings would not represent their most powerful deity as being a woman."[121] To some extent Ahmed is right, especially with the deep veneration accorded to *Ani* and the idea that 'mother is supreme' among Igbo people. From a broader perspective, and owing to the reality of how women are abused and oppressed in Igbo land, and especially in the unfortunate case of infertility, his argument becomes faulty.

On that note, I disagree with Ahmed, because when *Ani* refuses to yield harvest for the farms, Igbo people are never angry with *Ani*. Just in the same way they are never angry with *Igwe* (*Ani*'s husband and the god of rain and thunder) when it does not rain. Rather, they blame themselves, believing that someone must have annoyed *Ani*, and thereby looking for a way to pacify *Ani*. When a woman is unable to procreate, abuse and anger await her from the same society that venerates *Ani*.

---

118. Hiatt, "Role of Women."
119. Hiatt, "Role of Women."
120. Hiatt, "Role of Women."
121. Hiatt, "Role of Women."

SOCIAL AND MORAL UNDERSTANDING OF OFO-NA-OGU (THE IGBO SYMBOL OF JUSTICE)

The yearning for justice through the Igbo symbols of *ofo-na-ogu* is also a cultural value through which the ethic of *onye aghala nwanne ya* is sustained. Justice is a substratum on which Igbo values are built. Igbo prayers, greetings and wishes all tilt toward the "Igbo dual concept of justice and moral probity, *ofo-na-ogu*."[122] To work toward a perfect society, the rule of equity which manifests itself in social justice is the bed rock in the formulations of Igbo moral norms. The rule of equity "ensures that no one person or group of persons acquires too much control over the life of others."[123] This sense of justice finds a better expression in Stephen Mott's reference to John Rawls' theory of justice. Rawls' understanding is that "Justice provides the standard by which the benefits and burdens of living together in society are distributed. It regulates from an ethical as well as a legal and customary standpoint the apportioning of wealth, income, punishments, rewards, authority, liberties, rights, duties, advantages and opportunities."[124] This egalitarian principle is evident in the Igbo proverb which says: "Egbe bere ugo bere, Nke si ibe ya ebela nke (sic) kwa ya" which literally means, "Let the kite perch and let the eagle perch, whichever tries to prevent the other from perching, let its wing break."[125] This is a philosophy of tolerance and inclusiveness where no one should deprive the other of the comforts of life. This sense of social justice is in conformity with Anthony Appiah's sense of cosmopolitanism: "One truth we hold to, however, is that every human being has obligations to every other. Everybody matters: that is our central idea."[126] This idea of enough space available for everyone to operate is the core value of the Igbo norms of justice and sharing.

This sense of justice can still be understood in the proverb: "Nwata kwo aka ya, osoru okenye rie nri!" which means, "A young person can eat with elders, if he/she washes his/her hands!"[127] This depicts that with equal opportunity and fair play given to everyone in society, one can reach one's highest goal in life. A child can attain success and be raised to

---

122. Okorocha, *Meaning of Religious Conversion*, 95.
123. Uchendu, *Igbo of Southeast Nigeria*, 18.
124. Rawls, *A theory of Justice*, 4, 62, 259, as cited in Mott, *Biblical Ethics*, 78.
125. Amaechi, "Religion in the Political Culture."
126. Appiah, *Cosmopolitanism*, 144.
127. Igbo Contact Forum, "Igbo Idiom."

the pinnacle of exultation. However, there is a caveat here. Despite this sense of social justice and of the child's ability to ascend to the table of elders, there is respect for elders, and there are distinctions of age, sex, and wealth. However, with hard work, one can move from one's social ladder to another level. The emphasis here is on achievement based on social justice, in the understanding of egalitarianism.

In the cultural context of *ofo na ogu*, the Igbo people believe in a flourishing and a viable life hinged upon justice and moral probity. *Ofo-na-ogu* is the source of true life.[128] In trying to understand Igbo social justice, the true meaning of the symbol of justice is worth considering:

> The Igbo traditional *ofo* stick is made out of a small branch of a tree the same name—the *Detarium Senegalense*. The tree itself is a rare but has one significant feature: the branches when old and dried pluck themselves off the parent trunk without rotting. Consequently, they are thought to live forever. The branches of this tree are tough and the whole tree is held to be sacred. An *ofo* tree is never cut . . . *Chineke* (God the creator) created the *ofo* tree specially and that the natural shedding of the branches (without decay) is symbolic both of the natural proliferation and "pruning" of families in old age and of the continuity of life and after death. The *ofo* stick fashioned out of these fallen branches of the parent tree is an ancestral staff, emblem of authority, and the traditional symbol of justice and truth.[129]

We can see that *ofo* symbolizes many things in Igbo world: a symbol of worship, a symbol of justice, a symbol of unity, a symbol of truth and honesty, and above all a symbol of a sense of connection with God and the ancestors. These symbols portray how members of the Igbo culture are supposed to care for one another—*onye aghala nwanne ya*

Onye aghala nwanne ya is thus manifested in sacred symbols, where Igbo people communicate their unity both in the physical world and in the spirit world. "The *ofo* staff is believed to embody within itself the spirit and ethos of the ancestors and is at once the emblem of unity, verity and sanctity as well as the perpetuity of the family or group possessing it."[130] The aim of an average Igbo family is unity for all her members, perpetuity through procreation, and veneration of sacred institutions so

---

128. Okorocha, *Meaning of Religious Conversion*, 95.
129. Okorocha, *Meaning of Religious Conversion*, 96.
130. Okorocha, *Meaning of Religious Conversion*, 97.

as to appease the ancestors and the deities. With this, the maintenance of cosmic balance is paramount to all.

Having known the Igbo world-view, and its perception about gender and procreation, we are going to critically evaluate the condition of infertility, referred to as the "massive iceberg hiding beneath calm waters."[131] The next chapter will explore the scourging effects of infertility and investigate the medical and technological solutions to infertility in the 'technological world' and in a traditional African society. The reason for this is to see how infertility is tackled from different perspectives. To demonstrate the effect of infertility in marriage, this chapter will also explore the essence of marriage and the rigorous marriage procedure in Igbo culture, using Awo-Omamma in Imo State as a case study.[132] Further, in the rituals preceding marriage and within the marriage rite itself, one can clearly see another essence of marriage, whereby failure to attain any children brings much discomfort.

---

131. Schover and Thomas, *Overcoming Male Infertility*, 5.
132. Okoro, "Christian Marriage and Divorce," 16.

2

Infertility
A Problem among Igbo Couples

INTRODUCTION

THIS CHAPTER DESCRIBES THE extraordinary expectations and sacrifices imposed by infertility in an Igbo world in which indigenous forces subordinate infertile couples. Most severely, within this subordination, "women's social value will rest upon their serviceability in a male-dominated space."[1] Within this Igbo world, folklore and many other arts depict the thinking of the day. The following ancient poem is an embodiment of the mind-set and the dominant ideology of an average traditional Igbo woman about being a wife.

> Be you as beautiful as a mermaid, the beauty
> of a woman is to have a husband.
> Be you one who has been to the land of white people,
> the beauty of a woman is to have a husband.
> If a woman does not marry, her beauty declines.
> One who is beautiful is best to be in her husband's house.
> When you get to your husband's house, have
> a baby.
> After you look after the child, the child will
> look after you.[2]

---

1. Emecheta, *The Joys of Motherhood*, 1.
2. Amadiume, *Male Daughters, Female Husbands*, 72.

In the biblical injunction of *Shema Yisrael* "Hear, O Israel!" (Deuteronomy 6:4), parents are expected to diligently teach about the monotheistic nature of God, socialize their children into it, and repeatedly teach it to them and have them recite it in season and out of season. In the same pattern, Igbo parents recite wifehood to their daughters, and talk of it to them "when you sit in your house and when you walk by the way and when you lie down and when you rise up."[3]

The poem celebrates the essence of wifehood, underscoring the significance of fertility. This implies that infertility, or the inability to have a baby, is like a ship wreck for the woman and her family. "Childlessness is a personal disgrace. It is also felt as a kind of slur on the community, a social fault, and it often leads to divorce or polygamy."[4] It is equally a thing of shame for the man and his family as virility is a sign of prowess and wholeness.

As part of the comparative methodology of this book, this chapter will look at a Western (particularly Euro-American) perception of infertility, how it reacts to it, and some of the technologies advanced in providing some solutions to infertility, considered against an African/Igbo perception of infertility. The points of comparison are multiple. There is a similarity in the experience of infertility between Africans and people in the West, particularly, Euro-Americans. There is dissimilarity in the reactions of both cultures to infertility, and the different means they use to navigate the problem of infertility. For African culture, I am paying particular attention to Igbo culture. My specific comparative analysis is related to the Euro-American culture and their understanding, perception, and reaction to cases of infertility.

GENERAL OVERVIEW OF INFERTILITY

The World Health Organization (WHO), a leading global organization which focuses on health issues, provides six definitions of infertility. These include clinical, demographic epidemiological, "infertility as a disability," primary, and secondary infertility.[5] For example, a clinical definition of infertility focuses on a medical and a reproductive definition. The

---

3. See Deut 6:7; the essence here is the semblance of communication pattern which shows the importance of the message.

4. Bujo, *African Theology*, 116.

5. For more, see WHO, "Infertility Definitions and Terminology."

medical definition identifies infertility as "a disease," while the reproductive definition includes both female and male: "Infertility is the inability of a sexually active, non-contracepting couple to achieve pregnancy in one year. The male partner can be evaluated for infertility or subfertility using a variety of clinical interventions, and also from a laboratory evaluation of semen."[6] For this study, infertility is to be understood as "a medical diagnosis that can be made when a couple has been having unprotected intercourse for a year or more without conceiving a child."[7]

In traditional Igbo society, this definition is tenable. It is particularly so for the experiences of Efuru in her two marriages from the novel *Efuru* mentioned in the "Introduction" of this book. When pregnancy did not occur, "Efuru was very worried in her second year of her marriage."[8] This was the same in her second marriage, when she married Gilbert, "two years passed and Efuru was still not pregnant. Her mother-in-law could bear it no longer and so she called her one day to her bedroom. 'My daughter, doesn't your body tell you anything?'"[9] This means that when pregnancy does not occur within the first year of marriage with continuous unprotected sex, then a case of infertility is to be suspected.

Infertility here is not only limited to women, males are included. This is important because studies in the United States (and as we shall see later, in Igboland) show that ". . . about 40 percent of couples with infertility have a problem solely with the male partner. Another 20 percent of couples struggle with infertility problems on both the male and female sides. Only the remaining 40 percent of infertile couples have an exclusively female problem."[10]

From ancient times, and particularly from the biblical tradition, infertility was negatively viewed as a punishment from God. Women, who were the most affected by this "punishment," bore the blame of it, either by resigning to their fate or to the shame of the blame, until the day they were able to conceive.[11] John Byron, a New Testament scholar, writes,

6. WHO, *WHO Laboratory Manual*, as sited in WHO, "Infertility Definitions and Terminology."

7. Best, *Fearfully and Wonderfully*, 264. The above definition is the standard one used by many authors. For more, see WHO, "Infertility Definitions and Terminology."

8. Nwapa, *Efuru*, 24.

9. Nwapa, *Efuru*, 141.

10. Schover and Thomas, *Overcoming Male Infertility*, 5.

11. As there were infertile couples during biblical times, in some cases men must have been responsible for some couples' childlessness, just as they are today. The story

"Childlessness, in the Hebrew Bible, is presented as a particularly female problem. There are no biblical stories that center on an infertile man."[12] No medical treatment was recommended in the scripture as a solution to this "ailment." Since infertility was viewed during biblical times as a punishment, women who suffered it then felt, and even until today feel some sense of failure and anguish. This accounted for why the women who were victims lived in shame, and why some became jealous of those who could conceive. Others would even send their maids for sexual intercourse with their husband and bear children. The book of Genesis tells us that "[w]hen Rachel saw that she was not bearing Jacob any children, she became jealous of her sister. So she said to Jacob, "Give me children, or I'll die!" (Genesis 30:1).

On the other hand, the Biblical tradition is replete with the celebration of offspring, which confirms the understanding among Christians that "child-bearing is a good thing. It is not wrong to want to raise a family with your spouse. Christians believe that children are a gift from God."[13] Megan Best goes on to support this argument with Psalm 127:3–5, which says, "Children are a heritage from the Lord, offspring a reward from him. Like arrows in the hands of a warrior are children born in one's youth. Blessed is the man whose quiver is full of them." God designated child-bearing as a thing of joy and blessing when He promised and said to Abraham: "I will surely bless you and make your descendants as numerous as the stars in the sky and as the sand on the seashore" (Genesis 22:17). In juxtaposition with infertility, Megan Best further notes that Deuteronomy chapter 28 "presents the opposite of infertility as not just barrenness, but also a mayhem and exile. The passage anticipates the sacking of Jerusalem and the Babylonian exile in 587 BC, prophesying cursed offspring (v.18) and exile with loss of children."[14] Infertility is like a ship-wreck, and a calamity of monumental proportion.

Certainly, humans in our modern times have continued to have a penchant for having their own biological children, as that offers them a sense of wellness and a feeling of being whole. This, they try to achieve through modern medical technologies when the reproductive process of conceiving fails. Modern medical technologies have alleviated some of

---

of Abraham and Sarah could be a case in point. See Gen 15–18.

12. Byron, "Infertility and the Bible."
13. Best, *Fearfully and Wonderfully*, 266.
14. Best, *Fearfully and Wonderfully*, 266.

the anguish that is associated with infertility problems. With these technologies, couples can have children of their own, either in or out of the womb. In Vitro Fertilization (IVF) is one of the Assisted Reproductive Technologies (ART) that has brought this relief. However, in-as-much as the use of medical technology for "curing" infertility has great positive values; its end has raised many ethical questions, which we consider later. In the meantime, we consider the general effects of infertility and the implications in an Igbo family setting.

GENERAL EFFECTS OF INFERTILITY

There is almost always a high degree of joy when a new child is born. As Shuman and Volck write, "[w]elcoming children is a good thing. Wanting one's own children is part of the human experience."[15] On the other hand, infertility is nearly never a desirable situation. To some extent, infertility challenges a dominant feature of the Christian theology of incarnation. If God can come in the form of a baby, then, having a baby in a marital relationship is most desirable. Megan Best describes it this way, "Married Christian couples usually just assume they will have children, they do not anticipate any problems, because they have never tried to have a child before. If conception becomes difficult, they then realize they have no control over what happens."[16] When this happens, couples "don't sleep well and sexual intimacy starts to suffer."[17] In the long run, they begin to be traumatized. This can help us understand the anguish of infertile couples. There is anguish because "God made us as sexual creatures designed our sexual proclivities to be expressed in a loving marriage relationship, and established conception and childbearing as the ordinary fruit of the marital union."[18]

When couples fail to reach this goal, this evokes a sense of emptiness, because the urge to bear children in a marital relationship is a force that is innate in human beings. In some cases, this sense of emptiness comes because of the pressure from the socially constructed expectations of begetting children by couples. When couples go through the emotional pain of infertility, it is natural and a normal response to that innate

15. Shuman and Volck, *Reclaiming the Body*, 89.
16. Best, *Fearfully and Wonderfully*, 263.
17. Best, *Fearfully and Wonderfully*, 263.
18. VanDrunen, *Bioethics and the Christian Life*, 119.

desire to procreate. For some, this leaves them in a state of emptiness and sorrow, with a lack of self-esteem, and a lack of wholeness. Humans may try to fill this sense of void through ART like IVF.[19]

Because of this urge and near desperation to have one's own biological child, a great deal of money is spent on ART. In America, for example, the desperation among some couples to have their own biological children is not hard to find as "[r]ecent statistics about the number of people pursuing infertility treatment and the costs incurred annually are rather staggering."[20] In monetary terms, "[a] single round of in vitro fertilization (IVF) (which frequently does not result in a successful pregnancy) costs more than twelve thousand dollars."[21]

Apart from the monetary implication and expenditure, Best acknowledges that IVF medical technology takes another toll on the couple.

> In some ways, the advent of assisted reproductive technology (ART), such as In Vitro Fertilization (IVF), has increased the anguish of infertile couples. The availability of these therapies forces them to decide if they want to take on the burden of treatment, and it can prolong the struggle for years.[22]

In this case, modern reproductive technology looks like a double-edged sword. When it is successful, it has led families to be happy. But instances of its failure to work, and other ethical implications surrounding it, have led both to anger and to passion-soaked ethical debates.

In the Igbo context, the situation is not different in terms of being a double-edged sword. First, Igbo people love children, and an Igbo proverb shows why there is acceptance of a child conceived through IVF. This proverb summarizes the acceptance of such a child *Ebe nwa si lo uwa, ya hiri*, (some other dialects will say, *ebe nwa si bia uwa ya biri*) which literally means, however a child is conceived or came into existence, let the child live. This is because of Igbo people's love for children and because coming into existence is not the child's doing. The child should live, as he/she has a right to life. On the other hand, children conceived through

---

19. The first of its kind was witnessed in Nigeria on the February 11, 1998 with the birth of baby Hannatu Kupchi. Her birth has remained something of great joy that the hospital management says "Every year at Nisa, we never fail to celebrate this day because it marked the beginning of a new era for us. Subsequently, over 2000 IVF babies have since been borne." Nisa Hospital, "First IVF Baby in Nigeria."

20. VanDrunen, *Bioethics and the Christian Life*, 120.

21. VanDrunen, *Bioethics and the Christian Life*, 127.

22. Best, *Fearfully and Wonderfully*, 264.

IVF are almost classified as children who are adopted, or children from a female-husband marriage, as we will see in the later part of this chapter. Research conducted by Nneka Okafor brings out this point succinctly. Okafor and her study team "found that IVF is perceived as very expensive, unnatural, and not cultural. Children conceived through this method are equally regarded as abnormal or inferior to those conceived naturally."[23] The question of legitimacy comes out strongly. We see more of this in the following subsection.

MODERN TECHNOLOGICAL SOLUTIONS TO INFERTILITY

ART is an aid to the human procreation process. It "includes all techniques involving the direct manipulation of human eggs, sperm and embryos outside of the body."[24] The first and still most common form of ART is IVF.

Historically, "IVF has been with us since the birth in 1978 of Louise Brown, the first child born alive who was conceived in a petri dish or *in vitro* (Latin for 'in glass')."[25] As a definition, IVF is "[a] procedure in which eggs, matured through the use of fertility medications, are laparoscopically removed from a woman and mixed with sperm from a man, and the resulting embryo(s) is/are placed into the woman's uterus through the cervix."[26]

With this procedure, couples are capable of experiencing pregnancy and child-birth, and so have their own biological children, which will bring joy to their families who were previously in anguish because of infertility. This process allows couples to choose which embryo to implant in the womb of the woman (probably the one with little or no adverse health conditions), which embryos to possibly donate to couples in need and those to be destroyed.

Because infertility can lead to emotional stress, anguish and even divorce, IVF medical technology has saved marriages from distress and divorce. Because of IVF, couples who long for a binding force in marriage through having a biological child can comfortably have one. IVF

---

23. Okafor et al., "Perceptions of Infertility," 64–65.
24. Best, *Fearfully and Wonderfully*, 325.
25. Lysaught, "Assisted Reproductive Technologies," 846.
26. Rae, *Outside the Womb*, 26.

has demonstrated that humanity is still in the process of adopting new inventions that continue daily to express humanity's inventive skills and creative vision. It shows that human beings, through their inherent power of creativity, have widened the frontier of knowledge.

With the wave of new medical technologies, Christian scientists, ethicists and couples are learning to draw ethical boundaries in the field of reproductive medicine. John Brown,[27] one of the first beneficiaries of IVF, sees it "as merely 'helping nature along a bit.'"[28] Joseph Fletcher shares the same view, as he sees ART as a noble venture:

> Laboratory reproduction is radically human compared to conception by ordinary heterosexual intercourse. It is willed, chosen, purposed and controlled, and surely those are among the traits that distinguish Homo sapiens from others in the animal genus, from the primates down.[29]

One can agree with the above proposition that medical technology has really improved human lives. It has alleviated some of the anguish that follows infertility problems. Although with IVF medical technology couples are capable of experiencing pregnancy and having their own biological children, the destruction of embryos in the process has ethical implications which sometimes call into question the morality of IVF.

It must be noted that ". . . some of these procedures are not yet widely available in Africa or are prohibitively expensive, others are becoming available."[30] Despite being expensive, another African problem is the acceptability of IVF medical procedure; this is because of the question of legitimacy of children born through IVF. There are traditional solutions to the problem of infertility. We will see more of this in the subsequent sections.

Ethical Implications in the Use of Modern Medical Technology

There is no denying that there are good uses of medical technology. Modern medicine is a gift from God. Human wisdom and ingenuity, too, are gifts from God. Employing medical technology can honor life and allow people to be stewards of God's gifts. However, appropriate use of medical

27. John Brown is the father of Louise Brown, the first baby born through IVF.
28. Pence, *Medical Ethics*, 99.
29. Fletcher, " Ethical Aspects," 776.
30. Kunhiyop, *African Christian Ethics*, 204.

Infertility

technology for the beginning and improvement of human life and lifestyle has remained contentious for various reasons. One of the reasons for the contentious debate, in the case of IVF, is that an embryo, which in some ethical/religious traditions is considered life, may be destroyed:

> If more than three fertilized eggs are transferred at once, the likelihood of multiple pregnancies dramatically increases, which proportionately increases the likelihood of fetal loss and premature birth, with all its attendant costs. Moreover, multiple pregnancies can lead to selective termination, in which one or more fetuses are destroyed to improve the odds of successful development for the remaining fetuses or to reduce the risks to the woman, who cannot safely carry all of the fetuses.[31]

Life, in almost all civilizations and cultures, is considered sacred. The discarding or destruction of embryos remains a huge ethical problem. For the Roman Catholic Church, which protects and "witnesses to the sanctity of life 'from the moment of conception until death,'"[32] and some evangelical churches, who consider the embryo as human life, its destruction becomes an intrinsic evil.

Destruction of embryos is enabled because of the financial burden of IVF. In the process of using this medical technology, more than one ovum is fertilized, multiple embryos are created, and some weaker ones are discarded to give room for the greater possibility of the survival of other embryos. Considered as living beings, when embryos are destroyed, they suffer a loss of life which contravenes ethics of the sanctity of life. In the above-mentioned Roman Catholic and Evangelical traditions, every human life is intrinsically good and must be upheld. Upholding human life at every stage (embryonic stage to adulthood) will make humans attentive to their common destiny. Richard Stith puts it well when he writes, "... the sanctity of life grants us an appreciation of the dignity and meaning of human condition which we could not otherwise have."[33] In the light of this, the selection and subsequent destruction of embryos will be morally not acceptable.

It might be argued, however, that the early analysis of the embryo and subsequent disposal of 'surplus' ones, since it is evident that "about

---

31. Panicola et al., *Health Care Ethics*, 160.

32. John Paul II, "Address of October 29, 1983," 390, as cited in United States Conference Of Catholic Bishops, *Ethical and Religious Directives*, 20.

33. Stith, "Toward Freedom from Value," 742.

90% of IVF couples choose to discard surplus frozen embryos"[34] would be a relief from eventual abortion of a developing fetus. It can be argued on the other side that if an embryo is considered as life, making a distinction between values of life at its different stages is a discrimination against life itself.[35] Striking a balance and coming out with a sound ethical principle with best human values becomes the best option. The aspect of "human value" is important, because "[m]edical ethics deals with human values whenever and wherever they intersect with medical knowledge and technology."[36] Though IVF innovation looks good, it comes with its troubling ethical baggage, making humans look like commodities to be manipulated.

Furthermore, the use of modern medical technologies raises an ethical question as to whether it is morally acceptable to use everything that is technologically possible to produce a new life in the reproductive process. Where should humans, as mortal beings, draw the line on what is morally acceptable in the exercise of their creative knowhow?

Despite the joy IVF has brought to couples, it still raises ethical questions and principles. Should one have biological children by all means? Is every scientific research, path and every outcome which is scientifically possible and successful, morally right too? Should life be an object of experimentation? Does extensive experimentation with medical technology look like placing "the life and identity of the embryo into the power of doctors and biologists and establishes the domination of technology over the origin and destiny of the human person?[37] Are there no other ways to have contentment in a marital relationship without biological children? Do we not have happily-married childless couples who have used their resources to better the lives of children around the world? What are the appropriate principles that can be used to make decisions in situations of infertility?

Another ethical concern with technology is Pre-implantation Genetic Diagnosis (PGD).[38] With this, humans can now decide what kind of human beings they want. In this procedure, babies are considered

---

34. R. Browne et al., "Embryo Donation," 127–29, as cited in Best, *Fearfully and Wonderfully*, 407.

35. Van der Poel, *Ethical Principles*, 47.

36. Van der Poel, *Ethical Principles*, vii.

37. Congregation for the Doctrine of the Faith, *Donum Vitae*, II, 5, as cited in *Catechism of the Catholic Church*, 571.

38. Best, *Fearfully and Wonderfully*, 378.

as products which parents "customize," and aim at producing special characteristics in the babies and abolishing the coming into existence of certain kinds of human beings. Charles Curran, a noted Catholic theologian, writes, "[t]here is the definite possibility that in the future, and to some extent even now, we can eliminate deleterious genes from the human gene pool, and add desirable genes which will improve human individuals and the human species."[39] Humans have become real "manufacturers" of fellow human beings, and can technologically interfere in evolutionary development to "better" the human species.

Analysis of the general ethical implications of IVF is important, because it will help to weigh the enormity of the problems associated with infertility in Igbo land when we begin to evolve some kind of sociocultural construct to bring relief to infertile couples. To have a better picture of infertility in Igbo land will require the assessment of a broad picture of infertility.

ASSESSING INFERTILITY IN IGBO LAND AND ITS TREATMENT

From a clinical perspective, obstetricians and gynecologists notably Odidika Umeora and Gabriel.Igberase have adduced the following as major contributors of infertility among Igbo people: illegal abortion, poor treatment of sexually transmitted diseases, age before marriage, men's ego and failure to seek medical help, and the presence of spiritualists and unorthodox practices.

Infertility has been compounded by men living in self-denial in accepting their reproductive challenges. Research conducted at the University Teaching Hospital of Calabar in South-South Nigeria shows that "[t]he male partner of infertile marriages in Nigeria now recognizes that he could be the source of the problem. It is generally accepted that about 30–50% of infertility is due to the male causes, with female causes accounting for 50–70%."[40] With this staggering reality, one can ask why Igbo men are still living in self-denial. These statistics pointedly speak to Igbo men and culture, bringing to light their own contradictions, especially in blaming women for infertility in their marriage.

---

39. Curran, *Issues in Sexual and Medical Ethics*, 103.
40. Ekwere et al., "Infertility among Nigerian Couples, 35–36.

For clarity, we can make a distinction between primary and secondary infertility. Primary infertility is used to designate "a couple that has never been able to conceive a pregnancy after a minimum of 1 year of attempting to do so through unprotected intercourse."[41] In the case of primary infertility, the couple "has never" conceived, as against secondary infertility which is a failure in conception after one or more pregnancies.

The research of gynecologist Umeora,[42] shows that "[i]nfertile women are believed by the men to have lived unhealthy past with repeated cases of abortions and sexually transmitted diseases precipitating their current condition."[43] The case of Ogochukwu (not her real name), whom I encountered in pastoral ministry, is a clear example. She was a very pretty girl of light skin, but because of her inability to conceive she was called all sort of names. That she was extremely pretty made her a suspect of being an *ogbanje*.[44] Her mother in-law once called her "a man," and another woman in the extended family called her a "mermaid spirit."[45] Odidika describes a childless woman was once referred to by her mother in-law as a "worthless man in a female body."[46] To be childless is a huge cross to carry within the Igbo world.

---

41. Medline Plus, "Primary Infertility."

42. Umeora is a Professor of Obstetrics and Gynaecology at the Department of Obstetrics and Gynaecology at Ebonyi State University Teaching Hospital. He did extensive research on the plight of infertile women and the psychological trauma they pass through. See Umeora, "Dr. Odidika Ugochukwu Joannes Umeora."

43. Umeora and Obu, "Cultural Misconceptions," 5.

44. An *Ogbanje* especially *Ogbanje mmiri* is believed to be married in the spirit world to an aquatic spouse. Their physical characteristic is their comeliness and excessive beauty. This water spouse is always seen to be jealous. One of the ways for the water spouse to show his jealousy and disapproval of her marriage in the physical world is to make the woman not to beget children. This surely will cause a lot of pain to the woman and her husband in the physical world. See Okoro, "The concept of Ogbanje." Above all, *Ogbanjes* are also said to "have river spouses who intervene when the Ogbanje marries. They disrupt the marriage harmony." Achebe, *Healing and Exorcism*. 31.

45. Girls who are referred to as mermaid spirits are believed to have a husband in the spirit world. Their sea spirit husband sends them to the world to torment their human husband, first by not begetting children and eventually killing their human husband. See Amadi, *The Concubine*.

46. Umeora et al., "Cultural Misconceptions," 4.

CAUSES OF INFERTILITY IN IGBO LAND

There are factors that one cannot change about infertility. One such factor is that a person may have been born that way. This could either be a natural or a medical condition. As a natural condition, this will fall within WHO's category of "epidemiological definition of infertility."[47] Infertility, as a medical condition, is defined and classified by WHO as "infertility as a disability."[48] Regardless of being a natural or a medical condition, the Igbo worldview has an explanation for whatever happens. Anything that happens has a reason, and often has a spiritual connotation. Part of the explanation that will be given to a person with such a natural condition will be the Igbo belief in reincarnation, spiritual marriage, witchcraft, nemesis, or a vocational calling to be a priestess. There are many medical, spiritual and cultural reasons why infertility is rife in Igbo land. We now look at the causes of male and female infertility in Igbo land.

Unsafe Abortions

Researchers Abubakar Panti and Sununu Yusuf have identified unsafe abortion as one of the prime causes of infertility in sub-Saharan Africa in general, and in Nigeria in particular. Referring to the findings of Idris Audu, they affirm that the major cause of infertility "has been attributed to high rate of sexually transmitted diseases, complications of unsafe abortions, and puerperal pelvic infections."[49] This is so because of Nigeria's legislation on abortion. The abortion debate, with its numerous intrigues, always has controversies trailing it. The debate has remained complex, and to have a full grasp of its arguments, one must have knowledge of philosophy, biology, ethics, law, moral logic theory, women's studies, sociology and theology.

In Nigeria, not much conversation is heard about this topic, because it is treated as almost a "closed chapter." Abortion is not only illegal in Nigeria, but has stringent and draconian laws formulated around it. The Nigerian penal code prescribes punishments for abortion thus:

---

47. WHO, "Infertility Definitions and Terminology."
48. WHO, "Infertility Definitions and Terminology."
49. Audu, "Infertility," 333–43, as cited in Panti and Yusuf, "The Profile of Infertility."

228. Any person who, with intent to procure miscarriage of a woman whether she is or is not with child, unlawfully administers to her or causes her to take any poison or other noxious thing, or uses any force of any kind, or uses any other means whatever, is guilty of a felony, and is liable to imprisonment for fourteen years.

229. Any woman who, with intent to procure her own miscarriage, whether she is or is not with child, unlawfully administers to herself any poison or other noxious thing, or uses any force of any kind, or uses any other means whatever, or permits any such thing or means to be administered or used to her, is guilty of a felony, and is liable to imprisonment for seven years.

230. Any person who unlawfully supplies to or procures for any person anything whatever, knowing that it is intended to be unlawfully used to procure the miscarriage of a woman, whether she is or is not with child, is guilty of a felony, and is liable to imprisonment for three years.[50]

Since it is illegal, clandestine abortion is common-place which comes with a huge price seen in the fatal effects of unsafe abortions. When young women resort to clandestine abortions, the consequences include the complications and the negative effects it has on the reproductive life of the patient including the greater possibility of infertility in the future. On the side of men, fear of the after-effects of abortion, including the possible death of the woman, puts the man responsible for the pregnancy under pressure and trauma, as the knowledge of abortion will bring a lot of shame to him and his family. Clandestine abortion is always rife where abortion is illegal, and Nigeria has remained a case-in-point.

Poorly-Treated Pelvic Inflammatory Disease

Umeora's research[51] shows that in Igbo land, because of a lack of motivation for a doctor's visit, or clinical consultation, and because of poverty, there is a high prevalence of poorly-treated pelvic inflammatory disease, intra-peritoneal abscesses, and overwhelming sepsis,[52] which all have

50. National Assembly of Nigeria, "Chapter 21 Offences against Morality."
51. Umeora et al., "Cultural Misconceptions," 1–2.
52. These are diseases that induce infertility. "Peritonitis is defined as an inflammation of the serosal membrane that lines the abdominal cavity and the organs contained therein. The peritoneum, which is an otherwise sterile environment, reacts to various pathologic stimuli with a fairly uniform inflammatory response." Medscape,

Infertility

remained significant factors in the causes of infertility. Umeora notes, "tubal factors remain the commonest etiological issue in infertility in sub-Saharan Africa."[53] When these illnesses are not adequately treated, infertility often becomes the huge price paid.

There is infertility among Igbo men too, though they are almost always reluctant to accept it. Men's infertility is chiefly associated with an abnormality of semen volume, or "due to poor semen parameters."[54] Men's refusal to subject themselves to medical evaluation is another factor in infertility. They refuse such evaluation because they think it is always the woman's problem. They fear the stigmatization that is connected with sterility. The most common causes of infertility in men are low motility, oligospermia (low sperm count), azoospermia, (lack of sperm in the semen) and asthenospermia (decreased mobility of spermatozoa) semen parameter abnormality.[55]

Ignorance about Infertility

Infertility ignorance, poverty, and the unavailability or inaccessibility of medical institutions are other contributors to infertility in Igboland. Umeora's study team writes that "[i]lliteracy is rife in most communities in Southeast Nigeria. Medical knowledge is abysmal. Diseases and disease processes are interpreted variously to suit the different fora and situations. Many notions exist as to the etiopathogenesis of infertility."[56] With these different notions, people do not seek medical help on reproductive problems. Sometimes people think they have been bewitched, and so blame their reproductive problems on enemies. Instead of consulting with orthodox medical experts, they consult "herbalists, traditionalists and spiritualists in search of needed reprieve and solution."[57] These consultations most often end up complicating an already precarious situation with continued difficulty in conceiving children.

"Peritonitis and Abdominal Sepsis."
    53. Umeora et al., "Cultural Misconceptions," 5.
    54. Panti and Yusuf, "The Profile of Infertility," 7.
    55. Panti and Yusuf, "The Profile of Infertility," 10.
    56. Umeora et al., "Cultural Misconceptions," 1.
    57. Umeora et al., "Cultural Misconceptions," 2.

Consultation and Manipulation by Unorthodox Practitioners

Consultation with "herbalists, traditionalists and spiritualists" is often complex and pain-inflicting, since they have their own "etiopathogenic explanation." In a pattern very peculiar to them, "[t]hey make medical assumptions and diagnosis without clinical or diagnostic aids."[58] They give reasons for a woman's reproductive problem other than medical ones, such as linking it to "punishment for a social misdemeanor or attributed to other factors including witchcraft and the disaffection of one's ancestors."[59] A spiritualist once told a patient with a reproductive problem that "your problem is not your fault, but your mother annoyed some people before she delivered you and those people are now attacking you through witchcraft to make your mother unhappy. They have blocked your womb and kidneys."[60] In another instance, this explanation from a traditionalist is stunning: "[t]he fibroid you have is as a result of old and dirty blood you got when you were meeting various men in the past. This has now blocked your Fallopian tube and you cannot get pregnant unless I remove it."[61]

This is even worse because the female is blamed for her reproductive problem. That the traditionalist made medical assumptions and diagnoses without elaborate and verifiable medical or laboratory evaluation, and no physical examination or recourse to medical history, is the height of irresponsibility. Living with this kind of guilt surely complicates the woman's problem. Without seeking the attention of orthodox medicine, where laboratory results are verified, cases like this, which are numerous in Igbo land, contribute to the high level of infertility. Sometimes, too, wrong and poor diagnosis and prescriptions from orthodox medical practitioners have compounded the problems of infertility. This could be as a result of lack of sound ethical practice in the area of medicine and poorly equipped medical facilities in Igbo land.

Again, from the perspective of the ATR with a belief in reincarnation, "... misfortunes like physical or mental disabilities and irremediable bad character which would debar one from reincarnating are blamed on one's 'chi' received from God as punishment for one's conduct in the

---

58. Umeora et al., "Cultural Misconceptions," 5.
59. Panti and Yusuf, "The Profile of Infertility," 9.
60. Umeora et al., "Cultural Misconceptions," 3.
61. Umeora et al., "Cultural Misconceptions," 3.

previous or even those of his parents or relatives before he was born."[62] With this mind set, when a woman or a couple is unable to become pregnant, it could be concluded from this perspective that in their previous existence they were wicked to children, and as such punishment for their wickedness is to make them childless in this present existence.

The Age Factor

Age is another factor that leads to infertility in Igbo land, especially as marriage is often delayed. Such delays can arise because of economic considerations. Azubike Aliche and Stella Nwokeji write that the "[b]ride price has been blamed, often, for the late marriage among Igbo young men and women, in relation to other ethnic groups that have no place for bride price in the marriage process."[63] In Igbo land, a man is expected to start thinking of marriage when he has a job, and most often when he has a house of his own, even if his father has a big house. Better still, he should have the resources to cater for the expenses in the long process of marriage. This puts enormous pressure on him.[64]

With all these marriage requirements, young men delay marriage, marrying in their mid-thirties and early forties, and end up marrying women in their own age brackets. At these ages, clinical research shows that "[a] couple aged 30 with no infertility problems has an 80% chance of conceiving within 12 months; at 40, a 50% chance, at 45, a 10% chance."[65] Particularly for females, research result shows that "[b]y the time she is 40, a woman has only a few thousand eggs left. As the eggs age, they are harder to fertilize and less likely to produce healthy embryos. There is a drop in fertility and an increase in miscarriage rate . . ."[66]

As it is with the man, so too, it is with the woman in delaying marriage. Women can get married only when the men are ready, since the men are the ones expected to make the marriage proposal. Most often, before a young woman gets married in Igbo land, she has the hope of

62. Metuh, *Comparative Studies*, 260.

63. Aliche and Nwokeji, *The Culture Wars Within*, 15.

64. We are going to discuss in detail the laborious and expensive process of Igbo marriage in the later part of this chapter. We will see the list of what is to be bought and brought by a young man who is intending to marry in Appendixes 1 and 2. These are some of the factors that can cause marriage to be delayed.

65. Best, *Fearfully and Wonderfully*, 277.

66. Best, *Fearfully and Wonderfully*, 277.

having a university degree. Sometimes, with the intricacies surrounding the education system in Nigeria, she ends up graduating between the ages of 25 and 30, and by this time her fertility rate has begun to decline. As Megan Best writes, "a woman's fertility begins to decline at age 27. With regard to infertility there is only one message in the media: women are urged not to delay having children."[67]

The age factor has remained a significant challenge in Igbo culture, since there is always a public outrage at single motherhood. Culturally, women are not permitted to be mothers before marriage. On the part of the man, he is supposed to have some kind of economic stability before ever thinking of marriage. With this kind of cultural orientation and economic burden, marriage may be delayed, which affects the fertility of the newly-weds, because they marry at an age where they may be medically 'knocking at the door' of infertility.

TRADITIONAL SOLUTIONS TO INFERTILITY IN IGBO LAND

There is an Igbo proverb which says that *ihe ne enweghi ka esi emeya, ka esi emeya di adi* which means, when a problem seems not to have a solution, there is always a way of going around it. Theophilus Okere echoes this as he writes, "[t]he following Igbo proverb indeed aptly captures the local source of experiential and practical knowledge: *Nku di na mba na-eghere mba nri, The firewood in a particular context is good enough for the cooking in that environment.*"[68] This means that every culture and people have their own local ways to solve their particular problems. I agree with Okere, Njoku and Devisch that no culture, no matter how civilized and sophisticated it might claim to be, should arrogate to itself the monopoly of knowledge. They write that ". . . the glitter and efficiency of the cosmopolitan science and technology mediated and propagated by the West (or the North) in the last few centuries as the one-and-only valid about the one-and-only universe, may sometimes unduly veil the local roots, cultural origins, history, and limited epistemological assumptions of that very science production."[69] They argue that every "culture's

---

67. Best, *Fearfully and Wonderfully*, 270.
68. Okere et al., "All Knowledge," 276.
69. Okere et al., "All Knowledge," 275.

unique genius, and distinctive creativity"[70] become means through which people in that culture solve their own problems. Since infertility is a major problem in Igbo land that is hard to solve, there are some culture-based and traditional solutions that have been used to go around it.

'Women Marriages' or the 'Female Husband' Solution

One solution which is considered the lesser evil is 'women marriages,' or the 'female husband,' in which a woman marries another woman as a way of reducing or eliminating the pressure of childlessness. 'Women marriages' are the other side or extension of polygamy among Igbo people:

> While the traditional Ibos did not practice polyandry (a woman married to several men), they did accept woman-marriages—a woman marrying other women in order to establish her own household. Women who married other women were called 'female-husbands.'
>
> These marriages, for the most part, were not homosexual marriages. Ibo women married other women for several reasons. Some were barren women who married other women to bear children on their behalf. Others were older women who had lost all their children by death. The female-husbands adopted the children of their wives. Thus woman-marriage was a way childless women affirmed their value and secured their position in society.[71]

This practice was common during ancient times, and there are still pockets of it here and there in Igbo land. It solved the problem of infertility for the female husband with cultural pressure forcing women into this kind of practice. Since Igbo culture is shame-based, the Machiavellian principle of "the end justifies the means"[72] becomes the unspoken ethical principle most women use to arrive at such decisions. However, having arrived at any decision, especially, in bringing some kind of fulfillment to female husbands, there are ethical considerations.

---

70. Okere et al., "All Knowledge," 275.
71. Nnoromele, *The Way People Live*, 51.
72. Chadwick, *The Municipal Machiavelli*.

Ethical Implications of Women Marriages or Female Husbands

'Women marriages (female husbands)' reduces a woman to an object of another's ego and sense of fulfillment. Further, a woman engaged in this type of practice is at the mercy of lascivious and randy men in the neighborhood. The female husband gets an independent compound for her bride to stay in, and in most cases, different men acceptable to her attempt to beget children with her.[73] With that, she loses her sense of dignity and decency, since she is brought in as a children-bearing machine. In this way, it is morally unacceptable to use one evil to 'cure' another evil, especially among women themselves, who are yearning for emancipation. On the side of the man, while to some extent it constitutes an element of shame, on the other hand, men use it to boast of their sexual exploits as a sign of virility, valor and masculinity. This is at the detriment of the woman, who is sexually objectified. If the man is already married, his wife might even be blamed for his unfaithfulness. As Daniel Jordan Smith observes, "[m]arried women are in some ways complicit in enabling men's extramarital sexual behavior."[74] In most of these situations, the woman remains the victim.

Polygamy

Polygamy, and more particularly polygyny, involves a man having more than one woman as his wife. There are multiple reasons why men engage in such practice, including the traditional aim of polygyny:

> When a family is made up of several wives with their households, it means that in time of need there will always be someone around to help. This is corporate existence. For example, when one wife gives birth, there are other wives to nurse her and care for her other children during the time she is regaining her vitality. If one wife dies, there are others to take over the care of her children. In the case of sickness, other wives will fetch water from the river, cut firewood, cook and do other jobs for the family. If one wife is barren, others bear children for the family, so that the torch of life is not extinguished. Where peasant farming is the means of livelihood, the many children in a polygamous family are an economic asset—even if they also must eat plenty of food.[75]

---

73. Uchendu, *Igbo of Southeast Nigeria*, 50.
74. Smith, 2010 "Promiscuous Girls," 16.
75. Mbiti, *African Religions and Philosophy*, 139.

Having multiple wives has economic implications, affects the sexual satisfaction of the man, discourages women from being promiscuous, and aids in the situation of one of the women being barren. Polygyny confers respect to the man as a "manager" of a large household. It produces many hands to work on the farm since agricultural machines on the farms have been traditionally unusual and to some extent are still unaffordable today. Nnoromele, writes, "[t]raditional Ibo economy was based on subsistence farming, and each family's survival depended on how much it could produce on the farms. Polygamy assured that enough children would be born to help farm and sustain the family."[76] Above all, this type of marriage is a form of solution to childlessness in Igboland. With multiple women in a marriage setting, it gives a second or third wife a chance to bear more children for the man if the first is unable to bear children. As such, it is a kind of reprieve for childless women. Aylward Shorter summarizes the reasons for polygamy in Africa in a fine way:

> Ensures the bearing of many children so that the status and property may be passed on and the family may become extended in space and time . . . (polygamy) serves the prosperity and growth of the extended family and provides status and support for women in societies where they have no vocation other than marriage and the bearing of children to their husband's lineage . . . (Polygamy is) a way of catering for unsupported women in a society which does not tolerate the independent woman, . . . (and above all provides) a solution to a wife's infertility.[77]

With multiple wives, the problem of childlessness can be solved. What this does not take into account is any reproductive medical condition of the man. Again, as the Igbo proverb previously quoted says, "*Nku di na mba na-eghere mba nri, The firewood in a particular context is good enough for the cooking in that environment.*"[78] Every culture and its people always have their local means of tackling problems that seem to defy any solution. In this case, if the man is having a reproductive medical condition, he will certainly arrange for other men, most often from his family, to help him conceive children from his wives. He has to do this because failure to exhibit virility will be a sign of weakness, and this will constitute a dishonor for him.

76. Nnoromele, *The Way People Live*, 50.
77. Shorter, *African Culture*, 173.
78. Okere et al., "All Knowledge."

Ethical Implications of Polygamy

The ethical implications of polygamy are similar to those of female husbands. Here, women are at the beck and call of the man, and he can have them like property, just as he has yams in the barns. Also, it presumes that the woman is the cause of childlessness, and the only way to "cure" that is to get more wives. With other men helping an impotent man to beget children with his wives, this becomes a commodification of human beings. Thus, he sees his wives as his property, wherein he can give them out to others as he wishes because he wants to satisfy his own ego. In all, polygamy is morally unacceptable because it designates women as machines producing children, thus objectifying them instead of seeing them as humans.

The More Recent Solution of Adoption

There is no Igbo word for 'adoption.' Instead, there is only a description of the condition in which a child is brought to a family. Some Igbo people use the phrase "*ikuta nwa*" for this, while some use a more derogatory phrase "*izuta nwa*," which means "buying a child." The practice was abhorred, and still is to some extent, because the child adopted is always seen as a stranger since he/she does not share the same lineage with members of the large family.

There is a better understanding now, with married couples opting for adoption, and then through good nurture subduing any nature which might be a strange trait to the family of adoption. These traits (like stealing and madness which are highly dreaded in Igboland) may have been inherited by the adopted child from his/her biological parents. To a great extent, adoption is solving the problem of infertility in Igbo land, because "[a]doption serves as alternative option for infertility in marriage: In Igbo land where infertility and barrenness seem to blur the hope of having children in the family, it provides succor to the couples."[79] Despite this advantage of adoption, especially its ability to challenge the problem of infertility, it is not without its own ethical implications.

---

79. Nwaoga, "Socio-Religious Implications," 708.

Ethical Implications of Adoption

It is true that the word adoption is not in the Igbo lexicon, and it is true that children adopted are sometimes abused, since they are not entitled to a family inheritance. It is equally true that adoption has eased some tensions of infertility, because "when faced with infertility, many couples buy the idea of adoption because it saves the child and even the adoptive parents from physical or emotional trauma."[80] However, the abuse that emanates from it and its ethical implications are not hard to find.

Denial of inheritance is always a problem for adopted children to have to contend with. Like children born in the case of women marriages/female husbands, adopted children have no right to inheritance, and this injures their self-esteem and their feeling of acceptability in the family that adopted them. The issue of legitimacy is an important value for Igbo people, which as Nwaoga writes is viewed

> as evidence to paternal lineage which shows through generation to generation. The typical Igbo family is patrilineal. The implication of this is that the supreme authority that empowers entitlement to resources flows from the 'father figure' which is hereditary but restricted to only legitimate and truly biological sons of the father of the family. The bottom line is that in Igbo society, most people do not have regard for any child adopted by any family, and such adopted child is often regarded as 'bastard' and as such will not have right of inheritance. Adopted sons and daughters have no say in the village assembly and this is contrasting the freedom of expression.[81]

Furthermore, abuse can stem from a situation when the child behaves in an "abnormal" way, such as flouting family rules and values. In this case, he/she could be told to go and look for his/her real parents, because his/her life style is not in conformity with his/her adopted family's values. (It is dismaying that a child is held responsible for bringing himself/herself into his/her family of adoption). It is much easier to embarrass an adopted child in the community if he/she does not physically look like members of his/her adopted family. Most often, living in this kind of atmosphere, the child will suffer the loss of a supporting structure that would have enabled him/her to grow as a normal child. As a result of

---

80. Nwaoga, "Socio-Religious Implications," 708.
81. Nwaoga, "Socio-Religious Implications," 708–9.

this psychological tension, the child can suffer neglect or abuse; this often leads to the child withdrawing from others and thus becoming lonely.

However, Igbo people could be schooled on the biblical connotation of adoption, to make it more meaningful. While one can understand that the difficulties of infertility are not as easy as they may seem, counselling Igbo couples on the benefits of adoption of children could be the best route to take. Scripture may help us navigate through this. Ephesians 1:5 says, "Thus he chose us in Christ before the world was made to be holy and faultless before him in love, marking us out for himself beforehand, to be adopted sons, through Jesus Christ. Such was his purpose and good pleasure." If we are adopted into God's family, why should couples not adopt children who are not their biological children? Through adoption, our image of God can better be understood, since couples can adopt children from distant lands and nurture them well, as we are all adopted all over the world and nurtured by God. This understanding could help to eliminate the Igbo connotation of an adopted child as a "child that is bought."

THE GENERAL UNDERSTANDING OF MARRIAGE IN IGBO LAND

Having seen the traditional solutions proffered by Igbo people in cases of infertility, we shall now look into marriage, paying particular attention to its laborious nature, its resource-draining, and the general goal of marriage. The marriage process is laborious, because "no matter how the Igbo acquire a wife, the process of betrothing and marrying an Igbo girl is a long ceremonious one. It often takes years and is seldom accomplished in months."[82] This long process of negotiating marriage will help in understanding why infertility is considered a monumental tragedy in marriage. Furthermore, its importance can be seen from the way Igbo boys and girls are socialized in Igbo society.

Starting more than a century ago, and up till today, one will notice that "[f]rom the time that boys and girls are capable of thinking for themselves, marriage is set before them as the one object to be attained. During the earlier years, it does not assume a serious aspect, but question any boy or girl, and the answer is certain to be that, in due course, they must marry."[83] This penchant for marriage is in part a result of how people of

---

82. Uchendu, *Igbo of Southeast Nigeria*, 51.
83. Basden, *Among the Ibos of Nigeria*, 51.

Infertility

marriageable age who are not married are disrespected. Basden states, "[u]nmarried persons of either sex, except in special cases, are objects of derision, and to be childless is the greatest calamity that can befall a woman. Hence, a very high value is set upon marriage."[84] As a topic that raises a lot of debate, its goal too has generated heated conversations in Igboland, especially where a marriage could be termed fruitless or fruitful owing to the number of off-spring generated in that marriage. In this perspective, marriage, its goal and the understanding of the weight of infertility will be the focus of this part of the chapter.

In Igboland, marriage is never a private arrangement between the couple. "It involves the whole family (*Umunna*), and to some extent the whole village."[85] This can be seen in the way Igbo people communicate. "The expression: *Otu onye adighi alu nwanyi* meaning 'one person does not marry a woman' sums up Igbo people's attitude towards marriage."[86] This is an expression of *onye aghala nwanne ya*, wherein everyone is involved in the life of everyone. With marriage being a joyful thing, everyone participates in the formulation of the union. When a marriage is contracted, its goal is manifested in some family celebrations during the year. One of such celebrations is *ara na umu* among Awo-Omamma people, of which there are different appellations in other regions of Igbo land.

Among Awo-Omamma people, there is a traditional gathering and celebration of the gift of fertility, "*omumu.*" This celebration is called "*ara na umu*" which literally means "the breast and the children." "During this ceremony everybody tied to a given family from their mother's lineage gather to celebrate the gift of 'omumu' (children). They eat from the same pot . . ."[87] no matter how highly one is placed in the society. This communion reinforces and bonds the family well.[88] To a great extent, one can argue in this context that *ara na umu* is the celebration of the purpose of marriage which is the begetting of children, and thus the saying "the many the merrier" fully applies in a celebration like this.

---

84. Basden, *Among the Ibos of Nigeria*, 51.
85. Okoro, "Christian Marriage and Divorce," 12.
86. Okoro, "Christian Marriage and Divorce," 12.
87. Okoro, "Christian Marriage and Divorce," 20.
88. Okoro, "Christian Marriage and Divorce," 20.

Igbo Marriage as a "Journey of No Return"

When marriage has been traditionally contracted in Igbo land, a woman who returns home from her place of marriage because of the failure of the marriage is always taunted, except if there was a threat to her life.[89] She is somewhat considered a failure, because "a woman who ventures to return to her relatives is liable to receive but scant sympathy from them. She is accounted a nuisance, and they will do their utmost to persuade her to return to her husband, and will, failing to attain their object by persuasion, not hesitate to resort to forcible measures."[90] There is a huge 'stigma' and 'punishment' associated with divorce in Igbo land. Where there is a divorce, women are

> severely punished. The husband who, in most cases, is angry that his wife left punishes her by forbidding her from seeing her children or having any relationship with them. Society punishes her as well. If she occupies any position in the church or society, the position is taken away. She is considered an aberration and will almost never remarry.[91]

One can see the dilemma of women who are divorced or seeking to divorce. Compounding their problem is that ". . . if the woman dares return, she can't inherit any part of the family property, often reserved for male offspring."[92]

The huge financial commitments associated with marriage in Igbo land make a repetition of such an undertaking an uphill task. With this background, we can now review the marriage procedure among Awo-Omamma people. This will help us understand how infertility is treated as a calamity.

MARRIAGE PROCEDURE IN AWO-OMAMMA AS A CASE STUDY[93]

Marriage is not a private affair in Igboland. It has always been a family project, and it is expected to be so. In that sense, it is considered "a sign

---

89. Nnoromele, *The Way People Live*, 79.
90. Basden, *Among the Ibos of Nigeria*, 59.
91. Nnoromele, *The Way People Live*, 79.
92. Aliche et al. *The Culture Wars Within*, 14.
93. I use Awo-Omamma as a case study because it is my ancestral home which I

of an *efulefu* (a worthless man) to contract marriage without parental knowledge and affirmation."[94] Margaret Farley, a Christian ethicist, concurs with this, when she writes, "despite hundreds of years of colonial and missionary efforts to promote and even enforce a principle of individual choice, the arrangement or at least approval of marriages remains to a significant extent in the hands of the family."[95] In ordinary marriage circumstances, when a young man finds someone he wants to marry, he tells his parents. If a friend, another member of the nuclear or extended family sees "a wife material," he consults the prospective suitor of the family and a pre-nuptial investigation is initiated. This stage is what is called in popular Igbo expression *iju ese* which simply means "investigation" or "background check." This background check is important because "parents have to see to it that the girl to be brought home as the daughter-in-law is carefully chosen from a well behaved and decent family."[96] This investigation will entail checking the girl being morally upright and physically healthy, which means not having what could be termed as publicly-humiliating illnesses, such as epilepsy, leprosy, or tuberculosis or any trace of mental illness running in her family. The inquirers will also have to find out if they have any immediate or remote blood ties (consanguinity) with the other family.

They will seek to know about the fertility rate of the family. If girls from that family have fertility problems, this may likely bring an end to the inquiry and the marriage process will be discontinued. Also, "the inquiry will find out whether they are from clans of traditional enemies."[97] Any 'silent but always alive' membership in the Osu caste system (outcaste) always remains a fundamental point of inquiry before a marriage is contracted.[98]

---

know too well. See Okoro, "Christian Marriage and Divorce," 18–26.

94. Atado, *African Marriage Customs*, 36.

95. Farley, *Just Love*, 79.

96. Spitzer, "Marriage," 259, as quoted in Okonkwo, *Marriage*, 35.

97. Okoro, "Christian Marriage and Divorce," 21. In my native town in Awo-Omamma, oral tradition has it that people from Amaji do not intermarry with those from Umuawa (both are villages in Awo-Omamma). The reason adduced for this is the belief that people from Umuawa killed some people from Amaji during an ancient inter-village rivalry. With that, both villages remained longtime enemies, especially in the issue of intermarriage. However, while there might still be pockets of this skirmishes here and day, the rivalry has been relatively submerged with time, modernity and the advent of Christianity. Now people freely intermarry between both villages.

98. The *osu* caste system is a class consciousness or social stratification in Igbo

All of these inquiries are necessary because marriage is a communal affair, and if wrongly contracted it affects everyone, as everyone is involved in the life of everyone, and especially so when it comes to serious and major decisions like marriage. Again, the inquiry is important because Igbo culture is full of taboo lines that must never be crossed, as this might spell some misfortunes for the family. Crossing a taboo line also includes marrying someone who had defiled the land by committing murder, as we saw in reference to Okonkwo in *Things Fall Apart* in chapter 1 of this book. The purpose of the initial inquiry conducted by families at the earliest point of the marriage negotiations is to make sure that ritual and ethical rules are not broken.[99]

As soon as a prospective wife is found, and an investigation conducted for her suitability for the family is carried out, the next step will be to engage a middle man (called *onye akaebe*) who is a "go between" the two families:

> Once an acceptable bride is found, the groom's father may request a close and loyal friend to be the middleman in the marriage process. This man—*onye akaebe* (the middle man) guides most of the inquiries and arrangements. As a result, the girl's father receives the pledge that the union has the consent of the groom, who is willing to make payments. In every traditional marriage arrangement, there must be this *onye akaebe* (a witness).[100]

The role of *onye akaebe*, who is both a witness and the middle man, is very important. He is a bridge through which both families are linked. He becomes a consultant, especially when the new family begins to experience marital difficulties. If for some reasons the marriage is to

---

land. This is where some families within a section of the Igbos are considered to be slaves and were offered to the deities as sacrifice. As a ritual object of sacrifice, people dread marrying them, as they believe marrying them will conjure evil befalling the family that marries them. Those who do not belong to this *osu* family are called *nwadiala* which literally means "son of the soil." Nwadialas are seen as the masters, while the *osus* are people believed to be dedicated to the deities and as such considered as untouchables, likened to the untouchables in the Indian caste system. "*Osu* is a cult—slave, who has been dedicated to the service of the dedicator's deity ... the dedicator may be an individual, an extended family, or a lineage." Uchendu, *Igbo of Southeast Nigeria*, 89. See also Dike, *Osu Caste Discrimination*.Inc., 2007 The osu caste system is still present but highly subdued in Igbo culture. It does not represent true Igbo values. It has remained "the greatest contradiction to Igbo equalitarian ideology." Uchendu, *Igbo of Southeast Nigeria*, 89.

99. Uchendu, *Igbo of Southeast Nigeria*, 49.

100. Okonkwo, *Marriage*, 37.

Infertility

be terminated, he will be at the fore front of that process. Above all, as Okonkwo observes, "the handing over of the bride wealth is always done through him, since it is through him that it will be recovered if need arises."[101] When all these have been settled, then a date is fixed for the traditional marriage proper.

The Betrothal

Before the marriage proper, several trips must have been made to the bride's house. "Normally the young man and some of his kinsmen will go to the bride's home to collect the list *inara akwukwo*."[102] (Samples of such lists are attached in the Appendix of this book of what is expected from the groom and his family.) When everyone has arrived, the negotiation begins. Nnoromele writes that, "[a]fter eating and drinking, the bridegroom's father would use idioms and proverbs to announce the reason for their visit."[103] Then the "middle man" uses a proverb to initiate the process of negotiation, as stipulated in Igbo traditional marriage proceedings. This announcement is done in a proverb, "because among Awo-Omamma people marriage is regarded as too serious and sacred to be discussed in direct or common language."[104] This is important, because for Awo-Omamma people "to speak always in plain and simple language is to talk like inexperienced little children."[105] A serious business and contract like marriage has to be spoken about is some esoteric ways.

At this point, the groom's father will respond that he will seek the consent of his daughter. The seeking of his daughter's consent will take the form of asking the daughter if she knows the guests in their house. If she affirms that she knows them, then, the straight question will be "would you like to be part of their family?" if this is in the affirmative, then, the process of paying the dowry is initiated.

Traditionally and technically, when the "dowry is paid,"[106] the young people are now married, and "the girl cannot contract another

---

101. Okonkwo, *Marriage*, 37.
102. Okoro, "Christian Marriage and Divorce," 21.
103. Nnoromele, *The Way People Live*, 46.
104. Okoro, "Christian Marriage and Divorce," 22.
105. Arinze, *Sacrifice in Ibo Religion*, 3.
106. Okoro, "Christian Marriage and Divorce," 23.

marriage."[107] This dowry can be any amount. "The amount of the bride price will depend on the beauty, size, ability, social status and training of the girl."[108] The amount will further be determined by the level of education of the girl, as the amount paid for a university degree holder will be different from the amount paid for a girl who never went to elementary school. As Basden notes, while "[i]n the olden days the bride price was reckoned in cows, goats and cowries,"[109] nowadays that practice has changed. In modern times, most families just accept a token from the groom's family as dowry. This is to forestall the impression that they are selling their daughter to the groom and his family.

Part of the blessing which the bride's father imparts will be a blessing for fecundity. This is the joy of every family in Igbo land to have as a good number of children as they can possibly have.[110] In the past, Francis Arinze notes, "the traditional number which will make a couple content is nine children."[111] Mulhall Jones' use of simile to depict Igbo people's love for children as they love yams clearly drives home the point.[112] He says, "the main energies of the Igbo were and are devoted to raising as many as children as yams as possible."[113] Though the need for fertility is still a treasure, in modern times young couples do not have very large families. Now, since they want to give their children at least a modest life style, they limit the number of children they now have.

Traditional Marriage—*Alum Nwanyi*

Before the girl moves to the husband's house there is always a huge celebration in which almost all members of the community get involved. Obianuju Ekeocha, a culture of life activist, describes the celebration : "[t]he ceremony is picturesque in every way and so brings to life everything the world romanticizes about Africa—from the kola nuts to the freshly

---

107. Okoro, "Christian Marriage and Divorce," 23.

108. Okoro, "Christian Marriage and Divorce," 23.

109. Basden, *Among the Ibos of Nigeria*, 52.""number-of-pages":"300""source":"Amazon""abstract":"George Thomas Basden (1873–1944

110. Okoro, "Christian Marriage and Divorce," 24.

111. Arinze, *Sacrifice in Ibo Religion*, 2, as cited in Okoro, "Christian Marriage and Divorce," 24.

112. Okoro, "Christian Marriage and Divorce," 24.

113. Jones and Mulhall, "An Examination," 11, as cited in Okoro, "Christian Marriage and Divorce," 24.

tapped palm wine, from the colorful attires to the skillful drummers and agile dancers moving perfectly to the beat."[114] The more people, the more prestigious and the more honorable people see both families. The involvement of many people, with its electrifying scenario of joy bearing testimony to marriage not being a private affair, is an expression of the ethical principle wherein no one is left behind (*onye aghala nwanne ya*). Before this elaborate feast on the day of the traditional marriage, there is also a big feast a day before the traditional marriage:

> There is elaborate feasting and dancing on the eve of the girl's departure to her new home. This involves, among other things, summoning the girls age-grade companions, including males and females, to a special feast prepared by the girl with her mother's aid, after which gifts of raw yam, meat and, in present times, occasionally money are made to each member of the age grade. Among modern, educated Igbo, the custom still persists and is referred to as 'bachelor's eve.'[115]

All these indicate that marriage in Igbo land is expensive, elaborate, ritually dense and public. This makes a repetition of such proceedings difficult, thus making divorce difficult. It puts pressure on young men to earn enough money before thinking of marriage, thus making them delay marriage and marry when they are older. This can lead to the problem of infertility previously discussed, which can occur as a result of delaying marriage.

PROCREATION AS THE GOAL OF MARRIAGE IN IGBOLAND

Igbo people and their culture "are not ambiguous about the reason for a man and a woman to unite themselves in marriage. Fertility is considered central, so the entire village publicly prays for it right from the start of a marriage."[116] Some authors, such as Nnoromele, have suggested that "[t]wo words, however, summarize the Ibo concept of marriage: community and procreation. The Ibos believed that marriage was a community rather than individual event. People married, not necessarily for love and companionship, but to fulfill the social obligation of maintaining the life

---

114. Ekeocha, *Target Africa*, 119.
115. Agbasiere, *Women in Igbo Life*, 111.
116. Ekeocha, *Target Africa*, 120.

of the community through procreation."[117] This context of procreation as the goal of marriage is well expressed in socialization in Igbo land. The first moment an Igbo person emerges from the womb, the process of socialization, which sees procreation as the end purpose of marriage, sets in. First, at the birth of a child, the whole community is electrified with new life, as life is renewed, and energy is duly revitalized.

Second, at the birth of a new child, there is great joy that the union, which has brought the new child into existence, is fruitful. Since the parents of the new-born have generated life through marriage, the same is expected of the new born baby; else he/she will be considered a failure in life. So, from day one, the child is socialized to know that marriage is solely aimed towards procreation. This sense of joy at the birth of a child in Igboland is captured by Obianuju Ekeocha who writes, "[i]n the town I come from, a new baby is always welcomed with much joy. In fact, we have a special song reserved for births, a sort of 'Gloria in Excelsis Deo.' The day a baby is born, the entire village celebrates by singing this song, clapping their hands, and drinking."[118] This yearning to have a child and the joy that follows seem to be legitimate. After all, some education and psychology specialists, such as Elobuike Nwabuisi, say that different theories portray human beings as organisms that start preparing for their long or short terms of stay on planet Earth, and the preparation and subsequent internalizing of an existing ethos becomes the foundation of the neophyte's behavior, psychic health, and general optimism in longing to raise one's own children.[119]

The act of being socialized is manifested in different rites of passages such as the *ima ogodo* rite. Ima ogodo rite of passage celebrates the gift of pregnancy, in that way, marriage and then being pregnant becomes the primary goal for an average Igbo woman Metuh describes this rite thusly: "This rite, which takes place within the first months of pregnancy, is in fact the marriage festival, as different from *inu nwanyi*. (bring home a wife) which focuses on the agreement and payment of dowry."[120] This shows that before pregnancy, a marriage is said to be hanging on a balance. Failure to achieve pregnancy means the union will be regarded with disdain, or the woman will forever be taunted:

117. Nnoromele, *The Way People Live*, 44.
118. Ekeocha, *Target Africa*, 40.
119. Nwabuisi, *Religion and African Culture*, 11.
120. Metuh, *African Religions*, 124–25.

A woman without *nwa* (child) is almost nobody and her marriage is always questionable and in constant jeopardy. Hence in her grief, such a childless woman pathetically asks her *chi* (God): *m mere gini?*—what have I done? In the light of this, the prayer and wish of every woman is *chi awola m oke* (may my "*Chi*" not by pass me when sharing) or *chi m emegbule m* (may my God not cheat me).[121]

Regarding the woman's pain and vulnerability about childlessness, Mbiti describes this succinctly:

Unhappy is the woman who fails to get children, for whatever other qualities she might possess, her failure to bear children is worse than committing genocide: she has become the dead end of human life, not only for the genealogical line but also for herself. When she dies, there will be nobody of her own immediate blood to 'remember' her in the state of personal immortality.[122]

This situation is still very strongly felt among Igbo people, despite the advent of Christianity over a century ago on Igbo soil, and with over 75% of the Igbo ethnic group said to have been evangelized:[123]

The fault may not be her own, but this does not 'excuse' her in the eyes of society . . . the childless wife bears a scar which nothing can erase. She will suffer for this, her own relatives will suffer for this, and it will be an irreparable humiliation for which there is no source of comfort in traditional life.[124]

This is one of the humiliating aspects of infertility. It dehumanizes the couple and all those who taunt them. More so, on the woman, it reduces her to a mere machine of baby production. With the focus on procreation as the purpose of marriage, there is a difference from other cultures and particularly Western culture, in that Igbo male folk have a blaming attitude—they primarily see women as the cause of infertility, even if medically proven otherwise.

---

121. Amadi-Azuogu, *Biblical Exegesis*, 208.

122. Mbiti, *African Religions and Philosophy*, 107.

123. Victoria Ibewuike found "that more than seventy-five percent of the Igbo people today are Christians . . ." Ibewuike, *African Women*, 320.

124. Ibewuike, *African Women*, 109.

SHAME, EGO AND DOUGHTINESS AMONG IGBO PEOPLE

Marriage and child-bearing are complex issues; this is partly because Igbo culture is a shame-based culture. (If one can protect one's ego from fear of shame, guilt can be mitigated.) This fear of shame informs how couples make decisions, including those dealing with childlessness in marriage and all the ramifications that surround it. This accounts for why Duane Elmer says, "Western—individualistic—societies are more guilt-based while Two-Thirds World—collectivistic—societies tend to be more shame-based."[125] In this milieu of shame, most Igbo impotent men will not mind blaming their wives for childlessness, without considering the guilt of blaming an innocent woman. This is so because ego is a characteristic feature of an average Igbo man, in the light of that, he might go to the extent of covering up whatever that will expose his vulnerability including putting the reason of childlessness on his wife or on some spiritual forces even if he is aware of his fertility problems. Notwithstanding the blame marathon, there is always a way out.

Despite the complexity of the situation, Igbo people believe that there is always a way to go around a problem. An Igbo proverb characterizes such a situation well: *ejighi mma ekwu eyi ochiagha egwu* which means, "a war hero is never frightened with a mere kitchen knife."[126] A community and culture as rich, brave, doughty and powerful as Igbo culture cannot be bullied by a few traditional challenges. They have to approach and handle such challenges with courage and valor. This courage and valor are envisaged in the full application of the indigenous ethical principle of *onye aghala nwanne ya*. This full application will help to liberate Igbo couples from the problem of infertility so that they can live in dignity and with freedom.

CONCLUSION

Procreation has remained the main purpose of marriage in Igbo land. With procreation as the main and sometimes the only purpose of marriage, one can only guess what happens when this goal is not met, especially after the fanfare that is associated with marriage in Igboland. Childlessness is almost like a disease in Igbo land, of which the negative

---

125. Elmer, *Cross-Cultural Connections*, 173.
126. Onwudufor, *Mmanu E ji Eri Okwu*, 101.

impact has been devastating. The suffering of a childless married couple in Igbo culture is a huge contradiction in a culture that is supposed to care and protect them. It is a paradox that a culture that celebrates that no one should be left behind, in turn neglects one of its own when there is barrenness or childlessness.

We have seen the "moral weight" of modern medical reproductive technologies. We have seen that, notwithstanding the seemingly wide acceptance of ART, vexing questions still persist among many philosophers, feminists, and Christian thinkers, as well as secular and Christian bioethicists, on the ethical implications of IVF as an ART. We have seen how the marriage procedure is expensive, ritually buoyant, and ceremoniously rigorous in Igbo land.

The next chapter will critically engage the method, sources, theologies and ethical principles advanced by two prominent female African theologians: Mercy Oduyoye and Rose Uchem. This will lead us to see how Oduyoye and Uchem's theological and ethical methods, sources, and principles can contribute to the liberation of married couples suffering from infertility

3

Engaging African Female Theologies
The Thoughts of Mercy Oduyoye and Rose Uchem

INTRODUCTION

THERE ARE SEVERAL PURPOSES for this chapter. The first is to engage the thinking of two African women theologians, one Methodist and the other Roman Catholic. While they represent different denominations, they both seek to transform, in some way, the situation of African women. The second purpose is to apply the comparative method I identified in the introductory chapter. Various themes will be explored, including formation as an African female theologian, identifying the fundamental problems, their understanding of the social context of African women, their understanding of the church, the ethical principles which they perceive will contribute to the liberation of African women, and how those ethical principles can liberate Igbo couples from infertility in marriage.

First is the thinking of Mercy Amba Oduyoye who is originally from the Akan matrilineal tribe in Ghana. She is an African woman Methodist theologian, and an intellectual giant. Elizabeth Amoah, a professor of Religious Studies at the University of Ghana, writes of Oduyoye, "she is indeed a pioneering and a wise African woman theologian who has contributed tremendously in the area of theology, the study of religion and culture, missiology, and to academic life in general."[1]

---

1. Amoah, "Preface," xvii.

Oduyoye has also been designated as "a pioneer in challenging Third World theologians to put at the top of their agenda the concerns of women."[2] She worked for many years as youth education secretary in the World Council of Churches.[3] This widened her horizon as she tackles complex issues from religion and theology, in a field dominated by men. Her success is not only in the area of academics. Her family has been among the staunch members of the Methodist Church where her father "Charles Kwaw Yamoah, a trained teacher, later became a Methodist minister who rose to the office of presidency in the Methodist Church of Ghana."[4]

Oduyoye's theology has been described by her academic daughters as a theology of "treading softly but firmly."[5] Isabel Apawo Phiri and Saojini Nadal suggest that "the 'hammer and axe' theology is not always the most fitting tool when pursuing the cause of gender-justice and liberation of women."[6] The style, mission and vision of 'The Circle of Concerned African Women Theologians,' brings out this point succinctly. Oduyoye herself writes that as "The Circle" moves forward they will be:

> embarking on what we hope will be a liberative theology, going at our own pace, setting our own priorities and responding to our own contexts. Our immediate community of accountability is African women who seek a continent that is alive to God's mission in Africa and respond creatively to what God wills for Africans.[7]

An interesting dimension of Oduyoye's life is that she has no children of her own, "[i]n a country where motherhood is as sacred as it was in Israel, she managed to mother many, but bore no-children of her own."[8] Having no child of her own but being a mother to many probably widened her vision for motherhood. This enlightenment is important, as it can help make childless couples know that there is much they can offer in the flourishing of the human society. As Oduyoye writes, "[m]othering

---

2. Ferm, *Third World Liberation Theologies*, 73.

3. This is an Ecumenical movement which their website *oikoumene* captures well. "The World Council of Churches is a fellowship of churches which confess the Lord Jesus Christ as God and Saviour according to the scriptures, and therefore seek to fulfil together their common calling to the glory of the one God, Father, Son and Holy Spirit." World Council of Churches, "What is the World Council of Churches?"

4. Amoah, "Preface," xix.

5. Phiri and Nadar, "Introduction," 1.

6. Phiri and Nadar, "Introduction," 2.

7. Oduyoye, *Introducing African Women's Theology*, 20.

8. Letty M. Russell, "Mercy Amba Ewudziwa Oduyoye," 46.

is a term to encapsulate not simply biological motherhood, but all the nurturing, mentoring and life-enhancing praxis that make for humanity and human communities as women imagine God to have willed and of which the Gospel provides a glimpse."[9] This is essential because owing to hard work and education, Oduyoye is able to withstand the storm of childlessness in the African context. She has many children through teaching as she has "mentored several scholars in and outside the African continent."[10] Because of education and enlightenment, which she considers as a way forward, "[t]he women writers of Africa are shaking African countries out of their complicity."[11]

THE THEOLOGY OF MERCY AMBA ODUYOYE

The context that shaped Oduyoye's theology is the pathetic condition of women in the continent of Africa. She saw and researched that women are treated as the property of men:

> In Africa, the very idea of a "free woman" conjures up negative images. We have been brought up to believe that a woman should always have a suzerain, that she should be "owned" by a man, be he father, uncle, or husband. A "free woman" spells disaster. An adult woman, if unmarried, is immediately reckoned to be available for the pleasure of all males and is treated as such. The single woman who manages her affairs successfully without a man is an affront to patriarchy and a direct challenge to the so-called masculinity of men who want to "possess" her. Some women are struggling to be free from this compulsory attachment to the male. Women want the right to be fully human, whether or not they choose to be attached to men.[12]

These fundamental problems of women being identified and understood only through a male and women's yearning for "the right to be fully human," become the basis of Oduyoye's incursion into the field of women's theology and liberation. Oduyoye's vast areas of theological studies concern what it means to be a woman and a Christian in the Third World, especially in Africa. She resolves the above fundamental problems

---

9. Oduyoye, *Introducing African Women's Theology*, 37–38.
10. Amoah, "Preface," xvii.
11. Oduyoye, *Introducing African Women's Theology*, 127.
12. Oduyoye, *Daughters of Anowa*, 4–5.

by embarking on a form of liberation theology that is a protest theology against all unjust structures, and especially the unjust structures against women, and even more particularly of the patriarchy. She underscores this when she says "[t]he framework of patriarchy is constructed on many pillars. Each requires scrutiny, but patriarchy itself is defective and must be torn down."[13] As a practitioner of evangelization and a scholar, she looks hypocrisy in the face and rebukes it. She investigates the problems that lead to the subjugation of women, and proposes steps that can solve them. In her thinking, the fundamental problems have unfortunately, been retained and sustained through socialization:

> Gendered socialization has operated against women in Africa, resulting in high illiteracy rates and lower education levels and attainments. Even forms of Western education have been unable to break these "proper" pigeon holes for women and men. Proverbs of traditional culture are deterrents enjoining women not to attempt to reach the same heights as men.[14]

Oduyoye argues for a reorientation, if African women are to be able to live life to the full. Her experience as a Ghanaian living in Nigeria gives her adequate information to engage in her scholarly work of women's liberation. As a female child in her family, "I was a non-entity, or so I felt. As a child I had no place when members of my father's family met."[15] Now married to a Nigerian man, her experience is the same, "I discovered that among the patrilineal Yoruba of western Nigeria, a wife is a member of the work-force in 'her husband's house,' but not one of the decision-makers."[16]

Oduyoye writes from an African background replete with anti-female practices, including: patriarchy, poverty, lack of education for females, lack of female voices in the church and family, polygamy, maltreatment of widows, and male children syndrome. Some of these practices are perpetuated and justified on the authority of culture and tradition. The menfolk hide behind African custom to maintain an undue dominance over women. This power of African custom is described by Hanny Lightfoot-Klein:

---

13. Oduyoye, *Daughters of Anowa*, 153.
14. Oduyoye, *Daughters of Anowa*, 62.
15. Oduyoye, *Daughters of Anowa*, 7–8.
16. Oduyoye, *Daughters of Anowa*, 7–8.

> Custom in Africa is stronger than domination, stronger than the law, stronger even than religion. Over the years, customary practices have been incorporated into religion, and ultimately have come to be believed by their practitioners to be demanded by their adopted gods, whoever they may be.[17]

Since men have been hiding behind African custom, tradition, religion and culture to oppress women, Oduyoye theologizes to make a distinction between what one may see as the biblical allegory of the "the voice of Jacob and the hands of Esau" (Genesis 27: 22–23):

> Affirming the Bible as a source for God's word brings women into the arena of biblical hermeneutics. In addition, African women have to ask: "Whose voice is the voice of the ancestors, the voice of tradition?" and "Where is the voice for today coming from?" They raise a question on the authority that keeps religious rites, rituals, and demands in place even where they are dehumanizing and do not seem to confer any obvious benefit on the subject/object.[18]

In trying to 'unpack' African theology, to discern what culture, custom and religion are, Oduyoye—in line with women's experiences and stories—seems to inaugurate what can be seen as a moment of grace, equality, self-awareness and self-realization. Oduyoye captures this when she says, "[w]hat is central to our humanity, therefore, is that both female and male are akin to God, having received the same divine spirit. Gender does not define our worthiness, since it is not present in God."[19]

In trying to untie the strings of oppression, she advocates for a continuous speaking-out against forces of oppression, because "[a]ny strategy to achieve greater power must be accompanied by 'voicing,' for if we ourselves do not deliberately attempt to break the silence about our situation as African women, others will continue to maintain it."[20] This book is in part a response to Oduyoye's call for 'voicing,' in other words, speaking out against the forces of oppression in Africa. This book is thus speaking out against the oppression of infertile couples.

---

17. Lightfoot-Klein et al., *Prisoners of Ritual*, 47.
18. Oduyoye, *Introducing African Women's Theology*, 48–49.
19. Oduyoye, *Introducing African Women's Theology*, 42.
20. Oduyoye, *Daughters of Anowa*, 170.

Oduyoye's Life-Sustaining and Liberation Theology

Oduyoye's scholarly enterprise sees the need to unveil the authentic identity for women which African culture and men try to veil. She writes, "the language used in describing women in both traditional and modern social structures and the position of women in the economy and the society belie the statement of African men that women are not oppressed."[21] African women's theology is Oduyoye's response to the plight of the African woman who is "at the bottom of the scale. She is oppressed by her African brother, she is oppressed by other women who are not African, and she is oppressed by non-African men."[22] She exposes women's experiences, where she wants the Gospel message to be given and understood through their struggle and historical context:

> The liberation theology of African women underlines the hope in Yahweh that they find in the Hebrew Bible. It underlines the expectation that God will hear our cries and would come to our rescue. This is what keeps women going. From the Greek Bible they see their hope in Jesus' preaching of the coming reign of God and the signs of its presence among us even here and now.[23]

The Christology in this thinking remains promising and revitalizing. This is the hope of African women, that they will all be united in Christ as God's children, as Amoah and Oduyoye state, "[t]he Christian religion raised in Africa the hope of a future when all things would be righted and be 'gathered up' in Christ."[24] This revival and gathering up in Christ will announce a total liberation of women and men. This is a major contribution of Oduyoye in the field of liberation theology.

When women are free, their oppressors too will be free. That is the new spirit of revival which she advocates, a spirit of a joint project. As Oduyoye opines, "Liberation must be viewed as men and women walking together on the journey home, with the church as the umbrella of faith, hope, and love."[25] She does this by seeking a new quality of life for women. It is this new quality of life that will eventually transform the whole community:

---

21. Oduyoye, *Daughters of Anowa*, 157.
22. Tappa, "The Christ-Event."
23. Oduyoye, *Introducing African Women's Theology*, 119.
24. Amoah and Oduyoye, "The Christ for African Women," 37.
25. Oduyoye, *Daughters of Anowa*, 185.

Women's struggle for survival in Africa is not only a struggle to stay alive. It seeks a quality of life that can be truly and fully human not only for themselves but also for men. When women refuse to stay on the margins, they are making a statement concerning their understanding of what it means to be human. The spirituality of resistance therefore enables one to hold on to one's humanity. Resisting anonymity is an expression of the belief that our individual humanity is meant to find expression in community.[26]

It is worth reiterating that this cause for liberation is anchored in Christ, the ultimate liberator of all. The biblical stories in which Christ came to the aid of women prove Christ as the ultimate liberator. Let us consider some of these biblical stories of liberation. To the woman caught in adultery, who was to be stoned by men, Christ said, "Then neither do I condemn you." Jesus declares, "Go now and leave your life of sin" (John 8:1–11). Regarding Mary, the sister of Martha, who was to be confined to the kitchen, a role assigned to women by men, Jesus says to Martha, "Mary has chosen what is better, and it will not be taken away from her" (Luke 10:42). The situation of "the woman with hemorrhage," was a precarious and pathetic one. Louise Tappa argues, "[w]e are told that over a period of twelve years, she has spent all her money seeking help. She is poor, she has nothing left. In short, she is outcast not only socially, but also economically and religiously as well."[27] Jesus liberates her from the mire of religious and cultural debasing structures. In all these situations, Christ is not just the 'multiplier effect' of liberation, but the final liberator himself.

Oduyoye's liberation theology identifies with "[t]he Christ who is on the side of life as being on the side of God."[28] Here we see the Christ who reaches out to women and the most vulnerable effecting a positive change in their lives. Oduyoye further writes, "Christ is the liberator from the burden of disease and from taboos that restrict women's participation in their communities."[29] This is the society that Oduyoye, through her theological enterprise, wishes to accomplish; namely, a society where "[o]ur baptism into Christ compels us to see ourselves as the beginning of a new humanity modelled after Christ."[30] Oduyoye believes and looks forward to a society where "[t]here must be a resurrection in its wake—new

26. Oduyoye, *Introducing African Women's Theology*, 76.
27. Tappa, "The Christ-Event," 32.
28. Amoah and Oduyoye, "The Christ for African Women," 39.
29. Oduyoye, *Introducing African Women's Theology*, 55.
30. Oduyoye, *Hearing and Knowing*, 137.

life, love, peace and justice—a new creation, a new community, the household of God in which all things are made new."[31]

Oduyoye does not limit this search for liberation of African women only within African culture. She brings it also to the church, and specifically to the church in Africa. She challenges the oppressive structure in the African church by arguing that "whatever is keeping subordination of women alive in the church cannot be the spirit of God. The church is intended to be the ecclesia of all people, women and men, across all social barriers."[32] Unfortunately, this is not the case in African churches, which seem to close eyes and ears to this force of insubordination. Oduyoye says, "[t]his must change."[33]

Not wanting to achieve this alone, Oduyoye maintains that to 'purify' theology and the *imago Dei* concept, there has to be a full team, where female scholars of theology must engage with themselves in order to achieve a dignified whole. While advocating the importance of a full team, she reiterates the need for solidarity from different perspectives, solidarity with the church, and solidarity among women. By solidarity she means, ". . . walking hand in hand, developing strength through unity so that common interests are protected and common aims are achieved."[34] In this way she invites the church to be in solidarity with women, because "[t]he Church's participation in God's mission entails working for and with goodness; that is justice, love, peace and wholeness."[35]

Among Yoruba women in particular, and by extension African women, Oduyoye calls for ". . . standing in solidarity as women."[36] The advantage of this solidarity is not hard to find, because "[w]ith our collective strength—numerical, financial and cerebral—we can draw on this bifocal system to gain entry into political structures to help formulate laws under which we all can live as free and responsible human beings."[37] However, the irony in this solidarity among women will be its exclusive nature. In as much as Oduyoye is envisioning a situation where women support women in solidarity, even the best of intentions can have its own

---

31. Oduyoye, *Introducing African Women's Theology*, 119.
32. Oduyoye, *Daughters of Anowa*, 182.
33. Oduyoye, *Daughters of Anowa*, 183.
34. Oduyoye, "The Meaning of Solidarity," 116.
35. Oduyoye, *Introducing African Women's Theology*, 87–88.
36. Oduyoye, *Daughters of Anowa*, 198.
37. Oduyoye, *Daughters of Anowa*, 198.

little set-back. The problem one can envisage with this is that while the women in solidarity could have an impermeable structure, it would definitely alienate the men folks, and in that process the hope of achieving a dignified whole and "the new creation found in the risen Christ"[38] for all would only be a farce. On this premise one can argue that to arrive at this wholeness, a solidarity among women which excludes the men may not establish Oduyoye's image of "a new community, the household of God in which all things are made new."[39]

Gender equality is a project for all. Everyone has to be mobilized in the process, male and female. Some male scholars are even at the forefront of enhancing gender equality. Advocating this course, Amuluche Greg Nnamani argues that "gender inequality is not supported by human biology (nature) or by the creator. Nature has made male and female to be complementary and interdependent beings of the one human species, such that each is indispensable for the survival of humanity."[40] From a scriptural perspective, Anthony Umoren argues against any urge "to re-interpret some of the biblical passages that have traditionally been used, especially among Christians, to intimidate and oppress women, in the belief that it is a divine decree that they are not equal to men."[41] With this sense of advocating for gender equality, these scholars have succeeded in giving some attention to women in their various enterprises, although the steps taken are again sadly slow. Uzukwu sees this mire and challenge as a major concern "which all must join to save Africa and humanity from rigid masculinity."[42]

For women to take their destiny into their hands and in solidarity, Oduyoye suggests that, "[w]e must have the courage to challenge African men who refuse to acknowledge the threat that paternalism poses to the unity of humanity."[43] This challenge is important because "[g]ender can and does destroy hospitality and hence human relationship and community health."[44] I agree with Oduyoye that arming oneself with knowledge of the socio-cultural dynamics of a culture and an awareness of the way

38. Oduyoye, *Introducing African Women's Theology*, 117.
39. Oduyoye, *Introducing African Women's Theology*, 119.
40. Nnamani, "Gender Equality," 38.
41. Umoren, "Theological Basis of Gender Equality," in Uchem, *Gender Equality*, 87.
42. Uzukwu, *God, Spirit, and Human Wholeness*, 37.
43. Oduyoye, *Beads and Strands*, 106.
44. Oduyoye, *Beads and Strands*, 53.

forward could be an important route to freedom. When this is attained, there will be a new narrative about our common humanity which will "go beyond scientific or biological origins."[45] There will be a new myth which "focuses on human interconnectedness as part of becoming human."[46]

Oduyoye's Solution—Her Contributions to the Fields of Theology and Christian Ethics

African women's theology and a need for socio-cultural change have remained what maybe Oduyoye's biggest goal and dream—a community of love, respect and solidarity. She seeks to attain this by challenging structures of oppression, and passionately appealing to women, too: "My call to my sisters tells of my dream; it is a plea for solidarity and a cry to be free of imposed subordination."[47] She advocates for this because she believes that African women's theology will help in bringing change toward a humane and loving society. Her African women's theology is ". . . a theology of relations, replacing hierarchies with mutuality. It is therefore a theology that is 'society sensitive.'"[48] This dimension of theology brings a sense of fresh air and an important way forward which will entail a change leading to a new cultural and psychological orientation among African people and scholars.

Oduyoye's call for a new orientation and a socio-cultural change of African culture with its ultra-conservative traits is a huge step forward. No culture lives in absolute isolation, and in that regard cultures must embrace change, because any group that accepts a measure of change could gain advantage over those that cling to the traditional pattern. It is not as if groups should give away their core identity in the name of change, but any group that oppresses a section of its members poses a barrier to human flourishing, and this leads to a stunted growth of everyone in that group. Part of her call for change is the widening of the horizon of the conversation, especially regarding Christian anthropology, and the oneness of the human family which Africans need to critically engage with. This new orientation will be the beginning of the new world order which Oduyoye clamors for.

---

45. Oduyoye, *Beads and Strands*, 107.
46. Oduyoye, *Beads and Strands*, 107.
47. Oduyoye, *Daughters of Anowa*, 212.
48. Oduyoye, *Introducing African Women's Theology*, 17.

The new orientation and change must find expression in the church too. The church must not behave as if all is well. The church must be alive to these areas of oppression, too:

> [T]he church has not joined in the search for a new value system; rather, it has suggested that there is no issue, thereby demonstrating its complicity in the structures of injustice . . . The church should enable all people to enter in hope into the struggles of others, to seek creatively to suffer our way through contradictions, to cope joyfully with diversities and with the varieties of being human, and to celebrate them.[49]

Since Africans are religious and more or less belong to one of the many Christian traditions, a full liberation of women must be attained within the church and within African culture too. It will be a partial victory if the culture is deconstructed but the church remains unchallenged, with its tight-fisted rigidity of exclusion of women in its public life and organization.

An Appraisal of Oduyoye's Life-Giving Theology

The efficacy of Oduyoye's methodology and theology is a result of her ability to allow her work, and the experiences of all women, to contribute and formulate a resounding voice for Third-World women, and oppressed women around the globe. Oduyoye names the sources and structure of women's oppression, especially with her knowledge of Akan culture and her role as a Christian minister. By naming the sources and structures of oppression that exploit African women's vulnerability and powerlessness, she reinforces the idea that when oppression is internalized, it has a negative effect on women, in that "women have so interiorized the ideology of self-denial that they feel it is illegitimate and presumptuous to demand things for themselves."[50]

She developed a way to reconstruct Africa from its patriarchal Christian basis, in the process revealing the pathetic condition of African women, who have been dehumanized and marginalized. She has done this with utmost caution. She has done this through what her friends, Isabel Apawo Phiri and Sarojini Nadar call 'treading softly but firmly.' Her friends came to this assessment because "she related how, through

---

49. Oduyoye, *Daughters of Anowa*, 185.
50. Tappa, "The Christ-Event," 33.

all her years of being a theologian, she had come to realize the often ineffectiveness of confrontation as a means to an end. Linking this to women's struggles for gender justice in religious and cultural settings, she said that such head-on altercations only resulted in the equivalence of cabinet drawers being shattered."[51] This theological rationale (treading softly but firmly) has become for her a "more appropriate and effective means"[52] and this has helped her to demonstrate the knowledge of African women's awareness of who their oppressors are. Having known their oppressors, they tread cautiously and gently because, "[w]hen your hand is in someone's mouth, you do not hit that person on the head."[53] This approach of treading softly but firmly manifests the change she is advocating, since she proposes it as one of the major ways to heal Africa's psyche. Furthermore, it can foster a Christianity that is relevant, and which can lead to a deeper and more personal union with God for everyone, male or female. When this is realized, then God's gratuitous love for humanity will not only be made manifest, but will also be lived among humans.

However, while Oduyoye's liberation and African woman's theology can hold make meaning for the educated, one may ask: how does this understanding of liberation get to the local women in the village? This seeming lack of impact on village women tends to make theology seen to be an elitist exercise that does not have much effect on the multitude of African women who may not be able to read or write. Nonetheless, one can still argue against this point, in that what she has said in her books can be repeated in the pulpits where the common African women congregate every week, or at community meetings. This will entail her admonition to women when she says, "[w]e women must reread the Bible to seek guidance on how to listen to God and to recognize where God is at work in our world today."[54] The advantage of women who engage in the scholarly work of women's liberation like Oduyoye is that they are Church ministers, too. In that way, as ministers and scholars they blend and maintain a close relationship between scholarly work and the art of pastoring. The pastoring work helps the scholar to bring into practical form her intellectual introspection on the realm of the divine.

51. Tappa, "The Christ-Event," 2.
52. Tappa, "The Christ-Event," 2.
53. Oduyoye, *Daughters of Anowa*, 3.
54. Oduyoye, *Daughters of Anowa*, 191.

Oduyoye has succeeded in launching a process through which women can be liberated. In the later part of the next chapter, her contributions and those of Uchem and Bujo will be classified into different categories, while weighing their similarities and dissimilarities to unpack their contributions in the process of liberation. It is through this background that one can see that the Igbo indigenous ethic of *onye aghala nwanne ya* has all that is required to liberate Igbo couples who suffer infertility.

THE THEOLOGY OF ROSE UCHEM—RE-INVENTING THE PLACE OF WOMEN IN AFRICAN THEOLOGY

Rose Uchem is a Nigerian Roman Catholic nun. She belongs to the religious order of Missionary Sisters of the Holy Rosary.[55] Belonging to a missionary group, Rose Uchem has done mission and scholarly work in many parts of the world. She sees that as an advantage, writing, "my transnational and trans-cultural experiences of extended periods of living and interacting closely with people of different backgrounds in the United States, Sierra Leone, Nigeria and Ireland"[56] add much to her scholarly enterprise. As a scholar, she is now "a senior lecturer in Christian Religious Education and Comparative/International Education at the University of Nigeria, Nsukka."[57] Uchem has a wide range of intellectual and research interests. These are manifested in her passion for "contextual theological education with a view to eradication of violence against women."[58] These interests surface principally in her articulation of the status of Igbo women in the Roman Catholic Church and in Igbo culture.

Rose Uchem is known for her straight forward critique of Igbo culture and the Roman Catholic Church for the double tragedy of subordination of Igbo women. She has experienced and researched that "there is a pervasive negative perception of 'woman' in the church and in the society."[59] As a theologian and one who is interested in the liberation of African women, she anchors her theology on the salvific mission of Jesus Christ. She sees a huge contradiction in the church's social teaching, as

55. Uchem, "Rose Uchem."
56. Uchem, *Overcoming Women's Subordination*, 21.
57. Uchem, "University of Nigeria Staff Profile."
58. Uchem, "University of Nigeria Staff Profile."
59. Uchem, "Gender Equality in Africa," as cited in Maphosa and Morgan, *Layers of Inequality*, 2.

she wonders how "a young seminarian is set above a fifty-year old woman religious who might have taught him in school; and a theologically competent woman is deemed unsuitable to image an unseen 'male God.'"[60] This, Uchem argues, is not social justice. It is a subversion of social justice in the name of gender differences. Subordination of women in the African culture and the Catholic Church becomes Uchem's preoccupation. She sees:

> a relationship between women's subordination in the Catholic Church and in the Igbo culture, epitomized by male-headship model of family, civil and Church life; and ultimately symbolized by women's exclusion from celebrating public sacramental ritual [Eucharist] in the Catholic Church and [the Kolanut] in the Igbo culture.[61]

This is Uchem's articulation of the fundamental problem. She sets out to resolve this by envisioning an inclusive theology that will make every male and female feel like a child of God. Uchem argues that a radical change in the social teaching of the Catholic Church, and the full application of that teaching, will give the best manifestation of our understanding of the true God we worship. Uchem further argues that "only a change in the Catholic Church's stand on women's ordination will send out a message strong enough to initiate the kind of conversion and transformation required by a new evangelization in Africa and Igbo society."[62] Her attempt at a theological resolution of the fundamental problem is a courageous effort from her side through fighting a challenging 'war' on two fronts: with the patriarchal Igbo culture and the patriarchal Roman Catholic Church.

Though Uchem is celibate by choice, she underscores the importance and joy of the institution of marriage within the church and in Igbo culture. Marriage and the dynamism it adds to human society are critically important. However, she challenges Igbo culture and the Church in their perpetuation of the oppression of women, especially in society's preference for a male child:

> The root problem is the quest for the male child, society's attitude to childlessness in marriage; likewise, the whole issue of tying up a woman's identity and respectability with being married or not;

---

60. Uchem, *Overcoming Women's Subordination*, 121.
61. Uchem, *Overcoming Women's Subordination*, 20.
62. Uchem, *Overcoming Women's Subordination*, 12.

having or not having a child. Thus it needs re-examination. What is being said here is not to be understood as a negation of the value of marriage and procreation. Rather it is meant to highlight the injustice of the disproportionate social and cultural burden placed on women in comparison to that placed on men with reference to childlessness, male issue and being unmarried. The concern being expressed is society's double standards regarding women and the fact that this devaluation of women is, uncritically, condoned and reinforced by Churchmen.[63]

On the concept of *imago Dei*, Uchem writes, "[g]ender equality is rooted in the fact that men and women are equally made in God's image."[64] She sees the need for a reorientation and a cultural hermeneutic, where, "[m]en and women need to regard each other more as equals and work together as equal partners for human development and the growth of God's reign in this world."[65] From a Christian and a biblical perspective, this will entail re-interpreting the bible to strip it of some of its oppressive language. In fostering gender equality, her argument and analogy in this regard are forceful. Referring to Genesis 2:22, where "the Lord God made a woman from the rib he had taken out of the man," Uchem argues:

> Over time, the symbol of the rib, which was meant to convey a sense of one-ness became a tool of oppression. The symbol of the rib is taken to denote weakness, inferiority and a secondary place in creation. However, those who advance these views fail to reason that the woman who was supposedly made from 'human stuff' (the rib) might be superior to the man who was supposedly made from 'dust.' Moreover, those who argue that the man is pre-eminent because he was created before the woman need to remember that wild beasts were created before the man and would therefore be considered superior to the man.[66]

On Igbo culture, Uchem criticizes the practice of excluding women from the presentation and presiding of the all-important ritual of kolanuts which, ironically, is the symbol of Igbo unity:

> The Kolanut ritual is one of the few Igbo customs that have survived the onslaught of the Western cultural imperialism, which came along with the Christian message. It is so symbolically

63. Uchem, *Overcoming Women's Subordination*, 67.
64. Uchem, *Gender Equality*, 47.
65. Uchem, *Gender Equality*, 56.
66. Uchem, *Gender Equality*, 49.

significant that, in recent times, this ritual has been adopted by some of the other ethnic groups in Nigeria. Especially during social occasions among Christians, the first item on the program is usually the presentation and blessing of the Kolanut. I witnessed several cross-ethnic Christian gatherings in Kaduna, Nigeria where an Igbo elder was called upon to officiate at the breaking of the Kolanut. A popular national adage thus developed around the Kolanut to the effect that: "The Yorubas grow the Kolanut, the Hausas eat it, but the Igbos celebrate it."!67

Uchem traces this ritual discrimination of Igbo women from infancy by following a UNICEF report which found that "girls are less valued than boys, 'within the family', when girls are taught the inferior and stereotyped roles considered more appropriate for girls and women,"68 from whence women's subordination is bound to occur. Within this structure of discrimination, the unfortunate given is that "men are preeminent human beings and women are secondary, existing for men and not really human beings in their own right."69 Basden writes that in this milieu, "[b]etween boys and girls the comparison is all in favor of the former, the latter only counting as a useful accessory in the life of a man. From the outset a youth assumes the position of the 'lord of creation' as his rightful heritage."70

On marriage and childlessness Uchem underscores that the subordination of women has made it difficult for women to be comfortable in discussing marriage and everything surrounding it, especially the difficulties or challenges of marriage. This is evident in some of the interviews she conducted. Uchem notes, ". . . there are several reasons why some women may not want to be as open as they might otherwise decide to be. One of the reasons could be related to an unwritten taboo about discussing one's experiences of marriage with another person; out of a sense of loyalty, even unto one's own detriment."71 Part of this difficulty and challenge of marriage will be the case of infertility. Childlessness in marriage and the chain-like difficulties that follow it have remained a

---

67. Uchem, *Overcoming Women's Subordination*, 60.

68. UNICEF, "Girls for Sale," as cited in Uchem, *Overcoming Women's Subordination*, 15.

69. Uchem, "Gender Inequality," 276.

70. Basden, *Among the Ibos of Nigeria*, 61.""number-of-pages":"300","source":"Amazon","abstract":"George Thomas Basden (1873–1944

71. Uchem, *Overcoming Women's Subordination*, 75.

'teething problem' in Igbo land. Uchem is forceful about this, and calls for an elaborate conversation on it. She writes, "... these more fundamental issues of inheritance and the mental constructions of the importance of having children, especially male children, which underlie polygamy, need further reflection and revision. It is at this deeper root level that polygamy, as a solution to the problem of childlessness, must be tackled."[72]

On sexuality, Uchem quotes Anne Carr, a reformed theologian, affirming that "God is not sexual; the significance of Jesus is not his maleness but his humanness . . ."[73] As such, our sexuality should not be an underlying factor in fostering a good relationship with God and with one another. In that perspective, our sexuality must be understood as a gift from God. We know that God's gifts are always good. Uchem continues her affirmation of Carr that "women's sexuality is not evil or unclean but good in the goodness of creation and sanctified in the sacramental life of the Church."[74]

In all, one can see that Uchem's theological reflection is based on the socio-cultural condition of Igbo women. From this background, she unveils and analyzes the phenomenon of underdevelopment and of gender bias as pertaining to the dehumanizing oppression and abject poverty faced by Igbo women. In doing this, she pays attention to the critical function of theology, by dwelling on Christ's manifesto which is yet to be realized in full in the lives of women: "By his life, death and resurrection Christ is meant to have 'become all things to all persons,' whether male or female,' but in reality this is not yet so for women."[75]

In resolving the fundamental problem from the Catholic Church's perspective, she invites the church to be a grass-roots church, an all-inclusive church, and a church where God must be seen as present and joining in the struggle of the masses for liberation from all structures of cultural and patriarchal oppression. Her thought on the resolution of the fundamental problem is a passionate appeal to the culture and the church to mirror Christ in evolving an egalitarian society. In Uchem's view, "[t]he cultural practices which continue to manifest in our contemporary society and Church need to be transformed into practices of gender equality in

---

72. Uchem, *Overcoming Women's Subordination*, 67.

73. Carr, *Transforming Grace*, 23, as cited in Uchem, *Overcoming Women's Subordination*, 216.

74. Carr, *Transforming Grace*, 23, as cited in Uchem, *Overcoming Women's Subordination*, 216.

75. Uchem, "Becoming All Things," 3.

word and action in the light of the Good News of Christ."[76] In this way, her challenge to the Roman Catholic Church has the sound of a voice in the wilderness. Going down the lanes of suffering women in Igbo history and the Bible, she has succeeded in bringing before her readers the closeness of God to women, and to the entirety of humanity throughout history. She says, "the outrage these women feel in their bones is God's cry of anger and pain at the injustice of those humans who inferiorize them."[77] The oppression of women is against Biblical injunctions and values. "This is what the Lord Almighty said: 'Administer true justice; show mercy and compassion to one another. Do not oppress the widow or the fatherless, the foreigner or the poor. Do not plot evil against each other' (Zechariah 7:9–10).

An Appraisal of Uchem's Theology

When I was growing up, my parents taught my sisters what is expected of females in Igbo culture. Among other things, while "[b]oys were supposed to be strong,"[78] girls must do things akin to how young women are expected to do things and behave.[79] With this 'decorum,' there is a sensitization of gender differences, wherein one gender is socialized to think it is a 'super hero,' and the other gender has to be soft and gentle with the tendency to be trampled upon. Uchem sets out to deconstruct this style of socialization which is possible because culture is learned and since it can be learned, in the same way, it can also be unlearned.

Uchem's theology and deconstruction of Igbo culture and the Roman Catholic Church are what I may call a theology of "*Talitha koum*."[80] This is so because like the young lifeless woman whom Jesus told to arise, she invites the Roman Catholic Church and Igbo culture to arise into consciousness, into a space of life, a space free from subordination. Uchem calls the church and Igbo culture "to grow." She invites "Christians to grow, from merely saying kind words to and about women, to tackling the root-cause

76. Uchem, *Gender Equality*, 12.

77. Uchem, *Gender Equality*, 157.

78. Ugwu-Oju, *What Will My Mother Say*, 51.

79. They must never walk very close to a man who is not a relative or direct brother. These were the requirements for "decorum" that the Igbo culture put on their young females.

80. Uchem advocates for a new life for the Church, and thus my reference to the woman whom the Lord gives new life when he raised her by saying "Talitha koum." See Mark 5:35–42.

of women's problems, namely, their continued subordination to men."[81] In the same token, she challenges these two very powerful institutions, and in that way empowering African and particularly Igbo women to arise from the mire of insubordination through the command given to them by Jesus Christ when he told the young woman to arise. She has been able to achieve this feat through courage that came with education.

Education and courage have remained formidable forces to use to fight and conquer the evil of oppression of women. She has significantly argued her case as an academic and as someone living a life of liberation. Despite her life of liberation and some progress made, she reiterates that much needs to be done, and especially more action and fewer words. Uchem argues that "Church people have made very fine pronouncements about women's dignity and the equality of men and women. Yet negative attitudes towards women persist in our societies and Churches till today in spite of small improvements recorded already."[82]

Fighting a serious 'war' on two fronts has made her results significant. One must bear in mind that the powerful patriarchal structure always fights back, and because she is confronting a goliath, her voice is distinct and loud. However, while she aims at liberating women, she must aim to liberate men, too, because men are under the bondage of oppressing women. This is in consonance with the Igbo proverb which says, "*nwata si a nne ya agaghi arahura, yanwa agaghi arahura*" which literally means: "a child who says his/her mother will not sleep, will equally not sleep." In other words, if men say that women will not be free, they too will not be free.

There is a strong need to study and understand gender imbalance in Igbo society. The awareness of gender inequality can be the only way to remedy the imbalance. Uchem writes, "[a] way forward is for all to acknowledge that relations are not right between men and women and for all to take definite steps to correct the situation. Secondly, it is necessary to understand the true meaning of gender equality."[83] Public awareness through education is necessary, as Uchem notes in her scholarly publications. In describing her work on gender equality, Uchem writes, "[t]he purpose of this publication is to make available to the wider public resource materials for creating on-going awareness and changing negative

---

81. Uchem, *Overcoming Women's Subordination*, 19.
82. Uchem, "Becoming All Things," 110.
83. Uchem, *Gender Equality*, 10.

beliefs, attitudes and behaviours (sic) towards women into positive ones in all areas of life."[84] This means that there is a great need for women and men to avail themselves of ongoing formation and education. If Nigerian and Igbo people engage more in cultural and religious studies, their level of awareness will fill the lacunae necessary to revolutionize Igbo and African native social institutions especially in some of her biases against the female gender.

Uchem is right in seeing an outright contradiction and hypocrisy in the Igbo designation of the kolanut as a symbol of unity, in the utter exclusion of women in presiding over its ritual of presentation and breaking. How symbolic and wonderful if the Igbo kolanut could have been used to foreshadow the Eucharistic celebration. Uchem is forceful in making this connection, which is a huge gap in Igbo cosmology and ecclesiology:

> Traditionally in the Igbo culture, the blessing and breaking of the Kolanut by the family head and the partaking of it by all present constitute the family morning prayer. The blessing and sharing of the Kolanut signify and effect the communion of the living with each other and with the ancestors whose protection on the family is thereby invoked. People in enmity with each other do not share the Kolanut together until they are reconciled. In this way, it has overtones similar to those of the Christian Eucharist. It is so rich in symbolism of inclusion, hospitality, fellowship, blessing and reconciliation that I have often thought that if Jesus had been born into the Igbo culture, he would have used the Kolanut for the Eucharist.[85]

Uchem's ecclesiological and Christological principle is evident as she uses language that is understandable and faithful, both to Catholic social teaching and to the reality of life in Igbo land. She believes that Christ liberated us, for us to be free, and the church must continue to be a champion of liberation. Her Christological thesis provides a good framework for a total human flourishing:

> Jesus' teaching role was closely linked with his prophetic role, as well as his healing ministry. As a prophet, Jesus shattered the purity system of Israel in a number of ways: through his parables, healing deeds, prophetic actions and table fellowship. The parables of Jesus were aimed at reshaping peoples' imagination,

---

84. Uchem, *Gender Equality*, 14.
85. Uchem, *Overcoming Women's Subordination*, 60–61.

forcing them to consider possibilities they would otherwise never have imagined.[86]

Her image of a free ecclesial and Igbo community is not hard to find:

> The equality of women and men has been lavishly affirmed in many Church documents. Yet, it remains to be concretized in reality. In a new world order, modeled on Christ and not on androcentric ideologies, justified with the Adamic myth, which conflicts with empirical evidence, women's experience will be different. In this new order of creation, leadership in family, society and Church will not be a permanently 'inherited privilege' of one sex, the male sex. Both women and men will share leadership equally. There will be women priests in the Catholic Church and other Western Churches in Africa and elsewhere. Women will officiate at the inclusive Eucharistic table of Christ and will participate in the ritual blessing of the Igbo Kolanut with the full dignity of the children of God. Women will no longer be projected as "children of a lesser God."[87]

This equality of women and men, a central theme in her scholarship, will remove the conditioned mind-frame of women being housekeepers and domestic role-tenders in Igbo land. Education of men and women must be reinforced. She advocates that "[t]he myths of origins that portray women as existing for men's comfort need to be re-interpreted as men and women existing for each other."[88] Education, whether in the church or African communities, is paramount, and that is one of the ways forward.

> The first step to empowering people through education is to recognize that there has been a paradigm shift . . . earlier belief is no longer working, and a new one has begun to replace it, bringing with it new theories and new understandings of the underlying realities. Formerly, the image of the world was an immovable flat disc resting on the abyss of deep sea waters and supported by huge pillars. Now, it is a well known fact that the earth is spherical, rotating on its axis while revolving on its orbit around the sun; a new piece of knowledge unknown to biblical writers. Consequently, the former conclusions about the

---

86. Uchem, *Overcoming Women's Subordination*, 199.
87. Uchem, *Overcoming Women's Subordination*, 189.
88. Uchem, "Eradicating Women Trafficking," 117.

ascribed secondary place of women in relation to men, arising from literalist biblical views of the creation needs to change.[89]

Furthermore, with education there will be the "understanding of humanity as one stock . . . the noticeable (biological gender) differences are to be recognized as sources of enrichment for the human community rather than a basis for inferiorization or secondary placement of the female in relation to the male."[90] As an advocate of inclusive theology and gender equality geared toward the liberation of women, Uchem enriches theology with a repertoire of Igbo women's experiences. She not only pays attention to Igbo cultural oppression of women, but goes further to discuss and engage with her religious tradition. She perceives the Roman Catholic Church as an uneven playing ground for males and females. Her arguments are compelling as she links the freedom of women in particular, and human freedom in general, to the mission of Christ. Like Gustavo Gutiérrez, Uchem sees this liberation project as a divine mission. As Gutierrez writes, "[t]his radical liberation is the gift which Christ offers us."[91]

In the next chapter attention is given to who Bénézet Bujo is, his method, sources and the ethical principles which emerge from his theology. The chapter will explore his proto-ancestor and *palaver* ethics, evaluating how they can reinforce the liberative character inherent in the Igbo indigenous ethics of *onye aghala nwanne ya* identified as an ethical principle capable of liberating couples who suffer infertility.

---

89. Uchem, "National Christian Religious Studies Curriculum," 543.

90. Uchem, *Gender Equality*, 4.

91. Gutierrez, *Theology of Liberation*, 103.

4

Engaging African Male Theology/Ethics
The Thoughts of Bénézet Bujo

BÉNÉZET BUJO IS ONE of Africa's foremost ethicist and theologian particularly known for his theological engagement with African culture. A description by *U.S. Catholic* says, "Father Bénézet Bujo is a diocesan priest from the Democratic Republic of the Congo, he is professor emeritus of moral theology at the University of Fribourg, Switzerland."[1] Bujo has written many books and scholarly articles in different areas of theology. He has shaped the perspectives of ethics from an African cultural context. Bujo is a theological voice to reckon with. He ". . . is a leading African theologian who studies ethics from an African perspective."[2] He has used inculturation theology as a means of dialogue with the African worldview and African culture, with the intention "to bring together the fundamentals of both Christian faith and African tradition, so that the Africans may find their own way in the resulting Christianity and feel at home therein."[3]

Oscar Bimwenyi-Kweshi has said *L'église en Afrique est née vieille*, which means, "The Church in Africa was born old."[4] In this regard, Elochukwu Uzukwu, a foremost African ecclesiologist and liturgist, recounts that:

1. US Catholic, "Father Bénézet Bujo."
2. Maina, *Making of an African Christian Ethics*, ix.
3. Bujo, *African Theology*, 75.
4. Kwesi, *Religions*, 168, as cited in Uzukwu, "Birth and Development," 3.

the midwives awaited the birth, and the child itself readily had no choice in the matter. Thus, from the time of first evangelization by Western missionaries until and after the Vatican II Council, structures such as churches, primary secondary and catechetical schools; seminaries; convents; and hospitals sprouted. Foremost in the mind of the evangelizers was the establishment of a church and, naturally, they turned to the Western European Church structures and often transplanted them intact in Africa with remarkable effect.[5]

From all indications, it appears the Western missionaries' main intention was just "to plant the Church and to increase the number of its members in Igboland . . . proclaim the message of salvation and to provide the means of salvation—the sacraments—to those who accept this message."[6] This has made Christianity still alien to many Igbo people and Africans, alien because with the introduction of Christianity, the Igbo people now domicile in two different worlds of reality. They first live in the world of their culture, where ATR reigns supreme and second in the Christian world, where they were renamed, "baptized without proper conversion and reintegration into his former culture and religion."[7] We see a people living in a mire of confusion, not knowing where to turn to during life's crises.

The missionaries did a good work in their Igbo mission. Most of them left their comfortable base in Europe to come to Africa, which was a hostile terrain to them. Their courage was without comparison, especially in traversing Igboland, a strange and rugged place. They landed from the cold weather of Ireland, for example[8] to meet the enervating heat in Igboland and unfamiliar food. When they came, the terrain was rough, as there were few foot-paths. But in their zeal for evangelization, they continued to spread the Good News through endless mission trekking. The mission land (the Igbo Land) was infested with ubiquitous mosquitoes, which caused many missionaries to die of malaria during their first year in the mission.[9] It would be uncharitable for one to just dismiss the massive effect they had, or their own sacrifices in the field. The fruits of their missionary labor are still being harvested today in Igbo land.

5. Uzukwu, "Birth and Development," 3.
6. Ebelebe, *Africa and the New Face of Mission*, 95.
7. Obilor, *Doctrine of the Resurrection*, 229–30.
8. The emphasis here is the Irish Holy Ghost Fathers who evangelized Igbo land.
9. Ikenga, *Roman Catholicism*, 76.

However, despite their major contributions in evangelizing Igbo land, they missed the mark in not using some of the existing Igbo structural values in the propagation of the faith. Their lack of understanding of ATR did not help matters. The colonial masters and missionaries did not only use demeaning words to refer to ATR, but thought Africans that:

> their religion was 'paganish' and 'heathen,' their political system was fragmented and disorganized, their technical skill was childish, their art was crude, their tales naïve, their music cacophonous, their dance lascivious. In which case then, the only way toward cultural salvation was to wash themselves clean of every bit of their 'low' and 'inferior' cultural givens, in order to imbibe the perks of a 'higher' and 'superior' culture from the hands of the colonizer.[10]

With this, the colonial and missionary ideology derided Igbo traditional institutions and religious symbols, because they saw them to be "cosmo-centric," as against "theo-centric," and as such incongruous with Judeo-Christian tradition:

> As the traditional religion was seen to be substantially opposed to the tenets of Judeo-Christian religion, it was variously qualified as not only cosmo-centric, but also animistic, and therefore no religion at all. For the colonial missionaries, it was simply a primitive form of religion that had no knowledge of the true living God of the Christian religion. Just as the religion was thought to be cosmo-centric, the traditional Igbo man was regarded as a person without a true sense of God. With this type of religious qualification, his soul was considered as a colony of Satan. The first cultural sphere therefore, to be disassembled was the religious sphere.[11]

This derision from the colonial missionaries led to the abandonment of the indigenous religion, values and culture which negatively impacted the way people embrace and live out the Christian message, and even the way they live out their traditional Igbo cultural heritage. The missionaries, probably without knowing it, in spreading the Good News of salvation within the colonial era,

> were forced to operate within the framework of the colonial era, they were forced to operate within the framework of colonial

---

10. Ekwuru, *Pangs of an African Culture*, 40.
11. Ekwuru, *Pangs of an African Culture*, 37.

package of forced acculturation. And with this frame of mind, they took off with the same colonial presupposition of cultural inequality, which assumed the traditional man to be 'pagan' and 'barbaric' as the essential prerequisite for evangelization.[12]

Within this context and background, the missionaries failed to incorporate traditional religion in their delivering of the Christian message. Today this still leaves a huge lacuna.

It is in the above context of cultural alienation of Africans that Bujo's African theology and ethics emanate. He speaks of the need to contextualize theology, especially in re-expressing the Christian message to take root within African culture. Alienation of African Christians from their cultural roots becomes Bujo's theological focus and fundamental problem. He resolves this problem through his deconstruction of African theology and the African psyche, advocating a need for theology to be rooted in the culture through an in-depth understanding of ATR. He writes, "African theology, it is plain, must be contextual, that is, it must take into full account the actual African situation."[13] This deconstruction and allowing theology to take root within African culture and religion has necessitated the emergence of various concepts to address the superficiality of theology. Concepts like: indigenization, contextualization, incarnation and Africanization of Christianity. These concepts are geared toward the same goal, inculturation (the taking root of the Gospel message within African culture), which Bujo's theology and ethics embody. Robert Schreiter, a seasoned theologian emphasizes this point in a similar way as he writes, "all of these terms point to the need for and responsibility of Christians to make their response to the gospel as concrete and lively as possible."[14] These concepts have been frequently used to make Africans see Christ and His message within the purview of their culture and history. Bujo champions this course in most of his scholarly work.

This is what could be called Bujo's decolonization of theology. Bujo shows that Africa has a lot to offer within her theology, and to Christian theology at large, about the economy and mystery of the incarnation. Bujo gives theology a different face, a theology with an African context, and thus responds to some authors like Emil Ludwig,[15] who in trying

---

12. Ekwuru, *Pangs of an African Culture*, 43.
13. Bujo, *African Theology*, 70.
14. Schreiter, *Constructing Local Theologies*, 1.
15. Ludwig (1881–1948) was a German-Swiss historian. He was famous for

to denigrate Africans and their religions and culture asks, "how can the untutored African conceive God?" and cynically answers, "Deity is a philosophical concept which savages are incapable of framing."[16] The same Ludwig, and others who thought that Africans were incapable of conceiving the concept of God, used already-designated African names for the Divine when they were translating the sacred texts: "[t]he same missionaries later found names of the Divine among African languages, which they used in biblical translations."[17] This means that they did not pay heed to the caution of Max Warren[18] to missionaries when he said, "Our first task in approaching another people, another culture, and another religion, is to take off our shoes; for the place we are approaching is holy. Otherwise, we may find ourselves treading on men's dreams. More seriously still, we may forget that God was there before our arrival."[19] Many African scholars have insisted that "Christian missionaries did not introduce Africans to the true God. On the contrary, God through the centuries has been as active among African peoples as among the Jewish people."[20] Christian missionaries seem to forget African philosophy and ethos were in place before their arrival. Mbiti goes on to argue that:

> There exist many laws, customs, set forms of behavior, regulations, rules, observances and taboos constituting the moral code and ethics of a given community or society . . . Any breach of this code of behavior is considered evil, wrong or bad, for it is an injury or destruction to the accepted social order and peace.[21]

Given the interconnectedness between God and human persons, the African ethos becomes Bujo's preoccupation in his theological enterprise. This is why he reiterates that "those who still insist that African morality is concerned exclusively with human persons and that its

---

writing the biographies of many great political figures. He wrote and documented historical facts and fictions. See Lueberin, "Emil Ludwig."

16. Cited in Idowu, *African Traditional Religion*, 88.
17. Ntloedibe-Kuswani, "Translating the Divine," 79.
18. Max Warren (1904–1977) was born of Irish parents and was a veteran Anglican missionary. See Warren, "Approaching another people."
19. Cited in Thomas, *Attitudes Toward Other Religions*, 225–26.
20. Ferm, *Third World Liberation Theologies*, 70.
21. Mbiti, *African Religions and Philosophy*, 201.

perspective excludes a monotheistic God, have failed to comprehend African thought."[22] Put in another way:

> Besides African history, Bujo's theology also has its foundation in an African anthropology. According to Bujo, human beings occupy a central place in the understanding of the Africans' moral universe. God and the spiritual world of the ancestors are only understood as they relate to life in the community. African traditional religion(s) are indispensable to the understanding of the moral universe of African people.[23]

To drive home this point, Bujo's proto-ancestor "philosophical concept" becomes his core theological concept of Christology as he makes the person of Christ better understood using the structures of ATR. One can say this is the essence of inculturation. Bujo's proto-ancestor concept touches the heartbeat of inculturation, because it transforms the core actions that make up the Christian faith among Africans. For Bujo, inculturation shows an in-depth understanding of culture, allowing each culture to flourish in the word of God which he likens to the good soil:

> In the process of inculturation, the kingdom of God does not require replacing one set of cultural 'clothes' with a new one. I would prefer to compare the kingdom of God, in the perspective of inculturation, with good soil which allows the seed or grains to grow up at once, provided that these are healthy. God's field, which contains only good soil, accepts all the positive elements of every culture and allows them to grow up and bear fruit.[24]

Bujo uses the African experience with ATR as his resource for identifying the fundamental problem, and in resolving it. Bujo is one of the outstanding African scholars who have shown adequate understanding of some of the misunderstanding of European scholars of African culture, theology and ethics. Like other African theologians, Bujo has advocated in his ethics and theology ". . . a Christianity incarnated in Africa. This will mean growth, and hence enrichment, for the entire church of Jesus Christ."[25]

His theological method is established in a unitary, inter-penetrating world (physical and spiritual). In this method, he unveils African

22. Bujo, *Foundations of an African Ethic*, 1.
23. Maina, *Making of an African Christian Ethics*, viii.
24. Bujo, *Foundations of an African Ethic*, 157.
25. Bujo, *Foundations of an African Ethic*, 168.

existential reality, as it makes sense in an African moral universe. In this setting, Bujo's Christology finds a sound expression in his projection of Christ as a proto-ancestor. Within this ancestor Christology, the person of Christ becomes intelligible to Africans within the framework of their religio-cultural perspective and their understanding of ancestorship.

Bujo's method of argumentation is efficacious, using papal and conciliar documents to his advantage. He pays attention to the encyclical *Veritatis splendor*, bringing out his sense of orthodoxy and faithfulness to the magisterium, but in that process calling attention to Africa's peculiar experience, history and ethics. Critiquing the document, he writes, "*Veritatis splendor* employs a Western doctrine of natural law; but the precepts deduced from this doctrine are based on human reason, which does not necessarily exclude errors."[26] In a bid to make his postulations more practical, Bujo does not reduce his writings to a mere intellectual curiosity, but makes them practical exercises. He draws inspiration from lived experiences and from ecclesial communities, and invites those ecclesial communities to go into practice in seeing "Jesus Christ as Proto-Ancestor." In his call for praxis, he writes, "theoretical considerations are not enough. They must prove themselves in practice. Every member of the church, clerical or lay, religious or secular, young or old, must go through a conversion process which will enable them to draw the practical conclusions for Africa today of the theological concept of Jesus as Proto-Ancestor . . ."[27]

CHRIST AS PROTO-ANCESTOR

In the African experience of the universe, an African philosopher, Bartholomew Abanuka writes that "ancestors are those who have realised to a remarkable degree the values and aspirations of their communities or groups . . . (From another perspective) ancestors are those who have not committed any abominations against the land when they were in flesh and blood . . ."[28] Bujo captures it well in his picture of an ancestor, saying that "[w]hen we say that we want to use the concept of ancestor as the basis of Christology, we refer only to God-fearing ancestors who exercise a good influence on their descendants by showing how the force

---

26. Bujo, *Foundations of an African Ethic*, 83.
27. Bujo, *African Theology*, 96.
28. Abanuka, *A New Essay*, 37.

which is life is to be used as God wishes it to be used."[29] In a nut shell, there are specific qualities that allow one to be considered an ancestor. In an earlier work by Bujo, he enumerates four of these qualities: ". . . to have been married, been blessed with children, to have lived long, and not to have died a violent death."[30] Metuh concurs with this as he goes on to give more details on the qualification for ancestorhood: "old age (relatively speaking, life lived according to the accepted moral standards of the group and appropriate funeral rites . . . and good death. Death after ripe old age is regarded as good and natural death and in some places it is called God's death."[31] In terms of the hierarchy and their connection of ancestors to the living, Bujo writes:

> In this hierarchical and participatory concept of life, the basic principle is that ancestors live on in their descendants. It is this principle that structures society at its different levels: family, clan, tribe. At the level of the family, the father is the link with ancestors. At the level of the clan, the mandate of the ancestors is carried by the head of several families together. In the tribe or nation, it is the chief, or king, who represents the ancestors.[32]

One can see that the "cult of ancestor' is very much alive in every strata of the life of Africans. Therefore, designating Christ as a Proto-Ancestor who is always present in the lives of His people makes sense. In a more detailed understanding of who an ancestor is, Jesus fits well in the African concept. Ancestors are, as Abanuka says:

> those who not only performed great feats for the community, but also died in grand old age have the most noteworthy credentials for being ranked among the ancestors (since old age is partly regarded as a blessing given to those who keep the laws and traditions of the community). Secondly, those who died young, having carried out an extraordinary assignment, for example, realising a stunning victory in war or carrying out any other assignment that added to the community's self-esteem, can get immediate access to the rank of ancestors.[33]

---

29. Bujo, *African Theology*, 79.
30. Bujo, *Ethical Dimension of Community*, 16.
31. Metuh, *Comparative Studies*, 137.
32. Bujo, *African Theology*, 20.
33. Abanuka, *New Essay on African Philosophy*, 37–38.

Though Jesus died young, he accomplished certain feats in his community that were unheard of. When Jesus opened the eyes of the man born blind, people of the community testified: "Nobody has ever heard of opening the eyes of a man born blind." (John 9:32). Above all, he lived as Bujo says, "a virtuous life in accordance with certain norms, which were issued and confirmed by a common ancestor and his successors."[34] In trying to establish the importance of Jesus being the "Protor-Ancestor," Bujo writes:

> Jesus Christ is the ultimate embodiment of all the virtues of the ancestors, the realization of the salvation for which they yearned. Further still, Jesus Christ is the Proto-Ancestor, the Proto-Life-Force, bearer in a transcendent form of the primitive 'vital union' and 'vital force.' By his resurrection, Jesus is taken up once and for all into the glory of God. He not only has life, he is life, and awakens others to life.[35]

Bujo's perception of Jesus as an ancestor is taken from his perspective of Jesus as the liberator who injects life and some kind of flourishing into his followers.[36] He is a bridge-builder. In this case, between the Supreme Being and the people, between a "distant God" and the people, ". . . the gulf between the intense awareness of the existence of God and yet of God's 'remoteness' in ATR is bridged in Christ . . ."[37] Jesus, in this understanding, becomes a link between humanity and God. He becomes the epicenter for morality. This accounts for why Bujo designates Christ not just as a Proto-Ancestor but as "Model of African Morality." With Africa being a relational culture and with everyone being accounted for by the other, this is important because Bujo contends that Jesus "came so that fullness of life might prevail, but there is a pre-condition: people must agree to serve each other and show concern for human dignity."[38]

Africa is replete with many challenges, like poor governments, witchcraft, and all kinds of disease which need to be subdued with a revitalized life provided by a proto-ancestor. Surely the proto-ancestor, with his liberating force, will inject a vital force into the community. Christ,

---

34. Bujo, *Ethical Dimension of Community*, 16.

35. Bujo, *African Theology*, 81.

36. The story of raising Lazarus from the dead in John 11:25 is poignant, as Jesus tells Martha, the deceased man's sister, "I am the resurrection and the life. The one who believes in me will live, even though they die."

37. Bediako, *Jesus and the Gospel in Africa*, 25.

38. Bujo, *African Theology*, 90.

as a proto-ancestor, gives meaning in the understanding of salvation history. This is so because he is:

> not only one who lived the African ancestor-ideal in the highest degree, but one who brought that ideal to an altogether new fulfilment. Jesus worked miracles, healing the sick, opening the eyes of the blind, raising the dead to life. In short, he brought life, and life-force, in its fullness. He lived his mission for his fellow-humans in an altogether matchless way, and, furthermore, left to his disciples, as final commandments, the law of love.[39]

The proto–ancestor concept brings the message of Christ and the Gospel home to Africans, as it makes their culture and Christian faith fluid, tied together, and making sense. This is the essence of Christianity, bringing God home to the people, Emmanuel (God with us).

Jesus as the Epitome of African Sense of Morality

Scholars like Isichei, who have argued that "Igbo societies are governed by gods and ancestors . . ."[40] are to a large extent right, because Igbos and by extension Africans want to keep their laid-down moral ethos. From that perspective, the gods and ancestors help in modelling and enforcing them. Jesus then becomes a model for African morality, because through his life, ministry, suffering and death, he embodies those values that are necessary for the integral development of every human person, and the community. The motto of his life and ministry is straight and simple. "I have come that they may have life, and have it to the full." (John 10:10). This is the aspiration of African ancestors for the community. Jesus embodies this fullness of life among other places and times, when "[h]e vigorously defended the rights of the weak, of women, of children and identified himself with outcasts and sinners."[41] Seen as a Proto-Ancestor and an epitome of African sense of morality, there is a new dawn within African moral space:

> It is this new perspective which must be henceforth the constitutive principle of African Christian ethics. The history of the Crucified One must be subversive for the customs and practices of both traditional and modern Africa. From the standpoint of

---

39. Bujo, *African Theology*, 79.
40. Isichei, *History of the Igbo People*, 24.
41. Bujo, *African Theology*, 87.

tradition, the remembering of Jesus is a challenge to conscience, urging the elimination from life those mistakes which might be labelled "the specific errors of African group life."[42]

In this regard, ethical principles and values like love and tolerance emanate from communities because they help to regulate life to an acceptable standard. The standard becomes the goal which members of the community set for themselves. Jesus as a "Proto-Ancestor whose last will was an appeal for human love and untiring effort to overcome all inhumanity"[43] does not only help in attaining African moral goals which are geared towards the common good but, ". . . humanizes and purifies the African ethos."[44]

A Critical Analysis of Bujo's Proto-Ancestor Thesis

Bujo's articulation of Jesus as proto-ancestor is not without its pitfalls. Bujo's analogy of identifying Christ as a proto-ancestor limits the scope of Christ's nature. Though African ancestors can be divinized, their veneration is largely anthropocentric. This does not fully bring the reality of the divinity of Jesus to the fore. Jesus is God, and has the same substance as the Father. The ancestor is not the supreme deity in the Igbo cosmos. Actually, ancestors are at the base of the hierarchy of Beings in the African and Igbo religious world-view. The Igbo belief system, as previously noted "consists of three hierarchical layers of the supernatural world."[45] Picturing Christ as an ancestor is a demotion within this divine hierarchical structure:

> The Igbo, like other Africans traditionally recognize the existence of a Supreme Being whom they call *Chi-uk-wu* (the Greatest Chi) or *Chineke* or *Ezecchitoke* (the God of creation) or *Osebuluwa* (God, carrier of the world). Below *Chi-ukwu* the Igbo also acknowledge the fact that this Greatest Chi has at His service, many ministering spirits whose sole business is to fulfill His commands. Thus in the invisible world of the *Igbo* we have so many spiritual beings of differing qualities and roles, namely, *Amadioha* (the thunder god); *Igwe* (the sky god); *Anyanwu* (the

---

42. Bujo, *African Theology*, 90.
43. Bujo, *African Theology*, 91.
44. Bujo, *African Theology*, 91.
45. Nnoromele, *The Way People Live*, 21.

sun god); *Ala* (the Earth goddess); *Amosu* (Witches or sorcerers or wizards); *Ekwensu* (Devil); *Ogwu* (mystical and magical forces); *Akalogheli* (disgruntled dead men); *Ogbanje* (spirits born to die); *Ndi-Ichie* (the living-dead or ancestors): etc.; to name but a few.[46]

We can see that the ancestors are in the lowest part of the African/Igbo hierarchy of spiritual beings. Therefore, designating Christ as an ancestor is making him a lesser god.

Again, in an African context there are many factors that qualify one to be an ancestor, and in the case of Christ one can argue that He does not qualify. To be an African ancestor, marriage and having children are important, showing that one is completely human, successful and accomplished. Africans love children. Bujo writes, "Childlessness is a personal disgrace,"[47] and "the worse death is to die childless."[48] Christ never married and had no children, and so designating him as an ancestor is problematic. Christ died a violent and shameful death, and since Igbo/African culture is a shame-based culture, anyone who dies a violent and shameful death in Africa cannot be a model. "Ancestors who had lived well, died in socially approved ways, and were given correct burial rites, were allowed to continue the afterlife in a world of the dead."[49] This indicates that there are "socially approved ways" to die and "correct burial rites" completed after death. Christ's death was 'shameful,' and he did not receive "correct burial rites," as he was hurriedly buried because of the Sabbath.[50] Ripe old-age is a treasure for African people and it shows that the dead person has been blessed by the gods. But Christ died young, and worse still, He died before his mother. Children are expected to bury their parents in African culture, and not the other way around. Christ dying before his mother is incompatible with African culture.

Ancestors are mostly males. For females to be ancestors, they must be unique and remarkably powerful. The portrait of Jesus as an ancestor will, to a greater extent exclude women, since ancestors are predominantly

46. Mbaegbu, "A Philosophical Investigation," 146.
47. Bujo, *African Theology*, 116.
48. Bujo, *African Theology*, 116.
49. Saideman, "Explaining the International Relations," 721–53.
50. Since Jesus was buried in haste, the women had gone to the tomb to complete the burial rites only to realize that he has risen. "When the Sabbath was over, Mary Magdalene, Mary the mother of James, and Salome bought spices so that they might go to anoint Jesus' body." Mark 16:1.

males. Jesus is God, and every human is made in the likeness of God. Designating Jesus, who is God, as an ancestor within this African world view with its patriarchal agenda, and domination and subjugation of women, might be a misrepresentation of God, who is all-inclusive of gender.

African people travel with their religion. Dianne Glave, an African-American who writes on environmental issues, notes that "Africans carried their religious experiences with nature to the New World through the onerous Middle Passage and colonial and antebellum enslavement, which transformed them."[51] This is evidenced in the place of ancestors in African-American religion. This connection adds vitality to our argument:

> Ancestors in African and Caribbean traditional religions are a part of the heavenly council under the governance of the supreme deity, along with the divinities and spirits. They make up an important link between the living and the dead, the eternal and the here and now. Indeed, a case can be made that they were adapted by slaves in the United States to Christianity via black religion, as can be seen in some spirituals and gospel songs.[52]

From this perspective, the ancestor is not a supreme deity but a kind of messenger of the supreme deity. Though Jesus is a mediator he is fully God. Jesus being in a "divine relationship to the Father establishes his superiority over the ancestors."[53] As such, his designation as a proto-ancestor is a reduction of his status.

BUJO'S AFRICAN ETHICS: PALAVER AND COMMUNITARIANISM

Palaver, amongst its many applications, is the dialogical congregating together among families in Africa to commonly seek solutions to conflicts within the nuclear and extended family. This dialogical process is never an aimless and unproductive talk, as it may wrongly be misconstrued. According to Bujo, the word "*Palaver* is by no means superfluous talk or useless negotiation but an efficient institutionalization of communicative action. If an important decision is to be arrived at over matters that affect the people as a community the wisest representatives of the people are

---

51. Glave, *Rooted in the Earth*, 44.
52. Hood, *Must God Remain Greek?*, 217.
53. Hood, *Must God Remain Greek?*, 219.

called together for a *palaver*."⁵⁴ Apart from resolving communal problems, one of the *palavers* (the family palaver) "... takes in all the questions that can contribute to invigorating the vital force of the extended family of the living and the dead."⁵⁵ Like most African rituals which are geared toward the celebration of life, Bujo notes that "*palaver*, which sometimes lasts for several days, usually ends with a celebration, or at least with an informal get-together; the form of this concluding celebration will depend on the kind of question discussed."⁵⁶ This moral discernment process has the capacity of solving problems in the nuclear and extended family systems. *Palaver* and its dialogical method of solving a problem in Africa become one of Bujo's foundations of African ethics. Bujo writes that "African ethics does not stay at the level of formal principles, but is concerned with the application of the norms proposed in the course of palaver."⁵⁷

Bujo identifies three categories of *palaver*. The first category "is therapeutic *palaver*, which is a dialogue between the traditional healer and the patient, or his and her circle."⁵⁸ In this dialogical arrangement, the practitioner engages with his or her patient to find out the possible "causes of an illness."⁵⁹ In addition, medical and communal histories are investigated and then steps are taken within the context of the community to treat the infirm. The second form of *palaver* is "the family *palaver*"⁶⁰ where "behind closed doors people deal with problems of the family in its African sense, encompassing the living, the dead and the yet-to-be-born. Family *palaver* is the foremost place for developing domestic ethics."⁶¹ This kind of dialogical engagement delves into a wide range of issues, including topics about marriage, inheritance and "sharing family property."⁶² The last form of *palaver* is administrative. This "is called if a family *palaver* fails to solve a problem, or to address issues relating to the wider community. This *palaver* has a more political character and may

---

54. Bujo, *Ethical Dimension of Community*, 36.
55. Bujo, *Ethical Dimension of Community*, 36.
56. Bujo, *Ethical Dimension of Community*, 50.
57. Bujo, "Distinctives of African Ethics," 84.
58. Bujo, "Distinctives of African Ethics," 83.
59. Bujo, "Distinctives of African Ethics," 83.
60. See Bujo, *Foundations of an African Ethic*, 46–54.
61. Bujo, "Distinctives of African Ethics," 83.
62. See Bujo, *Foundations of an African Ethic*, 46–54.

apply to several clan communities."[63] Administrative *palaver* sounds like a court of appeal where aggrieved members who are not satisfied with the decisions arrived at family *palaver* take it to administrative *palaver*. It must be noted that the foundation of the three types of *palaver* is domestic and community-based.

This community-based engagement becomes the substratum of African ethics, which are different from Western ethics, with particular reference to Europeans and Americans:

> The concept and practice of palaver thus shapes certain distinctive (sic) of African ethics in relation to Western ethics. Following the Cartesian philosophy introduced above, with its emphasis on reason and individuality, Western ethics becomes grounded in natural law or moral law. In contrast, African ethics are derived primarily from the community and governed by what enhances abundant life for all.[64]

The multi-dimensional nature of Bujo's understanding and application of *palaver* has much to contribute to Christian ethics. The concept of *Palaver* strengthens Bujo's argument that theology can no longer be framed from only one perspective. Theology can no longer assume a universal cloak; rather, it has to be contextualized and understood to address a lived experience of a given people. Bujo's articulation of an African ethic grounded in the process of *Palaver* is his attempt to understand and interpret scriptures and theology in the light of the African lived experience of community, and what this experience contributes to the formulation of Christian ethics.

> The relationship between African communitarian and individual responsibility has immense implications for Christian ethics. On the one hand, Christians make very personal decisions before God. But on the other, they should not do so without regard for the faith community. The Christian is bound together with the Mystical Body. A good work is an important building block of this Mystical Body.[65]

This is one of Bujo's finest efforts, to see what Africa can put on the table in terms of Christian ethics. Africa, from his perspective, can no longer be ignored, because even its communitarian nature has immense

63. Bujo, "Distinctives of African Ethics," 83.
64. Bujo, "Distinctives of African Ethics," 83–84.
65. Bujo, "Solidarity and Freedom," 48–50.

implication for Christian ethics. Bujo's scholarly enterprise has done well toward regenerating, refurbishing and reactivating the immensity and richness of the African universe.

His arguments, like that of many African scholars, focus on the need to look to Africa for religious consciousness, with her rich cultural and religious heritage. Mbiti, who shares this view with Bujo, pointedly looks at Western Christians, and asks, "[w]e have eaten theology, will you now eat theology with us?"[66] Africa can no longer be theologically ignored, because "what happens in America, Europe and Asia has its impact upon Africa, so that the people of our continent are increasingly involved in the peoples of the world."[67] It is time for African theologians and scholars to tell their story. They must engage in a mission and in scholarly work that proclaim the hour and moment for Africa. Africans cannot undo the past but the experience of the past cannot be neglected in a bid to forge ahead. Bujo, who is quoting from Alistair McIntyre and apparently agreeing with him, says, "[w]e are, whether we acknowledge it or not, what the past has made us and we cannot eradicate from ourselves . . . those parts of ourselves which are formed by our relationship to each formative stage in our history."[68] African theologians and ethicists like Bujo have a mission to tell their own story. They must tell their success stories and the challenges therein, and formulate sound ethical principles to navigate through those challenges.

In the course of telling and enforcing an African story and theology, note the strong correlation between the individual and the community. Mbiti's timeless aphorism gives a better shape to this understanding: "I am, because we are, and since we are, therefore I am."[69] From this understanding of the individual in relation to the community, Bujo says that in this mutual encounter, the individual does not lose his freedom within this ethic. Bujo writes:

> As for Black African ethics, since individuals can only exist within the 'us,' it is impossible for them to fulfil their potential outside of the community. To grasp this concept, one must understand the notion of person in Africa, which consists in the interdependence between the individual and the community.

66. As cited in Bediako, *Jesus And The Gospel*, xvii.

67. Mbiti, *African Religions and Philosophy*, 284.

68. MacIntyre, *After Virtue*, 130, as cited in Bujo, *Ethical Dimension of Community*, 27.

69. Mbiti, *African Religions and Philosophy*, 141.

This interdependence goes beyond biological continuity and a shared spiritual heritage, to entail the uninterrupted interaction between all of a community's members—those alive, dead, and yet-to-be-born. Thus, to be called a 'person' does not simply require being a member of the community, but actively participating in mutual, interpersonal relations. In other words, individuals only become persons if they do not isolate themselves but act together with the entire community.[70]

Bujo draws a line between Rene Descartes' *cogito ego sum*, or in its French version *Je pense, donc je suis* (I think, therefore, I am), being the foundation of Western ethics and "African communitarianism." He argues that ". . . according to the African conception, the human being does not become human by *cogito* (thinking) but by *relatio* (relationship) and *cognatio* (kinship). The fundamental principle of this ethics is not *cogito ergo sum* (I think, so I am), but rather, *cognatus sum ergo sum* (I am related, so I am)."[71] This is the basis of Bujo's communitarian ethic. Bujo's understanding of an African ethic with communitarianism as its foundation stems from his perception of an African as a being in connection with others. Bujo insists that "without communal relationship one can neither find his or her identity nor learn how to think. Self-awareness presupposes somebody opposite to you in human form."[72] Since palaver is dialogical in nature, it is within this context of relationality that he articulates his understanding of African ethic which is "essentially based on communication."[73] The 'I' factor in Western ethics and the 'We' factor in African ethics creates a yawning gap between the foundations of the two.

A Review of Bujo's *Palaver*

Bujo's use of the word *palaver* raises its own problem. *Palaver* is a coinage from Portuguese '*palavra*' meaning "word, speech, talk."[74] Since it is not indigenous, it is bound to alienate those for whom it was coined. The term *palaver* has another application for some Westerners. The Oxford dictionary in United States English defines *palaver* as "prolonged and

70. Bujo, "Distinctives of African Ethics."
71. Bujo, *Ethical Dimension of Community*, 54.
72. Bujo, *Ethical Dimension of Community*, 54.
73. Bujo, *Ethical Dimension of Community*, 55.
74. Online Etymology Dictionary, "Palaver."

idle discussion."[75] Idle discussion or talk is unlikely to achieve any good result. However, those who call Bujo's understanding and embracing of *palaver* 'aimless talk' partly have a lack of understanding of African logic, and of Africans' perception of reality.

The lack of Western, and particularly, Euro-American, understanding of African logic seems to suggest that Edward Hall[76] is right when he says, "Western man sees his system of logic as synonymous with the truth. For him it is the only road to reality."[77] There is a difference between Western syllogism and African syllogism. African ways of logic, of solving a problem and arriving at a decision, are 'curved,' while the Western style is linear.[78] Calling *palaver* aimless talk is clearly a misunderstanding of the African mindset and syllogistic style.

Duane Elmer, a Western missionary, experienced this difference between Western and African styles of logic while on mission in Africa. He writes, "I was schooled in linear thought where one works in a straight line to the conclusion or decision."[79] 'Linear logic' is the Western style of solving problems, and in communicating a thought. This style of arriving at a decision is "efficient, direct, and precise."[80] This is not the thought pattern for Africans. The African form of reasoning can be said to be like a 'spiral' which entails "moving inward toward the center."[81] In this style, a linear thinker will find it repetitive and cyclic. This accounts for why *palaver* is seen as endless talk by some Westerners. It is not aimless talk; it is just a people's way of arriving at a solution to their problem through their inherent style of logic.

The juxtaposition and the difference that emanate from a Western style of conversation and an African style is a pointer to the argument that *palaver* is not an "idle discussion." In conversations, individualistic cultures (like most Western ones) are straightforward and use fewer words in communication. That is why, from a Western perspective, some will say that, "whenever individuals from different cultures come together

75. Oxford Dictionaries, "Palaver."

76. American researcher "Edward T. Hall was an anthropologist who made early discoveries of key cultural factors. In particular he is known for his high and low context cultural factors." Changing Minds, *Hall's cultural factors*.

77. Hall, *Beyond Culture*, 9.

78. Elmer, *Cross-Cultural Connections*, 149.

79. Elmer, *Cross-Cultural Connections*, 150–55.

80. Elmer, *Cross-Cultural Connections*, 150–55.

81. Elmer, *Cross-Cultural Connections*, 152.

and interact, they bring with them a whole host of different value orientations, cultural expectations, verbal and nonverbal routines . . . that often lead to communication problems and conflict."[82] This is because a collectivistic culture, like most African cultures, will use more words, entering into a relationship before they speak their mind on a given topic. James Neuliep puts it well when he writes that, "Direct styles are often used in low-context, individualistic culture. Conversely, an indirect style, which is often seen in high-context culture and collectivistic culture, is one where the speaker's intentions are hidden or only hinted at during interaction."[83] Here we see that language and its style of speaking can in part be what define a people.

Wilson Maina defends Bujo's thesis that *palaver* is not aimless talk. Maina writes, "'Palaver' does not mean unnecessary or meaningless talk. Palaver implies the discussion of an issue in a community where various people gather together, and share perspectives and arrive at the best solution. African palaver does not exclude individual decisions because everybody in the community is represented."[84] Once more, this points to the community-based ethic of Bujo.

THE POSSIBILITY OF A TYPOLOGY

Having now reviewed the theology and ethics of Oduyoye, Uchem and Bujo, this section identifies what may be considered a typology. The components of the typology reflect the contributions of Oduyoye, Uchem and Bujo in formulating a path toward liberation of couples who suffer infertility in marriage. The following themes, consistent with the comparative method identified in the introductory chapter of this book, will be discussed: denominational affiliation, reading the context, methodology, sources and approach, sexuality/marriage/child bearing/childlessness, Christology, the ecclesial role, education, and inculturation theology. The last section examines the theological and ethical principles which emerge from the three authors' works. Using their opinions and conclusions, we will be able to shed further light and a better understanding of the liberative force inherent in the Igbo indigenous ethic of *onye aghala nwanne ya*.

---

82. Neuliep, *Intercultural Communication*, 366.
83. Neuliep, *Intercultural Communication*, 249.
84. Maina, *Making of an African Christian Ethics*, x.

Denominational Affiliation

The three African scholars already engaged in this book are members of the Christian church. Oduyoye is a member of the Methodist church of Ghana and she is a lay theologian. She makes scant references to her denomination. She does not much invoke the authority of her Methodist tradition, but appeals to Christian leaders and elders of the church in general in driving home her points.

Uchem, on the other hand, is a religious sister in the Roman Catholic Church. She brings to the fore her denomination's exclusion of women from ordination to the priesthood. She advocates for a change in the policy. In the same vein, she invokes the authority of conciliar and post-conciliar documents on Catholic social teachings which advocate for the dignity and equality of all God's children. Particular reference must be made of her use of the papal document, *Gaudium et Spes, the Pastoral Constitution on the Church in the Modern World,* which talks about the pre-eminence of family and married life and the dignity of all who constitute this unit.

Bujo is a Roman Catholic priest who pays much attention to the structures in his church, which he perceives to be exclusive especially with regard to African experience and history in the life and theology of the Church. In all, the three scholars show a great depth of incisive scholarly research and pastoral zeal in driving home their points. In the process they invite the church and their denominations to wake up from slumber, and to be alive to existential human problems, especially those dealing with oppression of the most vulnerable.

Reading the Context

Oduyoye, Uchem and Bujo all pay glowing tribute to the missionaries who evangelized Africa. However, they are unanimous in saying that their missionary adventures had an ugly side. For Oduyoye, the activities and style of the missionary activity in Africa exposed a lacuna because of its lack of "root."

> The way Western churches that have been implanted in Africa look at women mirrors their Euro-American predecessors. As transplants that never firmly taken root, they have not yet grown free of the attitudes of their 'mother churches,' nor have

they been able to cope with reforms that have taken or are taking place in those churches.[85]

The idea of "implanted" and "as transplants" from Western paradigms itself constitutes arrogant alienation of Africans. For Uchem, "the missionaries effectively and uncritically implemented the colonial policies, which politically, economically and socially marginalized women. Consequently, women were deposed from their economic, political and social positions, which they had enjoyed in the pre-colonial, pre-Christian and pre-Islamic days."[86] Because of the ripple effects of the evangelization style of missionaries, and to forestall a repetition of the 'lord and master style,' Bujo for his part; advocates for an African church where "[m]issionaries must stop behaving like neo-colonialist bosses. They must be, not oppressors, but liberators, who bring good news."[87] All these critiques from these African scholars are a result of the missionaries not understanding African culture, and their imposition of their own ecclesial structures on Africans.

Methodology, Sources and Approach

Oduyoye and Uchem's methodology stems from their negative experiences as women and the experiences of Africans, especially those most vulnerable within the African patriarchal space. The pathetic conditions of African women, subdued and humiliated almost in every domain of African communities become the launching pad for their research. Bujo for his part uses the highly misunderstood and to some extent denigrated African cultural paradigm to re-express the Christian message.

The sources of these theologians show them as participant observers. They show a profound knowledge of scripture. Oduyoye shows a deep mastering of her matrilineal Akan culture, the use of proverbs, stories, fables and myths, all of which unveil the rich African ethos preserved through local and indigenous narratives. Uchem uses a variety of sources showing a clear understanding of the 'life-wire' of Igbo patriarchal life, like the ritual of breaking and eating of traditional kola nut. She also manifests a deep understanding of biblical narratives. She is a fine storyteller, as she makes the life experiences of the women she interviewed come alive for her readers. The richness of the interviews she conducted

---

85. Oduyoye, *Daughters of Anowa*, 172–73.
86. Uchem, *Overcoming Women's Subordination*, 46–47.
87. Bujo, *African Theology*, 111.

laid bare some aspects of Igbo culture's sweet-coated but bitter pills. She shows a deep knowledge of the teachings of the Roman Catholic Church: the *Catechism* of *the Catholic Church* is one of her major sources. Bujo's sources include philosophy and the African experience of their universe, and how it is intelligible to them. His use of Church documents (such as papal encyclicals) as a source, and his introspection into African culture make his arguments intelligible to a large audience.

In the manner of approach to her articulation of theology and ethics, as noted earlier, Oduyoye is known to 'tread softly but firmly.' Uchem is more straight forward. Both remain faithful to biblical narratives, especially in revealing the condition of African women. Like Oduyoye and Uchem, Bujo engages with ATR and African philosophy and culture to lay bare the African condition. These scholars' various approaches enrich the debate and widen the intellectual horizon.

Sexuality, Marriage, Child Bearing and Childlessness

Oduyoye, Uchem and Bujo hold in high esteem the institution of marriage. However, they each have a disdain for how childlessness is treated in Africa. Oduyoye says, "[p]rocreation is the most important factor governing marriages in Africa."[88] In that light, "[t]he fertility of the woman is the biological foundation of marriage and it governs male-female relations with the institution."[89] In that sense, procreation as the epicenter of marriage becomes the determinant of a successful marriage. From Oduyoye's perspective, this strong desire for having children entrenches polygamy within the African cultural space. She writes, "[n]evertheless, it is the importance of having children, more than anything else, that keeps both men and women from abandoning polygamy."[90] Uchem extols the essence of marriage and the valor of Igbo women, but maintains that the intricacies of marriage and women's attempt to save their marriages end up suffocating them. Uchem argues that "Igbo women are really strong and in control of affairs, but perhaps in order to humor their marriage partners, they let them feel good and in charge by acting subordinate."[91] Marriage, with reference to women, becomes paradoxical; in that context

88. Oduyoye, *Daughters of Anowa*, 141.
89. Oduyoye, *Daughters of Anowa*, 141.
90. Oduyoye, *Daughters of Anowa*, 52.
91. Uchem, *Overcoming Women's Subordination*, 54.

Uchem refers to women in marriage as "powerful yet subordinate." Uchem's critique of polygamy as a way of solving the problem of childlessness for a particular woman is significant. Polygamy, in her estimation, undermines the dignity of the woman. Uchem opines, "[t]hus, polygamy does not do justice to the actual experiences of those women both in the traditional and contemporary situations on whom a co-wife has been forced on account of their not having any child or a male child."[92]

Bujo succinctly, describes the shipwreck that can be seen in a childless marriage. He paints a picture of how the community turns its back and humiliates childless couples:

> A married couple with no children is like a dead tree in the eyes of the African community. Apart from their religious and eschatological ideas on survival, the partners are jeered at by their kin, friends and acquaintances. This public form of disgrace is an extra burden for the married people in question. Hence, in a good number of ethnic communities in Africa, it is the normal practice to conduct marriage "provisionally" until the wife is pregnant. Of course, other motives play a role as well: mutually getting to know one another better, assurance of sexual satisfaction, etc. Nonetheless, fertility appears to be the over-riding motive.[93]

This means that the success of a marriage will depend on how well the couples prove themselves to be complete human beings by begetting children. For Bujo, this accounts for the causes of polygamy: "[i]n this regard, three closely related situations should be mentioned: barrenness, lack of a male offspring, and the socioeconomic motive."[94]

On sexuality, Oduyoye and Uchem have similar views on the way men see themselves as a stronger sex and women as a weaker sex. Drawing specifically from African folktales, Oduyoye writes, "[i]n male-female relationships, as described in folktales, men see themselves under pressure to prove themselves; they perform heroic deeds, risking life and limb to win and retain the affection of the woman in their lives, usually mothers, wives, or mother-in-law."[95] Uchem shares the same view of the ugly issue of men legitimizing a woman's sexuality. Uchem agrees with the thoughts of Ranjini Rebera when she writes, "sexuality is still linked to temptation and sin, and female sexuality has always been the property

---

92. Uchem, *Overcoming Women's Subordination*, 72.
93. Bujo, *Ethical Dimension of Community*, 99.
94. Bujo, *Ethical Dimension of Community*, 109.
95. Uchem, *Overcoming Women's Subordination*, 45.

of men. A woman has no right to enjoy her sexuality; it is something she offers to the man. With this kind of imagery embedded in our psyche, it is not difficult to see how and why women become easy victims of prostitution."[96] Bujo, however, envisions sexuality in relation to the community, "African communities are interested in the sexual lives of all their members, since sexuality is not a private matter. The goal of sexuality is to keep together the community entrusted to us by our ancestors and to bestow ever new life on this community."[97]

With all the nuances of marriage and all its intricacies and the problem of childlessness in marriage, Oduyoye seems to suggest that the problem may never be solved, but women can change their attitudes toward the problem. This sounds like an overwhelming situation of 'live with the problem until when change comes.' She writes, "[a]bove all, I feel that real change will come about when women can say—with or without husbands, with or without children—that the most important fact is that women are human and will find fullness in reaching for goals that we set for ourselves."[98]

While Oduyoye is married, she has no biological child, and makes scant reference to that. Uchem and Bujo by virtue of the obligation of celibacy on the Catholic priesthood of the Latin rite and those in religious life are neither married nor have children.

Christology

Christology is the rallying point of these scholars, as they write of different forms of encounter with Christ through their variations on the theology of liberation. Their thoughts confirm the common impression that "Christology is undoubtedly the most advanced subject in African theology today."[99] The Christological import of Oduyoye and Uchem sets their mission on the course of immanent liberation of the oppressed (in their case the oppression of African women), which defines the mission of Jesus Christ. With a Christ-centered theology, they show the vital force that comes from Christ's reaction to the women who were oppressed in the scriptures.

---

96. Rebera, "Challenging Patriarchy," 105–12, as cited in Uchem, *Overcoming Women's Subordination*, 14.
97. Bujo, *Foundations of an African Ethic*, 37.
98. Bujo, *Foundations of an African Ethic*, 147.
99. Gibellini, *Paths of African Theology*, 70.

While Oduyoye and Uchem focus on women, the theology of all three scholars is Christ-centered. However, Bujo comes from a different angle. He enmeshes his Christology on the reconnection of African people to their culture. Thus, he espouses the proto-ancestor concept, depicting Christ as one who takes root in a culture, and in that process liberates and sanctifies the culture. In all, Christ is seen as the ultimate liberator of women and an African culture submerged in the mire of colonialism and Christianity.

Ecclesia

Oduyoye, Uchem and Bujo wear hats with two sides: one side is that of a scholar, and the other side that of a Christian minister. Oduyoye finds the church to be oppressive and a source of anxiety. She lays this bare when she writes, "[a]s one reads of women's lives in the Church, the evidence begins to emerge that 'women become dangerous' when we question 'the powerful and masculine models of the internal structures of the church,' and as such our presence has been construed as a source of tension."[100] In this regard, Oduyoye courageously speaks to the church and by extension speaks pointedly to African male intellectuals and theologians, inviting them and at same time challenging them to give "much attention to women in their various enterprises."[101] Uchem, in the same tone, challenges the church, particularly, the Roman Catholic Church, about the exclusion of women from the ministerial life of the church. She says, "[t]his situation is particularly disturbing, as it blocks possibilities of growth and conversion towards a greater sense of social justice required by the principles of the Catholic Social Teachings and called for in the new evangelization in Africa."[102] For Uchem, the structures of the Church have been oppressive to women, whereas it ought to be a paragon of liberation. She envisages a situation "where both the Igbo and the Church, must be sifted so that what is liberating for all, both women and men will be upheld and what is liberating for only men and not for women must be discarded or transformed."[103] Bujo's perspective hinges on the church being a listening one. For this to happen, ". . . the magisterium first *listens*

---

100. Fabella and Oduyoye, "Introduction," xiii.
101. Oduyoye, *Beads & Strands*, 108.
102. Uchem, *Overcoming Women's Subordination*, 18.
103. Uchem, *Overcoming Women's Subordination*, 30.

and develops large, broad ears."[104] Having listened, Bujo invites the church "... to enter into the sufferings of the poor and oppressed so that they may ease them in the name of Christ."[105] The point and similarity here is that all three think that the church has a serious role to play in the process of liberation. This commonality is significant.

Education

A common theme among the writing of Oduyoye, Uchem and Bujo is education. They attained the heights they have reached because of education, with each earning various academic degrees. The only way to dispel ignorance is through education. Education for them becomes a major tool in fighting oppression of women and subjugation of African culture and people. Education, both formal and informal (such as travelling into different cultures), widened the horizon of the authors. They recommend it as an important way to fight the scourge of ignorance and oppression. Oduyoye advocates for an equal opportunity for all in terms of availability of education, "Similarly, the numerical insignificance of African women in most professions reflects the global situation of women's lack of equal access to education."[106] Uchem has shown a great passion for this, as she teaches in the graduate level of higher institutions of learning. Bujo, in the family *palaver* context, establishes that parents can educate their young ones a lot through a family palaver. This didactic occurs within a *palaver* context "when the parents exercise their educational duty by calling their children to account for misbehavior: they do this by means of a clarifying conversation which permits an exact insight into the question at issue."[107] Education for all is necessary in sustaining the values of the community and in maintaining community equilibrium.

Inculturation

A crucial element of the work of the three theologians under study in this book is the issue of inculturation. While Oduyoye unveils her matrilineal Akan culture to holistically understand African women properly, Bujo

---

104. Bujo, *Foundations of an African Ethic*, 157.
105. Bujo, *African Theology*, 99.
106. Oduyoye, *Daughters of Anowa*, 93.
107. Bujo, *Foundations of an African Ethic*, 48.

and Uchem, from their Roman Catholic background, remain attentive to inculturation, which in their view is the bedrock of African theology. Inculturation emphasizes the need for making the Gospel message address each group in their particular experiences and history, and in that way bring the Christian message home. Inculturation focuses on the Gospel speaking in familiar language and symbols of the people. Uchem draws a connection between the Igbo ritual of the breaking of kola nuts and the Eucharist, suggesting "that there is a relationship between women's subordination in the Catholic Church and in the Igbo culture, epitomized by male-headship model of family, civil and Church life; and ultimately symbolized by women's exclusion from celebrating public sacramental ritual [Eucharist] in the Catholic Church and [the Kolanut] in the Igbo culture."[108] Bujo considers a proto-ancestor ecclesiology where the person of Jesus can be understood within the prism of African ancestorship. Bujo's appreciation of inculturation is apt and well rooted:

> I would prefer to compare the kingdom of God, in the perspective of inculturation, with good soil which allows the seed or grains to grow up at once, provided that these are healthy. God's field, which contains only good soil, accepts all the positive elements of every culture and allows them to grow up and bear fruit. Thus it is always the same field, but with a variety of plants which reflect the richness of the soil.[109]

Bujo's appreciation of inculturation is not without some nuances. There are challenges especially with some traditional practices in Africa like sorcery, female circumcision, polygamy and many others. While there are lots of good things in African culture, Bujo underscores the need to purify or change some of Africa's evil practices. He writes: "The inculturation of Christianity, however, should not hide the social relevance of African tradition, but rather challenge the African person to transform his/her world into a better place."[110]

THEOLOGICAL AND ETHICAL PRINCIPLES

The aforementioned eight themes constitute an application of the comparative method. This last section will now help us decipher the

108. Uchem, *Overcoming Women's Subordination*, 20.
109. Bujo, *Foundations of an African Ethic*, 157.
110. Bujo, *Ethical Dimension of Community*, 19.

theological and ethical principles that emanate from the thoughts of the three scholars, and how the identified theological and ethical principles can liberate Igbo couples experiencing infertility.

Mutuality and Voicing it Out

Oduyoye and Uchem advocate for mutuality, which leads them to propose that women and men be treated the same without regard to gender. They do this by pulling women out of the drain into which society has pushed them, and by advocating that women tell their stories themselves. Uchem speaks of "an inclusive theology, capable of overcoming women's subordination."[111] In this sense of inclusiveness, she envisages "equality of social, political, economic, cultural and religious opportunities for both men and women rather than to biological sameness."[112] Oduyoye, on the other hand, focuses on the submerged female gender, bringing them to that mutual dignity with men, which one can say, is God's will for humanity. As Oduyoye says, "[o]ur immediate community of accountability is African women who seek a continent that is alive to God's mission in Africa and respond creatively to what God wills for Africa."[113] When women tell their own stories, it is not only therapeutic, it is empowering and it also changes the narrative. This accounts for why Uchem's interviews are incisive and relevant, in which women recount their experiences in their own words.[114] Stories told by those who experience pain themselves are different. The case of first-hand experience narrated by Catherine, a nurse in the hospital interviewed by Uchem, shows the appalling situation of a female child in Igbo culture. Catherine says:

> Women were not valued. I remember when I was working in the maternity. Sometimes I had cases where some husbands did not even come to visit their wives after childbirth if it was a baby-girl. But if it was a boy, even if there was no money, they would go and borrow, to come and pay the bills and have the mother and child discharged. [Why was that.?] They prefer sons; ndi ga anochiri ha obi; those who would inherit their homestead.[115]

---

111. Uchem, *Overcoming Women's Subordination*, 12.
112. Uchem, *Gender Equality*, 47.
113. Oduyoye, *Introducing African Women's Theology*, 20.
114. Uchem, *Overcoming Women's Subordination*, 81–89.
115. Uchem, *Overcoming Women's Subordination*, 93.

This is significant because in the interview and other stories shared, we see that when women speak out, a healing process is initiated. They 'own' the story and experience, and in that process it is easier to find solutions to these problems even among women themselves. Though Bujo does not talk exclusively about women, he talks about African theologians speaking out. He says ". . . African theologians too must speak with a prophetic voice."[116] Bujo speaks about dialogue between cultures, which is in line with the principle of mutuality. Bujo goes further and says, "[t]here must of course be dialogue with other cultures; no one would wish African theology to be practiced in a ghetto."[117]

The Concept of *Imago Dei*

There is a similarity in the way Oduyoye and Uchem treat the *imago Dei* concept. They root their understanding of the *imago Dei* in Genesis 1:27. While Oduyoye states that ". . . we are beings created in the image of God,"[118] Uchem reiterates that ". . . men and women are equally made in God's image."[119] Both scholars assert that God duly created all of humanity in God's image. It is only through humanity's understanding of the true meaning of the *imago Dei* concept that the subordination of women could be eradicated. This is seen from a different angle in Bujo's perspective. The West and Africans must all be treated as God's children, without any race or culture feeling that it is superior over the other. To treat all human beings as God's children becomes the centrality of Bujo's thinking on the *imago Dei* concept. From a Thomistic viewpoint, he argues"[t]hat the relationship between the human person and God is that of an *imago* to its *exemplar*."[120] According to him, "God can only be experienced as a liberating God if he penetrates deep into the cultural roots of the people. This is because the human person thrives in these roots in the struggle for identity."[121] Whether the African continent or African women whom

---

116. Bujo, *African Theology*, 72.
117. Bujo, *African Theology*, 72.
118. Oduyoye, *Introducing African Women's Theology*, 48.
119. Uchem, *Gender Equality*, 47.
120. Aquinas, *Summa Theologica*, I–II, cited in Bujo, *Foundations of an African Ethic*. 97–98.
121. Bujo, *Ethical Dimension of Community*, 141.

Oduyoye and Uchem advocate for their liberation, there is a dire need to allow God's saving grace to permeate the inner core of their beings.

Solidarity Embellished in Love

In the face of oppression and exclusion, solidarity (alignment from different perspectives) rooted in love is important for ameliorating a bad situation, since solidarity can foster peace and freedom. Oduyoye writes about women and the church being in solidarity with women to bring about a greater and flourishing whole. Uchem invites all of humanity to "work together" to achieve God's purpose for the world: "[o]ur call as Christians, both men and women, is to conversion, toward being more like Christ. Men and women need to regard each other more as equals and work together as equal partners for human development and the growth of God's reign in this world."[122] This "working together" will entail companionship in the spirit of love. In terms of marriage, Uchem's perspective is that "[l]oving each other and adapting gender roles in this practical way makes for more harmony and happiness between couples."[123] With regard to solidarity in love from an African communitarian perspective, especially with reference to a suffering member of the community, Bujo writes:

> They speak with the dying and give them in various ways the feeling and the awareness that they are included in the *process of personal growth* even as their physical strength declines. Through this solidarity of the community in suffering and at the hour of death, in a communication that may take the form of a nonverbal "palaver," the sick and the dying find fresh courage and learn to face suffering and death with greater human dignity.[124]

In the same token of solidarity, Bujo calls on the universal church (particularly the Roman Catholic Church) to march hand-in-hand in solidarity with the church in Africa, which has long suffered from exclusion. This principle of solidarity, which cuts across the thoughts of all three scholars, will surely achieve the human community which they all yearn for—a community of peace, unity, love and harmony.

---

122. Uchem, *Gender Equality*, 56.
123. Uchem, *Gender Equality*, 46.
124. Bujo, *Foundations of an African Ethic*, 89.

In the next chapter, the nature of the indigenous Igbo ethic of *onye aghala nwanne ya* will be explored as an ethical principle that can liberate Igbo couples from the pains and struggles of infertility.

5

Onye Aghala Nwanne Ya
An Alternative

INTRODUCTION

THE AFRICAN ETHICIST SAMUEL Waje Kunhiyop understands African ethics as a tripartite construct:

> African ethics is intensely personal, communal and religious. It is personal in the sense that it is deeply rooted in the being of the person, affecting not only the mind, but also the heart, body and spirit . . .
>
> African ethics is communal in that it seldom thinks in terms of individual ethical decisions that do not affect other people. Whatever affects individuals also affects their immediate family as well as their distant relatives, both those who are living and those who are dead . . .
>
> African ethics is also religious. God, the spirits of the departed (the ancestors), the good and evil spirits have a pervasive influence on the morality of the people.[1]

In bringing out the essence of African ethics, Bujo is more forceful as he shares the same view with Kunhiyop: "[i]t follows—if one looks at the entire panorama—that ethical conduct not only is based on individual, but is realized primarily by means of a relational network that is equally anthropocentric, cosmic, and theocentric."[2]

---

1. Kunhiyop, *African Christian Ethics*, xv.
2. Bujo, *Foundations of an African Ethic*, 2.

African ethics, as espoused by these two African ethicists, fits well within the framework of Christian ethics. One dictionary definition of Christian ethics cites "four base points," which helps to make sense in our understanding of the fundamentals and the particular case of African Christian ethics:

> The base points are: (1) theological interpretation in a restricted sense—that is, the understanding and interpretation of God. God's relations to the world and particularly to human beings, and God's purposes; (2) the interpretation of the meaning and significance of human experience and history, of events and circumstances in which human beings act, and of nature; (3) the interpretation of persons or communities as moral agents, and their acts; and (4) the interpretation of how persons and communities ought to make moral choices and judge their actions, those of others, and the states of affairs in the world.[3]

From these "four base points" and the peculiarity of the African community, one can say that African ethics must be looked at from a multidimensional perspective, with many disciplines incorporated for a holistic understanding. Since patriarchy is embedded in Africa, African women's theology must affect the understanding of its ethical principles. Being largely an evangelized people, Christian theology and the Bible also have a bearing in African ethics. Since Africans are a religious people, ATR and cultural customs have a prominent role in the understanding of Africa's ethical principles, and the wider spectrum of the African continent. Incorporating all these will mean understanding and fully applying the indigenous ethic of *onye aghala nwanne ya* in the liberation of Igbo couples who suffer infertility from communal oppression.

In his 'Social Contract,' the Genevan philosopher Jean-Jacques Rousseau notes that, "Man(sic) is born free, and everywhere he(she) is in chains. One man (sic) thinks [of] (themselves) himself the master of others, but remains more of a slave than they are."[4] To some extent, this desire to be "the master of others" suggests that in the nature of humans, domination, selfishness and survival of the fittest are widespread. In this milieu, some humans, characterized either by gender, color or other affiliations, try to assert themselves by subjugating others, and using them to serve as ladders to affirm their 'superiority.'

---

3. Childress and Macquarrie, *New Dictionary of Christian Ethics*, 87.
4. Rousseau, *The Social Contract*, 1.

According to Thomas Hobbes, in this state of nature, individual lives are allergic to the fields of solidarity, and spheres of public participation become oppressive and high-handed:

> In such condition there is no place for industry, because the fruit thereof is uncertain: and consequently no culture of the earth; no navigation, nor use of the commodities that may be imported by sea; no commodious building; no instruments of moving and removing such things as require much force; no knowledge of the face of the earth; no account of time; no arts; no letters; no society; and which is worst of all, continual fear, and danger of violent death; and the life of man, solitary, poor, nasty, brutish, and short.[5]

Humanity reduces itself to this state whenever it arrogates to itself the master narrative. The same happens when a sub-set of the human race, such as those who identify on the basis of gender, race, religion or culture, assume the master narrative. Accordingly, Igbo men reduce themselves to this state when they think of themselves as masters over women, and in the long run remain themselves more as slaves. This narrative of the role of master "distorts *humanity*, which not only inhibits liberation for women but also obstructs genuine liberation for men."[6] This master narrative is not only limited to Igbo men, but may include Igbo women, too, who have willingly accepted to be slaves. In that case, Uchem suggests the goal of gender equality, "whereby both men and women are equally recognized and respected as human beings both in fact and in practice."[7]

Rousseau's unvarnished truth of "man is born free, and everywhere he is in chains" is an apt description of the situation of Igbo couples, especially when it comes to the case of infertility in marriage. Men, and by extension the Igbo culture, believe that it is their right to 'lord it over' women or infertile couples, but when they do this, they lose their freedom and become prisoners themselves. This is apparent in the Hausa proverb which says "*kowa ya hadiya tabarya kwana tsaye*," meaning "the one who swallowed a pestle will sleep standing [implying that] evil recoils on the

---

5. Hobbes, *Leviathan*, XIII 9.
6. Harrison, "Forging community," 140.
7. Uchem, *Gender Equality*, 47.

evil doer."⁸ Freedom for men and Igbo culture is inextricably tied to the freedom of couples with infertility problems.

The Igbo philosopher and cultural anthropologist George Ekwuru refers to this subjugation of the vulnerable as "*uwa ndi Igbo yaghara ayagha*" meaning the "Igbo world in disarray."⁹ He sees the lord and slave anomaly in the Igbo socio-cultural world like "a ship of which the set of the sail decides the way it goes, and not the calm or the strife of the sea."¹⁰ He goes on to criticize the oppressive forces in Igbo culture warning that "we are treading on a dangerous socio-cultural path of hate and injustice that might lead to a type of racial extinction."¹¹ An amelioration of this hate and injustice is largely what this chapter will engage with, as it advocates for the full application of the indigenous ethic of *onye aghala nwanne ya* as a constructive alternative to the theological and ethical principles of Oduyoye, Uchem and Bujo.

Greek philosophers understood every human person as being in search of freedom and happiness. The Catechism of the Catholic Church corroborates this truism for the human search for freedom, saying: "Freedom is the power, rooted in reason and will . . . by free will one shape's one's own life. Human freedom is a force for growth and maturity in truth and goodness."¹² This growth and maturity is the yearning and aspiration of every human person. Since men and women are in search of freedom, growth and maturity, anyone who oppresses the other loses his or her own freedom, and risks stopping their own growth and maturation.

In search of this freedom and growth, one cannot afford to stand aloof on the fence, because being indifferent in the face of injustice makes one an accomplice. This accounts for why Dr. Martin Luther King Jr., and Archbishop Desmond Tutu were right in their postulations of the implication of indifference in situations of injustice. Archbishop Tutu says, "If you are neutral in situations of injustice, you have chosen the side of the oppressor"¹³ In the case of the injustice and oppression of infertile couples in Igbo land, we cannot afford to be neutral as human persons to any case of injustice to any part of our human family especially those

---

8. Pachocinsk, *Proverbs of Africa*, 227.

9. That is the name of one of his books where he 'X-rays' the condition of Igbo society. See Ekwuru, *Pangs of an African Culture*, iii.

10. Ekwuru, *Pangs of an African Culture*, xi.

11. Ekwuru, *Pangs of an African Culture*, xiii.

12. *Catechism of the Catholic Church*, no. 1731.

13. Tutu, "If you are neutral . . ."

most vulnerable. In the same way, Dr. King says, "injustice anywhere is a threat to justice everywhere."[14] This means that in the persistent sense of injustice and victimization of infertile Igbo couples, injustice looms everywhere, and this has to be tackled.

To initiate the process of justice, freedom, growth and maturity for men and women, which are some of the values inherent in the indigenous ethical principle of *onye aghala nwanne ya*, this chapter undertakes a deconstruction of the Igbo psyche, aiming to show that *onye aghala nwanne ya* can liberate Igbo couples suffering from infertility. Full societal application of this principle would be a major contribution of this book in the field of ethics.

THE ROLE OF ETHICS IN MOTIVATING ACTIONS AND DECISION MAKING

The role of ethics in human society has remained a determinant and pivotal factor for people's judgment, behavior and moral strength. This is true both among themselves, and in their relationship with the supernatural. Since humans live in a cause-and-effect space, every human action has some consequences in the well-being of others. Richard Paul and Linda Elder write that, "[h]uman behavior has consequences for the welfare of others. We are capable of acting toward others in such a way as to increase or decrease the quality of their lives."[15] Human action or inaction can always affect the equilibrium of society. Drawing specifically from an African perspective, and because of the inter-penetrating nature of the Igbo physical and spiritual universe, Bujo goes beyond human actions and inactions in the physical world to include effects on and from those in the spirit world. Bujo writes, "[i]t has already been underlined that African ethics is essentially based on the community model which includes the living as well as the departed family members."[16]

Ethics (as part of the moral principles of humans) has a fundamental role in enhancing or diminishing human flourishing. Ethics "highlight(s) acts of two kinds: those which enhance the well-being of others—that warrant our praise—and those that harm or diminish the well-being of

---

14. King, "Injustice anywhere . . ."
15. Paul and Elder, *Miniature Guide*, 2.
16. Bujo, *Ethical Dimension of Community*, 29.

others—and thus warrant our criticism."[17] Since we are dealing largely with Christian ethics, within an African context, it is difficult to consider ethics here without a connection to religion and theology.

With a religious basis, one can fully step into the Igbo world and its behavioral patterns. Elechi Amadi writes in *Ethics in Nigerian Culture*, about the role of religion in fostering moral codes, "[r]eligion has played a particularly important role in ethical philosophy all down the ages because it has been a useful instrument for enforcing moral codes . . . [m]uch of the ancient and medieval philosophy of the Western world hinged on religious precepts."[18] Since it is hard to talk about a people's "moral weight of their culture" without talking about religion, the thought of the British philosopher and logician Bertrand Russell can help when he writes that, "many traditional ethical beliefs are hard to justify, except on the assumption that there is a God or a World Spirit or at least an immanent Cosmic Purpose."[19] This religious and ethics connection will be seen at work in our discussion of the ethics of *onye aghala nwanne ya*.

Every culture is evolving, some slowly and some with a 'supersonic' speed. This evolution of culture gives room to different ethical theories to respond to moral and social problems. Within the African continent, as seen among some African scholars, some ethical theories and theologies have emerged as attempts to solve particular human problems. In their search for liberation of African women, Oduyoye and Uchem argued for an inclusive theology and an African woman's theology that emerge from the context of Africa and African women's experience and thinking. To enforce and sustain African relationality and communality, Bujo came up with *palaver* as a way of solving some of Africa's problems, because *palaver* gives room to everyone to ventilate and air out their thoughts in the process of conflict resolution. However, having reviewed and weighed some of their theologies and ethics in chapters 3 and 4, I am convinced that the ethical principle of *onye aghala nwanne ya* will be most suitable in addressing the Igbo question of the oppression of infertile Igbo couples.

Failure to fully apply *onye aghala nwanne ya* as a means of liberation would be like imitating the temple priest and the Levite who were insulated and felt indifferent to the pain of the man who was maimed by robbers

---

17. Paul and Elder, *Miniature Guide*, 2.
18. Amadi, *Ethics in Nigerian Culture*, 3.
19. Russell, *Human Society*, 27.

in the parable of the Good Samaritan (Luke 10:29–37). Jesus did not approve of their indifference in the face of aggressive subjugation (though they were probably guided by Levitical laws). Rather, he approved the counsel and action of the Good Samaritan, and invites the ethicist to "Go and do likewise." The work of the ethicist is then to help formulate, advocate and fully apply sound principles that will help set humanity free from bodily, emotional and psychological pain. And, in this particular case, liberate infertile Igbo couples from shame and oppression.

THE IGBO INDIGENOUS ETHIC OF ONYEAGHALA NWANNE YA

The Igbo indigenous ethic of *onye aghala nwanne ya* (no kith or kin should be left behind or abandoned) is expressed in all facets of Igbo traditional life. It is seen where parents take care of their children, where children take care of their parents when they are old, and where the healthy take care of the infirm without counting the cost. In this milieu, "[a] moral person in the African view must, in addition to these categories and freedom, also have the requisite attitudes, emotions, principles, values, and norms that give credence to caring, sympathy, and relationships."[20] This is love manifested through interconnectedness and sacrifice, where every member of the Igbo community strives hard for the common good, and in the process maintain some kind of cosmic cohesion and communal harmony.[21]

Interconnectedness as a Way of Life

Solidarity, fellowship and mutual coexistence among Igbo people and with other communities are highly prized. One can never be completely cut off from his/her lineage. He/she will need them one way or the other, especially when he/she is in trouble, or is in search of social justice. In all, Igbo communal living is anchored on the premise, "Together we stand, and divided we fall."[22] Put another way, "A hand does not tie a bundle," meaning everyone is an active participant and collaborator in community living. This perception of Igbo and generally African interconnectedness is explained by Elia Tema:

20. Ikuenobe, *Philosophical Perspectives*, 54.
21. Nnoromele, *The Way People Live*, 23–24.
22. Murchison, *The Cost of Liberty*, 66.

> An African is never regarded as a loose entity to be dealt with strictly individually. His being is based on or coupled with that of others. Next to—or behind—or in front of him there is always someone through whom he is seen or with whom he is associated. The concepts of plurality and belonging to is always present, e.g., a person is always viewed as: "Motho wa batho" (person of persons or belonging to persons). "Motho weso" (Our person or person that is ours).[23]

It is therefore innate in Igbo people to open themselves to others, to learn of others as they learn of themselves and above all to know that all belong to a greater whole. With this knowledge, everyone works hard to preserve and sustain this greater whole, and above all not leave anyone behind. The following Igbo proverb is significant here: "*onye na-agbara ikwunaibe ya oso aghaghi igbakwuru ha otu ubochi o ga-acho enyemaka ndi nke ya*" which means "there is no time a person can run away completely from his kinsmen, as he will surely need their help and intervention someday."[24] Put in another way, everyone needs the other; one cannot completely isolate oneself from the whole, which is the community. This is so because there are many things one cannot do alone, including traditional marriage, and seeking for social justice in the community. This interconnectedness brings about increased harmony within the Igbo world. It promotes a kind of patriotism; best expressed in the principle of *onye aghala nwanne ya*. In all, being a loner in Igbo culture is almost like not existing.

This interrelatedness and care for the other is described by John Mbiti who defines a person in the African context as: "I am because we are and, since we are, therefore I am."[25] Desmond Tutu echoes this interrelatedness from his South African background: "I am what I am because of who we all are."[26] The questions that may arise because of this kind of interconnectedness will be ones of autonomy and personal freedom of the individual in relation to the Igbo community. Bujo, who argues for a holistic understanding of African ethics, writes that "[t]hese questions about solidarity and the people are posed in Black Africa in terms of the relation between community and individual."[27]

23. Mashai, "Pastoral Counseling," 21, as quoted in Paris, *The Spirituality of African Peoples*, 101.
24. Onwudufor, *Mmanu E ji Eri Okwu*, 53.
25. Mbiti, *African Religions and Philosophy*, 141.
26. Tutu, *No Future Without Forgiveness*, 70.
27. Bujo, *Foundations of an African Ethic*, 85.

In the Igbo community and Africa at large, an individual does not completely give up his/her identity in the community. The individual has freedom. Bujo, in his desire to show the relationship between an individual and the community, tells one of the many fairy tales in African culture. He writes that "the individual may not blindly follow the group. Life in the community demands alertness and the maintenance of one's own individuality."[28] Maintaining this individuality has a marked difference in Western perception. Bujo further argues that "[a]s Africans see it, it is impossible to define the human person in purely secular or purely religious terms, since he (sic) is both at once. Where one of these two dimensions is lacking, one can no longer speak of the human person *qua* human person; and this means that one cannot speak of 'autonomy' and 'theonomy' in the Western sense."[29] Despite this autonomy and identity, the community and culture define the individual. This is a kind of chain, whereby everyone relies on another, even when minor decisions in life are to be made. In this communal setting, Igbo families like all 'collectivistic' families are "generally cohesive and well integrated. Familial relationships are caring and warm but also hierarchical"[30] Love, care and sacrifice become the watch words for everyone.

This care and warmth account for the use of this popular Igbo saying: "*onye nwanne ya no n'elu osisi n' aracha ube jiri eji,*" which literally means, "He/she whose brother/sister is on top of the tree will be sure of eating the best of fruits." The Jukun speaking people of the middle belt in Nigeria have a similar proverb: "*nwuzau ma ninyinara waji anyunyun*" meaning, "If your brother is on top of the tree you can eat ripe fruits."[31] This means that in the *onye aghala nwanne ya* spirit of community and sharing, no one is left behind in the use of earth's resources. It is firmly believed and expected among Igbo people that one's brothers and sisters will always be there for him/her during times of need and pain, including the pain and anguish of infertility. This again accounts for why Igbo people use an aphorism like "*O nurube nwanne agbala oso,*" which literally translates to mean, "One who hears the cry of a brother/sister should not ignore it (i.e. walk away, or show apathy)."[32]

28. Bujo, *Foundations of an African Ethic*, 90.
29. Bujo, *Foundations of an African Ethic*, 95.
30. Neuliep, *Intercultural Communication*, 218.
31. Pachocinsk, *Proverbs of Africa*, 33.
32. Okafor and Appel, *Toward an African Theology*, 156.

The Igbo indigenous ethic of *onye aghala nwanne ya* is a deep and passionate principle, one which appeals to Igbo people not to abandon or leave anyone behind. The ethical principle calls for the caring for one another, which by its nature and principle will enhance human flourishing. This goal of human flourishing is compatible with Bujo's understanding of the objectives of African ethics. Bujo asserts that "[t]he main goal of African ethics is fundamentally life itself. The community must guarantee the promotion and protection of life by specifying or ordaining ethics and morality."[33]

On a celestial level, the theology of the relational aspect of Igbo community life has deepened their value and understanding of the Triune God. This is so because in Christian tradition, God does not exist in solitary individualism, but in a collective nature. This makes sense because, ". . . Christian spirituality can be genuinely personal only to the extent that is practiced communally."[34] In this way, the Igbo people's connection with God points to their traditional understanding of God, who lives in relationship. As Mbiti asserts, "[t]raditional religions are not primarily for the individual, but for the community of which he is part."[35] This idea of fellowship gives Igbo people an eschatological idea about the God they worship.

The term *nwanne* (brother/sister) taken from the ethical principle of *onye aghala nwanne ya* has a neutral gender. It literally means "my mother's child," and more simply refers to a sibling. This means *nwanne* could mean a brother or a sister. To strengthen the understanding of *nwanne*, it is worth noting that there is no Igbo word for nephew, niece or cousin. In a general understanding, every Igbo person refers to another Igbo person as *nwanne*. In a particular understanding, someone to whom one is related to is simply referred to as *nwanne* implying that he or she enjoys some kind of affinity like one's siblings, thus motivating a human action of caring for the person. Therefore, in its meaning and application, "the word '*nwanne*' is not just meant to communicate knowledge of someone, but to state an existential truth of being (*facticity*) and, of course, to motivate human action—'*being for*,' or '*Dasein*.'"[36] This implies that caring for the other has no gender implication. It is an implicit call

---

33. Bujo, *Foundations of an African Ethic*, 2.
34. Battle, *Ubuntu*, 88–89.
35. Mbiti, *African Religions and Philosophy*, 67.
36. Okafor and Appel, *Toward an African Theology*, 159.

to care first and foremost because the person is *nwanne*. In other words, "*nwanne* could be anybody, indeed everybody whose image of his or her 'self' is authenticated in his or her empathy for a suffering other—i.e, his or her needy *'otherself'*"[37] This means that the sense of compassion and care that guides the association of members of the Igbo nuclear and extended family is sustained by the core principles of *nwanne*.

This sense of *nwanne* and the whole ideal of bonding and caring for *nwanne* are entrenched in Igbo cosmology and the Igbo lexicon, expressing the power and strength that emanate when *umunne*[38] are bonded. This value finds meaning in "*Igwe bu ike,*" an Igbo axiom which means "Unity is strength." In other words, *nwanne* can only achieve success in collaboration with *umunne*. When a problem arises in an Igbo community, *umunne* are summoned, and a deliberative process is started to find the most appropriate solution to the problem.

Bujo echoes part of this in his *palaver,* in the sense of people congregating to dialogue and find solutions to family problems. Uchem advocates for it in her inclusive theology wherein everyone, male and female, should be taken into consideration when policies are formulated and decisions made, in the Catholic Church and in Igbo communities. This *igwe bu ike* philosophy gives credence to the success of an individual being measured in the light of the success of the community. Where an individual succeeds, then the family or community has succeeded. The individual is not expected to fail, because he/she is not expected to work alone. If the individual fails, the community can be said to have failed.

Amplifying this further, one sees this "unity is strength" in the lifestyles of Igbo people. A visual expression of this can be seen in the way houses are built—in Igbo land, one does not build one's house in a desert or isolated on a hill. Rather, one builds his home in connectedness with other homes. This is different from Western culture, where one can build his home in an isolated terrain or on a mountain, and live there all alone. Doing so in Igbo land would make the occupants of such a house people to be feared or to be held in suspicion, because life ought to be lived in connection with *umunne*.

The *onye aghala nwanne ya* principle invokes a picture of "affection, trust, equality, and mutual dependence. It is within this family setting that we learn to love without reservation, to quarrel without animosity,

---

37. Okafor and Appel, *Toward an African Theology*, 159.
38. *Umunne* is the plural of *nwanne*, an English equivalent for 'siblings.'

to forgive and be forgiven, to care and to be cared for and to give without counting the cost."³⁹ In this *umunne* atmosphere, any pain or suffering of one person is soothed in relationship. In this closely-knit community of shared values and beliefs, the community itself remains at the center of every activity, practice, and belief.⁴⁰ In a nut-shell, there will be no existence without this kind of community orientation. It is of little wonder, in understanding this community life and solidarity among Igbo people, that a proverb captures it well: "*onodu otu onye na-aka mma naani n'ime afo*" which means, "the only place where a person may enjoy staying alone is in the womb."⁴¹ In this way, the community and her life become an embodiment of love, which is lived, professed and shared. Here love becomes meaningful "when it is externally reflected in one's good deeds to others, a belief that reinforces Igbo philosophical values in shared communal well-being and hospitality to strangers in their midst."⁴²

Having seen the power and influence that *nwanne* has among *umunne*, one can now look at the advantages of *onye aghala nwanne ya*. The principle has its own merits, and these merits are what put it ahead of other principles and theologies in the process of liberating Igbo couples from the subjugation and oppression caused by of infertility in marriage.

THE LIBERATING QUALITIES OF ONYE AGHALA NWANNE YA AND ITS INDIGENOUS NATURE

Unlike Bujo's development of an African ethic which has *palaver* as a process, the term *palaver* is alien thus having its own implication. *Onye aghala nwanne ya* is indigenous especially in nomenclature. *Onye aghala nwanne ya* being indigenous is effective as it appeals and speaks to the core values of the people. It is common knowledge in Igbo land that when people want solutions to some of life's problems, they always look for indigenous ways to resolve them, and the impact is always lasting. Kalu, writing in *The Embattled Gods* observes that "Igbos resort to indigenous solutions at points of life crisis—an indication of where the heart is."⁴³ This accounts for why when people are in trouble, it is common for them

---

39. Tutu, *No Future Without Forgiveness*, 158.
40. Ikuenobe, *Philosophical Perspectives*, 53.
41. Onwudufor, *Mmanu E ji Eri Okwu*, 53.
42. Chuku, *The Igbo Intellectual Tradition*, 15.
43. Kalu, *The Embattled Gods*, 324.

to go to what is known as 'spiritual houses,' or to diviners, to find out what is wrong with them or their families. This is evident in that even with the advent of Christianity over a century ago in Igbo land, "traditional religion still rules the minds of most Igbos (sic) to a greater extent than has generally been realized notwithstanding outward manifestation to the contrary."[44] These places of refuge are traditional and indigenous in their style and nature. People go to such places during crisis situations like sickness, inability to build one's own house, childlessness, successive deaths in the family, and even students' inability to pass examinations. Other occasions may include young people's inability to get suitors for marriage, fatal accidents, or even having dreams that are of ill omen. In such situations, many do not come to the Christian churches to seek solutions, as the church will appear not to have answers to their problems. The church's language will appear to be different from the realities they face. Looking for an indigenous way to solve problems is inherent among Igbo people. This means that since *onye aghala nwanne ya* is indigenous and culturally linked, it will speak to the soul of an Igbo person, and thus they will naturally respond to the ethical demands of the *onye aghala nwanne* principle. Their response to this cultural and traditionally-based principle is feasible because Igbo people ". . . have difficulties adapting to situations that clash with their most steadfast beliefs."[45]

THE BIBLICAL AND RELIGIOUS CONNOTATION OF ONYE AGHALA NWANNE YA

Like all aspects of African ethics, *onye aghala nwanne ya* is also religious. This is so because taking care of *nwanne* is needed to maintain cosmic equilibrium. Harming *nwanne* unjustly may invite the wrath of the gods or ancestors, which can be very dangerous because at every point in time, ". . . every precaution must be observed in order to keep the spirit of the departed in a state of peaceful contentment."[46] With all being conscious of supernatural forces playing out within the Igbo world-view, this influences relationships among *umunne* and serves as a guide in the formulation of ethical codes. I believe Kunhiyop is right in writing that "God, the

---

44. Ubah, "Religious Change," as quoted in Kalu, *The Embattled Gods*, 324.
45. Suglia, "Receptive yet Grounded."
46. Basden, *Among the Ibos of Nigeria*, 100.

spirits of the departed (the ancestors), and good and evil spirits have a pervasive influence on the morality of the people."[47]

A scholar has said that Africa "is incurably religious."[48] Igbo people are contagiously religious, which could account for why an anthropologist says that "Igbo societies are governed by gods and ancestors. This is so because to Igbo people, the secular, and the sacred, the natural and supernatural are a continuum."[49] Being indigenous, *onye aghala nwanne ya* resonates with Igbo religiosity, and appeals to their sense of the supernatural. Arthur Leonard writes about African religiosity: "they eat religiously, drink religiously, bathe religiously and dress religiously."[50] In this divine connection, something indigenous will always have a religious dimension, and will thereby appeal to the people. This is important, because religiosity "permeates into every department of traditional society, any appeal made to traditional values and practices is ultimately a religious appeal."[51] *Onye aghala nwanne ya* is de facto religious.

In its religious undertone, the indigenous ethic of *onye aghala nwanne ya* has a biblical connection. With the expectation of being everyone's keeper, especially in doing good and protecting one's brother/sister, we see that when Cain had harmed his brother Abel, God asked him "Where is Abel your brother?" (Genesis 4:8–10). Doing good to one's brother or sister will mean giving a good account of him/her, but when one does evil to his/her brother/sister, he/she asks a rhetorical question like Cain: "Am I my brother's keeper?" Biblically speaking, we ought to be our brother's/sister's keeper. Failure to be one's brother's/sister's keeper attracts some kind of punishment. In the case of Cain, who killed his brother, the Lord told him, "And now you are cursed from the ground, which has opened its mouth to receive your brother's blood from your hand" (Genesis 4:11). This punishment is for the extreme case of murder, but the point we are making here is that the principle of *onye aghala nwanne ya*, has a biblical appeal. There is an expectation that everyone has to be accounted for (no kith or kin should be left behind). Furthermore, the New Testament admonition "carry each other's burdens, and in this way you will fulfill the law of Christ" (Galatians 6:2) is a true reflection of the principle of

47. Kunhiyop, *African Christian Ethics*, xv.

48. Ela, *African Cry*, 39.

49. Isichei, *History of the Igbo People*, 24.

50. Arthur, *Lower Niger and its Tribes*, 429, as cited in Metuh, *Comparative Studies*, 12.

51. Mbiti, *African Religions and Philosophy*, 358.

onye aghala nwanne ya. Having a biblical undertone makes the ethical principle more appealing to Igbo Christians.

THE ALL-INCLUSIVE AND GENDER-NEUTRAL NATURE OF ONYE AGHALA NWANNE YA

Mercy Amba Oduyoye and Rose Uchem argue rigorously for the liberation of African women. They do that by being passionate, with a focus on African women telling their stories of oppression on the basis of their gender. Through their theological and biblical analysis, they create a sense of rediscovery of the Gospel message, stripping it of its patriarchal and political powers and interpretations. However, this act of 'stripping' has its own drawback: the tendency of fighting the men-folk is itself against the principle of *onye aghala nwanne ya*. Their target can be said to be gender bias, since their "immediate community of accountability is African women . . ."[52] A neutral call for liberation of all will appeal to males and females. This is what the emotional appeal of *onye aghala nwanne ya* does. Since "*nwanne*" is of neutral gender, it has and will propel every Igbo person into an action of salvaging a bad situation, especially in making everyone accounted for.

It is not the aim here to pretend that Igbo culture and tradition have always been like a paradise and some sort of golden age. In other words, the intention is not to present an Igbo socio-cultural sanctity as if it is a culture without blemish or some challenges. Hence, there were murderers in Igbo communities, people who stole their neighbor's property, and people who fought and poisoned one another. All these are still being done today. The existential question is: why do people in such a beautiful culture, with beautiful norms engage in these forms of evil?

The response to this is, first, what is considered to be part of the problem of evil, which no generation of humans has ever been able to fully unravel its intricacies. Second, it is because the ethical principle of *onye aghala nwanne ya* has not been fully applied on those problems. With the qualities and appeal of this principle, however, one can confidently say that if fully applied, it can liberate infertile couples from the subjugation of Igbo culture. We do this by evolving an argument of the ethic being a constructive alternative to the principles outlined by Oduyoye, Uchem and Bujo in the face of infertility among Igbo couples.

---

52. Oduyoye, *Introducing African Women's Theology*, 20.

THE VALUES OF ONYE AGHALA NWANNE YA: CONSTRUCTIVE ALTERNATIVES AS A CATALYST INITIATING CHANGE

Segun Gbadegesin, in his research on the role of ethics in a culture, asserts that ethics play a significant role in the way a people live life, according to an endowed cultural paradigm. Living life within a defined moral space has a major purpose, which is largely "the promotion of human flourishing."[53] This flourishing does not apply only when one is alive (since Igbo people have respect for the dead), it applies too in death. We will now briefly look at some of these customs and oral traditions, with the aim of affirming some traditions, establishing new orientations, a cultural construct and a deconstruction of the Igbo psyche, in a bid to enhance human flourishing, for the liberation of Igbo couples from the oppression of childlessness.

Igbo Hospitality, Sacrifice and Total Self-Giving

As previously stated, in Igbo land, to be human entails being an active and integral member of the large community. Being a member of the community places a responsibility and loyalty of the individual to the community. It entails sharing and getting fully involved in the life of the community. Mbiti writes, "[t]o be human is to belong to the whole community, and to do so involves participating in the beliefs, ceremonies, rituals and festivals of that community."[54] Within this community, one can truly be protected and realize his/her potential:

> If any member was in need, he turned to his patrilineage (sic) members, who would contribute money to help him. Everyone was expected to participate in the activities of others. Anyone who suffers a mental breakdown would be assisted by others through the contribution of money towards medical care. They also contributed money to help very poor members build a house. Those unable to afford marriage expenses were also assisted by their patrilineage (sic) group.[55]

This is the life essence of a true Igbo community. This act of sharing sustains the dignity of the community, and that is what makes the

---

53. Gbadegesin, "The Moral Weight of Culture in Ethics," 33.
54. Mbiti, *African Religions and Philosophy*, 2.
55. Amadiume, *Male Daughters, Female Husbands*, 58.

community 'tick.' In its practical application, we see *onye aghala nwanne ya* playing out in ordinary Igbo family life. It was once common, and still is frequent now, that a member of a family will suspend his or her education to take care of an ailing member of the family. This might mean missing an academic year or more. An external care-giver was abhorred, and to a great extent is still detested. When the natural process of aging sets in, children who previously lived in the city may have to return to the village (abode of the grandparents) to live with their grandparents. The intention is to care for them through basic things they can help with, and give the grandparents a continued sense of parenthood. In this context, no one is left behind or unattended to, irrespective of age and medical condition. In this setting, children are their parents' pension, health insurance and 'benefits' in old age.

Even in death, Igbo hospitality, sacrifice and total self-giving are still seen at work. When an Igbo person (male or female) dies while outside of Igboland or in another country, other Igbo people living in the area always task themselves to ensure that the remains of the deceased are taken home to Igboland for burial. This accounts for why Igbo people will say "*ozu nwa igbo anaghi ato n' mba,*" which literally means, "the corpse of *nwanne* is never 'stranded' abroad." It has to go home to commune with the ancestors and those who have gone before them. In life and in death, hospitality and sacrifice have remained a road map for the Igbo people in their expression of the unique way they are bonded.

These values of care and self-giving must be sustained. In other words, a return to this sacrificial and total self-giving of one to another is important. The unbridled selfishness and individualism now prevalent in Igbo culture, probably because of her encounter with other cultures and civilizations, and especially where the need of *nwanne* is no longer taken care of, are alien to the culture.

A rebirth that will make the Igbo people take their rightful position within the continent of Africa is of utmost importance. The lack of this renaissance and unhealthy material competition will continue to impede the development and cultural progress of the Igbo people. This new phase of rebirth, which could also subdue the suffocating forces of injustice against couples suffering from infertility, can be initiated now to set an example in the African continent. This is important because, "the Igbo tribe known and recognized throughout the world as one of the tribes in the world gifted with rare qualities of high mental capacity, unflagging spirit of enterprise, and stubborn will for originality, creativity and novelty must be at the vanguard of this continental renaissance."[56] This renaissance can be achieved only if Igbo culture returns to the primordial spirit of sacrifice and total self-giving enunciated in *onye aghala nwanne ya*. Only when this is realized would Igbo culture be true to the words of the timeless ode of an illustrious Igbo son and Nigerian nationalist, Nnamdi Azikiwe (Zik) who said: "the God of Africa has specially created the Igbo nation to lead the children of Africa from the bondage of the ages."[57]

With this sense of hospitality, accommodation and renaissance, infertile married couples can find a home in their cultural space, Igbo land. When hospitality is truly enacted, no one, not even the distressed and childless, will feel alienated.

Renewal of a Life of Covenant: Food Fellowship and Kolanut in Perspective

When food is prepared by an Igbo family, it is not cooked only for those in the household. When someone shows up at meal time, without prior notice, the visitor is welcomed and "immediately greeted with an invitation 'to come and eat.'"[58] This is different from the Euro-American style, where there are strict boundaries and expectations of privacy, and where ". . . the individual reigns supreme."[59] In the Western setting, the individual is the chief determinant of things around him/her and his/her household, and there is great respect for autonomy and privacy. In understanding a person, one can say that "one nation under self" has been built; in this way the individual is construed as a national deity. Within North American context, especially among White Americans, Elmer says, the act of 'popping in' unannounced "causes many North Americans discomfort. First of all, you don't just stop by—that is rude according to our etiquette experts . . ."[60] It is considered rude, because, ". . . Americans value privacy so much that they have made it a law."[61]

---

56. Ekwuru, *Pangs of an African Culture*, 132.

57. Isichei, *History of the Igbo People*, 229, cited in Ekwuru, *Pangs of an African Culture*, 132.

58. Basden, *Among the Ibos of Nigeria*, 254.

59. Elmer, *Cross-Cultural Connections*, 135.

60. Elmer, *Cross-Cultural Connections*, 100.

61. Neuliep, *Intercultural Communication*, 148.

This is different in Igbo culture where friendship and acceptance of others have several ways of being exhibited. Again, one can stop by at any time at someone's house. If one happens to stop by at mealtime, even though unannounced, the host will welcome the visitor saying "*ukwu gi amaka*" which is loosely translated to mean "your legs are good," or "you meet me at the best time." Kilba-speaking people have a similar proverb, saying, "*U wotr azah lilat*" which literally means, "you hit your leg at the right time."[62] The host is delighted if the guest joins in the meal.

Though this custom was in place before the advent of the Christian tradition, one sees the same tradition of generosity and hospitality having bearing in Christian literature. Hebrews 13: 2 says, "Do not neglect to show hospitality to strangers, for thereby some have entertained angels unawares." 1 Peter 4:9 instructs us to: "Show hospitality to one another without grumbling." To share a meal is truly to open one's heart to the other. It is a manifestation of love because most often to share a meal is to accept others, and "[t]o accept others is to love them."[63] However, Igbo food fellowship is fading away because of Westernization, and the Igbo culture interacting with other cultures. The Igbo food fellowship must be revitalized. A good starting point would be a return to the ancient celebration of *ara na umu* festivity, which was mentioned in chapter 3 (on the marriage procedure in Awo-Omamma). This celebration brings out in a fine way the egalitarian nature of Igbo culture. Here everyone eats from the same pot, not minding one's status in the community. This shows oneness in the scheme of affairs in the Igbo project.

Living out the rituals symbolized in the kola nuts will bring positive changes in Igbo land. An understanding of the Igbo kola nut will make this point clearer. Okorie describes it this way. "The Kolanut itself is about the size of a chestnut and grows in a pod on the trees of Cola acuminata and Cola ntiga."[64] The pictorial image created by Basden of a kola nut tree is apt: "Tree twenty to thirty feet in height, both indigenous and cultivated, in most parts of West Africa . . . it thrives on all soils, and is found at all heights, from sea-level to three thousand feet and more. The nuts, which are bitter in taste, are highly esteemed by the natives."[65] The kola nut and its number of cotyledons and the way they cleave to

62. Pachocinsk, *Proverbs of Africa*, 396.

63. Elmer, *Cross-Cultural Connections*, 95.

64. Okorie, *Oji Igbo*, 9, as cited in Uchem, *Overcoming Women's Subordination*, 60.

65. Basden, *Among the Ibos of Nigeria*, 251.

one another have significant meanings. They all point to the celebration of life, and the unity of Igbo life with one another. Anthony Ekwunife describes the kola nut thusly, "morphologically, all the cotyledons including the thin central axis and the shape of each cotyledon, symbolize one reality or the other."[66] This reality is the central connection of all Igbo in one root of care, love and unity. Ekwunife further continues, "[t]he Igbo kola-nut (kola *acuminata* or *atrophora*) is quite different from the Hausa or Yoruba type of kola. Its social importance can only be fully appreciated by one quite conversant with Igbo culture since it filters its way through all the key moments of social interactions (reception of visitors, marriage alliances, settlement of cases, political alliances and so on)."[67] In all, for Igbo people, "the ritual kola nut expresses, communicates and unifies Igbo ideas of friendship, acceptance and approval, achievement, productivity and wealth, joy and sorrow, family, village and clan; unity and diversity of Igbo world..."[68]

Furthermore, as a foreign missionary in Igbo land, Basden acknowledges that what "impresses the average foreigner more than any other is the ancient custom of sharing kola nut."[69] Igbo unity, fellowship and love are visibly symbolized in the Igbo ritual of the presentation, breaking and eating of kola nuts. As another African scholar writes, "[t]he kola nut is the greatest symbol of Igbo hospitality. It always comes first. It is the king in hospitality culture. To be presented with a kola nut is to be made welcome and accepted."[70] The popular greetings that follow with the offering of kola nut to a guest in an Igbo household is "*onye wetere oji, wetere ndu,*" which literally means, "those who bring kola nuts bring life."[71] The presentation and all the rituals around kola nut are the celebration of unity and life and as such should be revitalized and celebrated with that "symbolism of inclusion, hospitality, fellowship, blessing and reconciliation..."[72] that it portends. This ritual must resist the aggressive wind of change that is blowing so fast across Igbo culture.

---

66. Ekwunife, *Consecration*, 109.
67. Ekwunife, *Consecration*, 108.
68. Ekwunife, *Consecration*, 109.
69. Basden, *Among the Ibos of Nigeria*, 250.
70. Uchendu, *Igbo of Southeast Nigeria*, 74.
71. Pachocinsk, *Proverbs of Africa*, 393.
72. Uchem, *Overcoming Women's Subordination*, 60–61.

In a bid to re-enact what the kolanut symbolizes and which finds expression in *onye aghala nwanne ya*, Igbo culture, with its rich ritual symbolism, must deepen its self-understanding with the ritual of kolanut. The ritual and symbolism if well-articulated and internalized, will not only accelerate cultural change, but will enhance the logic of progress and collective flourishing. To accelerate this change, there is a need to sustain and re-invent the ritual breaking of kolanut to engage in its socio-ethical reconstruction. When this is done and everyone assimilates its rich values, there will no longer be discrimination in Igbo religious and cultural spaces. The first step to begin this rebirth is through resocialization. With the rich symbol of celebration of life through the ritual of Igbo kola nut, the line of separation between couples who have children and couples who do not have children will be effaced. This is so because every human person will be treated as living and as a gift whether they are fertile or not. This deconstruction and resocialization will be an indication that everyone has been accepted in the community as they are, barren or fruitful. This deconstruction will entail women and men participating in the ritual of breaking of kola nut, which is now exclusively performed by men. We can now make an argument in that regard as a constructive alternative.

The Socio-Ethical Reconstruction of the Igbo Ritual of Breaking of Kolanut

The Igbo kolanut ritual, if it is to move toward positive cultural change, needs to be revisited. Making it an inclusive ritual, which Uchem advocates, would help Igbo people understand the powers of some of the female deities in Igbo land, and the role of priestesses who preside over significant rituals in the Igbo religious sphere. For example, in Igbo tradition, the Mammy water priestess is known for her valor, and has significant control over marine spirits. She casts such spirits out if they malignantly interfere within human space. The powerful activities of Mammy water, like casting out mermaid spirits and delivering men said to be married to aquatic spouses show that women are not new to leading religious rituals, and can effectively discharge such functions. After all, as Nnoromele writes, "[t]o traditional Ibos, a priest and a priestess were equal, and the words of the gods the priest or priestess presented were unquestionable and binding."[73] Doing this will significantly affect the

---

73. Nnoromele, *The Way People Live*, 24.

way women are appreciated within Igbo cultural and religious terrains. It will positively affect the dignity of men and, in the same vein, it will surely accord more respect and dignity to women and this can translate into abandonment of the abuse of infertile women.

The presentation and breaking of kolanut, and all it signifies, should be properly reconsidered, from theological and ethical perspectives. An Igbo proverb says, "*Oji bu ndu. Onve wetara Oji. wetara ndu,*" which is to say, "The Kolanut is life [Whoever] brings Kolanut, brings life."[74] Women buy the kolanut from the market, they process it, they trade on it, and they are referred to as 'bringers of new life,' through child birth. However, they cannot preside over the ritual of breaking of kolanut which is believed to be a sign of life. There is no formal reason given for this exclusion. The only reason might be that, 'it has been done that way from Adam.' This aspect of socialization needs to change, so as to bring out the immensity of the life-giving component inherent in women by having them begin to preside in the rituals of breaking kolanut. The Igbo Morning Prayer said with invocation with kolanut is profound, but ironic given that women—who bring a human forth in birth—cannot preside over such a life-giving prayer:

Chineke taa oji	Chineke (God creator), eat kola
Chukwu Abiama na Ezenu Ekene	Chukwu Abiama (God Almighty) take sweet white chalk
Obasi di n'elu Ekene!	Lord of Heaven, greetings!
Anyanwu, na Ezenu Ekene	Sun, King of Heaven, greetings!
Ala Nnewi taa oji	Earth-deity of Nnewi, eat kola!
Edo taa oji	Edo (a water spirit), eat kola!
Ndi Ichei ukwu, ndi ichei nta tanu oji	Great and small ancestors, eat kola
Onye wetara, oji wetara ndu	who brings kola brings life!
Ndu ka anyi na ario	we are asking for life!
Ndu nwoke, ndu nwanyi	life of man, life of woman!
Ndu anyi n'ayoabughi ndu osisi akpu	the life we are asking for is not the life of a cassava tree
Chineke nyere aku oyibo mmiri ona anu	God, you who gave the coconut the milk it drinks
Nye anyi ndu n'ihe eji akwado ya	Give us life and the wherewithal to sustain it
Gi bu Chinenke n'ata n'ogbe	You, God eat whole!
Ma anyi n'ata n'ibe	we eat in pieces!
Chineke bia nara anyi ojia waa	God, come break this kola for us

---

74. Okorie, *Oji Igbo*, 31.

Maka a'anyi enweghi aka	for we have no hands.
Asi nwata nya ghuba aru	if you tell a child to wash
Oghuba so n'afo	himself, he washes only his stomach
Ma oku agunyere nwata n'aka	But the fire given to a child
Adagh arughu ya	does not hurt it.[75]

Again, if women could preside over these life-giving rituals, their status in Igbo culture would be uplifted. This would mean that no one could look down on them because they are unable to conceive. For this to take place, there is a need for a resocialization which must be championed by men, but also by women, and applied in the raising of children. This has to begin from birth, because "[i]f we don't place the straightjacket of gender roles on young children, we give them space to reach their full potential."[76] From infancy, children must be taught the distinct nature of their biological differences, but without any supposition or statement of one gender's superiority over the other. The 'gender superiority syndrome' is a social construction, which needs to be deconstructed through re-socialization and re-orientation. This deconstruction is important, because Nigeria's gender equality index (which includes discrimination against women and stereotypes) is abysmal. According to a 2012 survey by the British Council, "Nigeria ranks 118 of 134 countries in the Gender Equality Index."[77]

Another change to the patriarchal structure that could help Igbo people in improving conditions for women is the better treatment of widows. Most often women are at their best in Igboland when they lose their husbands. Cursory observation of a typical village in Igbo land shows that there are more widows than widowers. In most cases, when the man dies, the woman lives longer and still holds the family together. Women have not failed in giving a good account of themselves in the running of African homes when the man passes on. After all, the biblical tradition is replete with women who successfully headed households. Igbo culture should give them a chance, because even the Bible, which Igbo people cling to so much "... is no stranger to women-headed households—Hagar and Ishmael; Martha, Mary and Lazarus; Lydia and her household."[78] A more human engagement with widows would send a strong signal that

---

75. Metuh, *African Religions*, 144–45.
76. Adichie, *Dear Ijeawele*, 18.
77. British Council, "Introduction."
78. Oduyoye, *Introducing African Women's Theology*, 79.

all humans are equal at every stage of their lives, whether they are barren, widow or widower.

For the spiritual and material well-being of its members, the Catholic Church in Nigeria and across the world forms different associations which are attentive to the needs of its members and society at large. The intention of forming such associations is, first, for administrative convenience, since the church is large and second, for its members to have a sense of belonging to the church. The Catholic Men's Organization (CMO) is one of such association. They have positively affected their members, and the Catholic Church in Nigeria. From its motives and its mission statement, the aim for setting up this association tells it all. Bishop Badejo writes that, "[t]he CMO vision statement defines it as a platform through which Catholic men collaborate with others to work for evangelization and serve humanity. Its mission is to mobilize Catholic men for spiritual development, effective leadership and service in the home, the church and society."[79]

Like the CMO, there is a counterpart for women, the Catholic Women's Organization (CWO), which supports the argument that women have often thrived when allowed to determine their destiny. The CWO is a powerful association of Catholic women that has done well in carrying out parish developmental projects, opening and managing skill-acquisition centers, running CWO parish schools, and having annual study sessions and seminars (such as 'August Return') for their own empowerment and for the protection of indigent women. Their organizational skills, and managerial and financial prowess, remain as proof that women can achieve much if given the chance. The objective of the CWO says it all:

> to provide a channel through which Catholic action may be brought into the current life of the people; to maintain a vigilant watch on the forces that endanger the society's well-being or threaten the fundamental Christian foundations of the country; to acquaint Catholic organizations for women throughout the Archdiocese with national legislation of interest to them as Catholics and as citizens; to study and promote Christian social principles; to provide seminars and conventions for the discussion of common problems and through publicizing these deliberations, to place the Catholic attitude before the general public; to assist, through affiliation with the World Union of

---

79. Badejo, "Catholic Men and Social Transformation."

Catholic Women's Organizations, in world-wide dissemination of catholic principles of social action, to provide representation at meetings of national and international character where matters concerning women are under discussion.[80]

One can see the sincerity and commitment of this group. One can see that they have brought solace to suffering people through funding projects in parishes. One can confidently say they achieve these feats because the church and Igbo culture allowed them to be. Their achievement is not based whether they are childless or not. It is the inherent skill and power in them. If men and the Igbo culture are capable of giving them a chance, "then, the journey towards the great synthesis of cultural renascence must have begun."[81]

Two other traditional women's groups in Igbo land that have distinguished themselves are: *umu-ada* and *ndi nyom*. They are organized and peaceful. They are well-known for their prowess in conflict resolution and developmental strides in the community. Their origin is significant, being "the daughters of the lineage. This group consists of women born in the same lineage, who, based on their common birthplace, form an organization known as *Otu Umuada*."[82] Because of their levels of organization and strategy, they are no pushovers in Igbo land. Though the *umunadi* group (men's group) is strong in protecting the lineage especially from external aggression, the *umu-ada* group is efficient in conflict resolution. They are so powerful that if there is conflict in the community and if they come to intervene, it is always successful, partly because of their record in settling disputes where a men's group had failed. Again, if they can achieve this feat, it becomes paradoxical as to why the same culture looks with disdain on them when they are unable to procreate. With this in mind, we can now make some significant proposals.

In Vitro Fertilization and the Igbo Question

Since a majority of Igbo people are Roman Catholics, any socio-religious construct will engage mainly with the Roman Catholic tradition. The Catholic Church has stringent rules around reproductive technology. M. Therese Lysaught, referring to *Donum Vitae* (the 'Instruction' of the

80. *Catholic Women's Organization Magazine*, 20.
81. Ekwuru, *Pangs of an African Culture*, 140.
82. Ibewuike, *African Women*, 64.

Church's Congregation for the Doctrine of Faith) writes that the church "... rejects all forms of 'artificial fertilization,' partially on the basis of the respect due to persons as embodied, partially on the basis of a specific understanding of marriage and the interconnection of marriage and sex, and children."[83] One of such arguments is the act of fertilizing the egg out of the marital union of sexual intercourse. *Donum Vitae* says, "[h]omologous artificial fertilization (that is, any technique used to achieve conception using the gametes of the two spouses joined in marriage) is prohibited when it separates procreation from the marital act in its unitive significance."[84]

The Second Vatican Council brought in many changes, including the church's understanding of sexual ethics. Leonard Nelson, who identifies threats to the Catholic understanding of healthcare, writes, "[t]he Church has traditionally used a natural-law methodology in addressing medico-moral issues. Until the 1960s, this traditional natural-law approach was seldom questioned within the ranks of the church."[85] Specifically, Catholic sexual moral law, based on natural law theory speaks of "the goal or design that has been built into the nature of things or persons. Self-realization or self-unfolding must occur in accordance with this design."[86] Natural law theory has guided the formulation of the Church's ethical and theological principles, including her teachings around the use of reproductive technologies.

The corpus of the church's sexual moral teaching is well spelt out in the encyclical *Humanae Vitae*, promulgated by Pope Paul VI on July 25, 1968. *Humanae Vitae* explains the nature and goal of marriage thus:

> The reason is that the fundamental nature of the marriage act, while uniting husband and wife in the closest intimacy, also renders them capable of generating new life—and this as a result of laws written into the actual nature of man and of woman. And if each of these essential qualities, the unitive and the procreative, is preserved, the use of marriage fully retains its sense of true mutual love and its ordination to the supreme responsibility of parenthood to which man is called.[87]

83. Lysaught et al., *On Moral Medicine*, 847–48.

84. Congregation for the Doctrine of the Faith, *Donum Vitae*, Part II, B, no. 6, as cited in United States Conference of Catholic Bishops, *Ethical and Religious Directives*, 22.

85. Nelson, *Diagnosis Critical*, 23.

86. Van der Poel, *Ethical Principles*, 23.

87. Paul VI, *Humanae Vitae*.

Onye Aghala Nwanne Ya

In this respect, the encyclical speaks about the limit of the power of humanity including the process that leads to the use of IVF reproductive technology:

> Consequently, unless we are willing that the responsibility of procreating life should be left to the arbitrary decision of men, we must accept that there are certain limits, beyond which it is wrong to go, to the power of man over his own body and its natural functions—limits, let it be said, which no one, whether as a private individual or as a public authority, can lawfully exceed. These limits are expressly imposed because of the reverence due to the whole human organism. and its natural functions, in the light of the principles We stated earlier, and in accordance with a correct understanding of the 'principle of totality.'...[88]

This near-total rejection of reproductive technologies, and especially IVF, by the Roman Catholic tradition opens up some challenges in the present 'moral climate,' which is pluralistic and diverse.

Part of this varied social moral atmosphere is the peculiar case of infertility in Igbo land. The scourging effects of infertility in Igbo land is a great evil. Despite the rejection of IVF medical technology by the Roman Catholic tradition, the case of IVF in the context of the indigenous ethical principle of *onye aghala nwanne ya* for Igbo couples needs further introspection. The need for further introspection aligns with Bernard Haring's assertion that:

> [t]he church's social teaching as well as its sexual ethics—the statements of individual theologians, theological schools, and also the magisterium—requires a hermeneutic. One must consciously and systematically inquire into the "Sitz im Leben" or life context "at that time" when the teachings were formulated, and into the life context of a Church which seeks to preach the Gospel to all cultures.[89]

In other words, Catholic sexual ethics as pertains to IVF requires adaptation. If this adaptation is done, it would serve as a catalyst in inaugurating a new way of life that could guarantee the overall well-being not only of infertile couples, but also the Igbo race as a whole. The need for adaptation could be deduced from the way Igbo people view conception and life, the fact that a new life is generated (through reproductive

---

88. Paul VI, *Humanae Vitae*, 17.
89. Haring, "The Curran Case."

technology) and this new life is to some extent accepted seems to suggest a new thinking among Igbo people. This new thinking viewed from the prism of theology and ethics needs to be further explored. Though IVF is an expensive medical procedure, when Igbo people go for it, are they not suggesting a new orientation and some kind of thanksgiving for an innovation which satisfies their inner-most quest for child birth? Wouldn't the suggested hermeneutics to the church's sexual ethics be seen in the proposal already amplified by Megan Best as it relates to the concern of masturbation and the unitive aspect of marriage? Megan Best writes, "some clinics have developed a system where condoms can be used—either a sterile condom for collection during intercourse (if masturbation is opposed), or a 'holy condom' (a condom with a pinhole in the end) for those couples that oppose contraception."[90]

As earlier indicated, ART are not widely available in Igbo land, and where available the cost is exorbitant. However, *onye aghala nwanne ya* beckons members of a family to do all there is in their power to aid any member of the family who is in pain. In this case, infertility is a condition through which a member of the family suffers pain, and where the resources are available, *onye aghala nwanne ya* invites the family to do what is needed to soothe the pain of their members. If IVF is affordable to an Igbo family, what then should be the appropriate response of an Igbo family in solving a problem like this? What should be the most loving thing to do by an Igbo family in the face of IVF option starring them on the face as a very challenging option? What ethics should guide the indigenous ethical principle of *onye aghala nwanne* wherein families are expected to collectively contribute the resources necessary to engage and benefit from reproductive technologies for the good of one or more of its own in pain?

Adoption—Appropriate and Open

'Baby factory' is a common term used by other ethnic groups like the Yorubas, Hausas and other tribes in Nigeria to denigrate Igbo people for the way some Igbos operate clandestine homes where babies are sold to desperate childless couples. The reflection of Azuka Onwuka, of Igbo extraction who went to Yoruba land for the National Youth Service Corps

---

90. Best, *Fearfully and Wonderfully*, 330.

(NYSC)[91] is instructive. Something profound happened to him when he arrived to serve in the NYSC program after graduating from the university. "A few months later, while discussing with a Yoruba friend on our small street (a close in which almost all of us knew one another), one of the teenage girls on the street passed by with a protruded stomach. I was shocked that she was pregnant."[92] This was a shock to him because it is not a common sight to behold in Igbo land. He continues:

> Given my background as someone who grew up in the South-East, it was strange to me, but I kept quiet to avoid being accused of bigotry. The Yoruba friend asked me with surprise: "Why is it that I have never seen a pregnant Igbo girl? Is it that they don't do what other girls do?" I laughed heartily but knowingly. I explained to her that Igbo girls engage in premarital sex like girls from other ethnic groups, but because of the stigma associated with teenage pregnancy, an Igbo girl would do everything to ensure that she is not seen to be pregnant.[93]

This situation gives rise to baby factories, because if Igbo girls become pregnant they most often become victims to those who operate these baby factories. Premarital pregnancy has always carried a stigma in Igbo land. Being a shamed-based culture, when a young girl gets pregnant before marriage, there are five options for the girl and her parents: the girl, sometimes without the knowledge of her parents, gives herself up to a 'baby factory;' her parents marry her off quickly to an old man or a man who is a widower; the parents get the father of the baby to marry her; the parents send her to a motherless-babies home to have the baby there, or, finally, they have the child aborted. Another, rare option is for the girl to have the baby for her family. The baby would belong to the girl's family, since no bride price was paid. If she is to have the baby for the family, most often the pregnant girl will stay indoors until she gives birth. With that birth, her chances of getting married are reduced, as is the possibility of her going back to school.

Another dimension of the 'baby factory' issue in Igbo land is its being patronized by some infertile couples. Situations abound where dangerous and unethical disguises are used to make adopted babies appear

---

91. NYSC is a mandatory one-year program of service that every Nigerian who graduates from polytechnic or university undertakes. The student serves others in an ethnic area different from his/hers.
92. Onwuka, "How Stigmatisation."
93. Onwuka, "How Stigmatisation."

as biological births. Women wear fake pregnancy outfits and some even take pills that bloat their abdomens for nine months, at the end of which they go to 'adopt' (buy) babies from a 'baby factory.' The baby is nocturnally brought home, and it is declared that the woman has given birth to a child. The process of taking medication to produce bloating is surely both dangerous and ethically troubling.

Given the centrality of biological conception and the culture of shame that abhors premarital pregnancy, Igbo culture must be attentive to the values of tolerance, love and forgiveness inherent in *onye aghala nwanne ya*, especially when a person is in a serious crisis like premarital pregnancy. Legal adoption must be accepted to ease the pain of girls who become pregnant before marriage. Given that Igbo people claim religiosity, one can ask: where is the spirit of forgiveness for a young woman who becomes pregnant before marriage? Why should baby factories thrive in a culture which values loving one another? Why should a woman take the pains of faking pregnancy when the same culture can show understanding of her situation and stop shaming her? If the husband is aware of all these, why should the man keep quiet or be part of these dangerous processes carried out by the woman he loves? If *onye aghala nwanne ya* is a voice that says no one should be left behind or neglected, then the culture ought to rally around those who have babies before marriage. Though being mindful of not giving out wrong signals to young people or condoning a laissez-faire style of life, Igbo culture can still give women who become pregnant before marriage the right disposition to keep their babies, or give their babies out for legal and appropriate adoption, without shaming them. Appropriate and open adoption can ease the pains of childless couples. It would curb 'abandoned-baby syndrome,' reduce dropping out from school by teenaged mothers, reduce the number of abortions, and reduce the number of deaths associated with clandestine abortions.

ECCLESIA AND LIBERATION— THE ROMAN CATHOLIC VISION

The mission and vision of Jesus Christ and His body, which is the church, is that He has come for His people to have life, and have it in all its fullness (John 10:10). It is clear from His mission that He came to establish the reign of God's Kingdom. The Church continues in her mission in making this Kingdom felt by all God's children. As it is written in the Catholic liturgy,

Jesus came to establish a "kingdom of truth and life, a kingdom of holiness and grace, a kingdom of justice, love and peace."[94] This new kingdom has to be different from existing mundane kingdoms. It is a kingdom of God, which is to permeate and transcend the secular order by transforming it, and transforming its culture and the world from within. In this regard, this kingdom is biblically referred to as salt, as yeast, and to an unobservable growing of the plant.[95] All members of this kingdom, male and female, are replicas of an image of the founder of that kingdom, Jesus Christ, who came that we may have life, and have it more abundantly.

In her bid to establish this kingdom, the Church has issued numerous encyclicals and documents, castigating discrimination, and celebrating one human family, proclaiming that everyone is equal. *Gaudium et Spes* affirms this when it states, "[t]hus we are witnesses of the birth of a new humanism, one in which man is defined first of all by this responsibility to his brothers and to history."[96] This responsibility calls for a mutual and loving relationship amongst all. Above all, it calls for freedom of God's children. "Only in freedom can man direct himself toward goodness."[97] An infringement in this freedom defaces the image of God in humans. This is so because, ". . . authentic freedom is an exceptional sign of the divine image within man."[98]

A full implementation of the Church's social ethical teachings would help to protect those who are vulnerable. A call for a new humanism, for a new person who transcends the self, is the only option to have a foretaste of God's kingdom here on earth. Pope Paul VI's encyclical *Populorum Progressio* poignantly brings this out:

> If development calls for an ever-growing number of technical experts, even more necessary still is the deep thought and reflection of wise men in search of a new humanism, one which will enable our contemporaries to enjoy the higher values of love and friendship, of prayer and contemplation, and thus find themselves. This is what will guarantee man's authentic development—his transition from less than human conditions to truly human ones.[99]

94. See the "Preface" for the feast of Christ the King, *Sunday Missal*, 79.

95. Pontifical Council for Justice and Peace. *Compendium of the Social Doctrine of the Church*.

96. Paul VI, *Gaudium et Spes*.

97. Paul VI, *Gaudium et Spes*.

98. Paul VI, *Gaudium et Spes*.

99. Paul VI, *Populorium Progressio*.

Though the Church is patriarchal in style, her teaching here cannot be ignored, because when men abuse power in the name of tradition, then the tenets of the culture should be an area to be illumined by the light of the Gospel. In the same way, this light of the Gospel has to penetrate, for example, the domain of men who oppress women. It has to illumine the minds of African women who are complicit in patriarchy in the church and in the culture. Oduyoye observes this when she writes, "[o]ften one finds that African women have so internalized this low esteem of women in the church and other prevailing values that they become accomplices in the suppression of their own gender."[100] Above all, the Gospel has to challenge areas of the culture that are not in consonance with freedom, love, peace and other values of the kingdom of God.

Reform of oppressive political structures, especially the Igbo political structure which results in the oppression of infertile couples, remains an urgent and important social duty which the light of the Gospel and Church must challenge. This injustice cries out loudly for God's attention. The urgency and courage to confront the status quo and effect social change is further enunciated in *Populorum Progressio*:

> The present state of affairs must be confronted boldly, and its concomitant injustices must be challenged and overcome. Continuing development calls for bold innovations that will work profound changes. The critical state of affairs must be corrected for the better without delay.[101]

Social change can only be possible when there is an eschatological and sacrificial understanding of the love of Christ. "Greater love hath no man than this, that a man lay down his life for his friends" (John 15:13). This is a call for everyone to participate and be fully involved in realizing the needed change. Oduyoye is right when she says, "[e]veryone must lend a ready hand to this task, particularly those who can do more by reason of their education, their office, or their authority."[102] This call for change, built on love, is the substratum on which the encyclical *Caritas in Veritate* of Pope Benedict XVI is written:

> Charity in truth, to which Jesus Christ bore witness by his earthly life and especially by his death and resurrection, is the principal driving force behind the authentic development of every

---

100. Oduyoye, *Introducing African Women's Theology*, 81.
101. Oduyoye, *Introducing African Women's Theology*, 81.
102. Oduyoye, *Introducing African Women's Theology*, 81.

person and of all humanity. Love—*caritas*—is an extraordinary force which leads people to opt for courageous and generous engagement in the field of justice and peace. It is a force that has its origin in God, Eternal Love and Absolute Truth. Each person finds his good by adherence to God's plan for him, in order to realize it fully: in this plan, he finds his truth, and through adherence to this truth he becomes free (cf. Jn 8:32).[103]

The Church teaches in its *Catechism* that, "every form of social or cultural discrimination in fundamental personal rights on the grounds of sex, race, color, social conditions, or religion must be curbed and eradicated as incompatible with God's design."[104] Since Igbo people are mostly adherents of Catholic tradition, this teaching by the Church should be fully inculcated, so as to set free those who have been held in bondage, and especially Igbo couples suffering from infertility.

Though the teaching of the Church is plausible, the Church herself needs to do some self-criticism and evaluation. The Church has to be, in the words of then Cardinal Gionanni Montini of Milan (later Paul VI), not only in search of herself, but of a church in search of the world.[105] This is so because the world is changing so fast. This is seen from the major changes that have taken place in other religious institutions and traditions, especially in the realm of their socio-political and moral teachings. On the other hand, changes in the Roman Catholic Church have progressively remained slow, especially, in introducing major changes.[106] The Roman Catholic moral principles, especially her sexual ethics as espoused in *Humanae vitae*,[107] may need to be adapted a little bit. The Church needs to be a bit more flexible and pragmatic regarding the signs of the time. Despite this need for change and adaptation, one cannot down play the contents of her teachings. These teachings call for social change, which can introduce much-needed liberating insights for modern civilization. Igbo culture stands to gain more if adherents of Catholicism hearken to the voice of the Church, shunning discrimination and allowing their

103. Benedict XVI, *Caritas in Veritate*, 1.

104. *Catechism of the Catholic Church*, no. 1935, quoting Paul VI, *Gaudium et Spes*, no. 29.

105. Linden, *Global Catholicism*, 82.

106. Waters, *From Human to Posthuman*, 79.

107. *Humanae Vitae*, as previously mentioned, is a papal encyclical which is like a compass that should guide the procreative, marital and sexual life of every Catholic.

infertile couples to be as they are and enjoy the fruits of their marital union even if they are childless.

REINFORCING THE CHRISTIAN LOVE OF AGAPE—WHICH CONQUERS ALL

The bible is replete with exemplary instances of sacrificial love. There is no way one can talk of Christian love without talking about sacrificial love, which Jesus himself embodied. "There is no greater love than this: that a person would lay down his life for the sake of his friends" (John 15:13). It is this Christian love that invites us to outdo each other in doing good. It therefore means that doing good to the other is not just a natural principle but the core foundation of Christian tradition. In this way, every Christian is invited to wear as cloak the act of sacrificial love—*agape*, the totality of self-giving. This is manifested in everyone imbibing the spirit of responsibly going an extra mile for the sake of the other. This sense of *agape*, the responsibility of going an extra mile in the indigenous ethical principle of *onye aghala nwanne ya* and Christian tradition, must be rooted in what the foremost Christian ethicist, Paul Ramsey calls the 'preferential ethics of protection,' especially the protection of the most vulnerable. When this becomes the guiding principle of Christians, then, we can be said to be living out in full the tenets of the Christian message. It is in sacrificial love that humanity can build up and fully live out its vocation of attaining a flourishing human family. "Love build up others and so doing it also builds up its own unlegislated self-discipline in personal living. Variable as the neighbor's needs, love is constantly engaged in tearing down where need be, and again building up, directives as to how better the neighbor may be served."[108]

Where sacrificial love exists, the boundaries of freedom, peace and harmony widen. In that way, the rights and integrity of not just infertile couples, but all *umunne* become secured and protected. This protection can insulate everyone from shaming, discrimination, impoverishment and isolation. Where this ethic of protection is at work, one can go a long way in doing good for the other, in doing good for *nwanne*, and not only because he/she is *nwanne* but because the love of God commands us to do so. With this love in place, we will find Christian love and the principle of *onye aghala nwanne ya* coalescing. Not only will they rise up in

---

108. Ramsey, *Basic Christian Ethics*, 89.

unison against stigmatization, oppression, discrimination, and injustice, but usher in a great renaissance of what it means to be loving and truly African and Christian. This then will give credence to the Igbo proverb of "*Egbe bere ugo bere, nke si ibe ya ebena nku akwana ya mana ya gosi ya ebe o ga ebe*" which literally means, "Let the eagle perch and let the kite perch and the one that says the other should not perch should not lose its wings, rather it should show it where to perch."[109] This is a kind of 'live and lets live' philosophy, where no one should deprive the other of any comfort of life. This idea of enough space available for everyone to operate will surely be a true expression of *agape*.

THE CHURCH IN IGBO LAND AND A NEW PRE-NUPTIAL LAW

A proverb in Hausa says, "*rashin sani yafi dare duhu*" which means, "lack of awareness is darker than night."[110] Lacking in awareness or living in self-denial, or worse still to be aware and then work against what one is aware of, is a palpable and dangerous darkness. Every adult in Igbo land is aware that the process of conceiving a child is never the sole responsibility of the woman. It involves the man and the woman. Men must take up the responsibility of checking their own medical condition and checking their fertility status before marriage and within married life. Igbo men must learn to conquer their ego. As Oduyoye and Uchem advocate, women too must learn to voice out their concerns. They can collectively lay out some conditions and requirements before marriage. Presently in Igbo culture and in most cultures in Africa, for the man, "having children brings social status and proof of virility, an attitude that boosts the male ego . . . the infertile man more often than not, has a deflated sense of self-worth and self-fulfillment and might be looked down upon and often taunted by his peers in society."[111] In this case, Igbo men must face the reality and extricate themselves from a shame-based cultural bondage.

Since the Church is a powerful social institution in Igboland, and since she already makes a mandatory request for HIV status and genotype from couples intending to marry, she can request from intending couples particularly men a medical report stating their virility status.

109. Amaechi, "Religion in the Political Culture."
110. Pachocinsk, *Proverbs of Africa*, 225.
111. Ekwere et al., "Infertility among Nigerian Couples," 35–40.

This is necessary since the aim of an average Igbo man is to have children in marriage. This is important because of the loyalty of an average Igbo man to the Church. This demand would help to clear the clouds of knowing who is really infertile. It must be noted that this practice can lead to discrimination and stigmatization of someone medically verified to be infertile, however, the stigmatization will be a lesser evil compared to one being aware of one's fertility problem but then goes on to accuse the other spouse of being responsible for their childlessness. With this in mind, the Igbo Catholic Church, and especially the two ecclesiastical provinces of Onitsha and Owerri, should ground their mission on "the transformative reality of Jesus' transcendence of the violence of his passion and rising into new life predicating a new order for all of creation."[112]

As a moral and spiritual institution, the Church in Igbo land can be part of this liberation and spiritual movement. They can respond to this crisis with Jesus' mission in mind, and interpret and apply his teachings in the case of the suffering of childless Igbo couples. Apart from enacting new prenuptial laws, or enforcing traditional *iju ese* (a traditional background check before marriage in the Igbo marriage procedure), the Church can further challenge unjust cultural structures. She can even implement new pastoral strategies in every parish, such as having a team of consultors whose membership will comprise physicians, psychologists, and pastoral workers, whose main apostolate would be to engage with infertile couples. This pastoral strategy, done in an atmosphere of trust and goodwill, would address the heightened needs of vulnerable Igbo couples, thus responding to their existential realities.

From the Igbo cultural perspective, the *iju ese* could include medical inquiries into the probability of fertility on both sides. Sometimes laws are enacted not to punish anybody but for the need to put the record straight. A medical condition stated in a marriage *iju ese* is an act of love, and should be embraced by anyone who loves his/her *nwanne*.

TOWARD A NEW HUMAN SPIRITUALITY

A new form of mission and spirituality could be the resuscitation of the true spirit of the Igbo principle of *onye aghala nwanne ya* in the practice of Christianity. A spirituality encompassing all human experience and activities, as they relate and connect with the divine, would be a

---

112. Uchem, *Overcoming Women's Subordination*, 189.

well-entrenched spirituality and ethic of inclusion with "the depth dimension of all human existence."[113] When this ethic and spirituality are duly reenacted, a flourishing Igbo humanity can be re-created. A real understanding of liberation would be in practice, where everyone who is holding anyone in bondage would love to free the person, and thereby hearken to the commands of Jesus: "Untie him and let him go" (John 11:44), and "Let any one of you who is without sin be the first to throw a stone at her" (John 8:7).

REVIVING THE SPIRIT OF 1929 (THE ABA WOMEN'S RIOT)

Vulnerable women's emancipation from oppression is important today. If this is not done, women will continue to be weakened under the weight of cultural and men's chauvinism. This in consonance with the thoughts of Alfred Adler, an Austrian medical doctor and psychotherapist who writes:

> The obvious advantages of being a man have caused severe disturbances in the psychic development of women as a consequence of which there is an almost universal disaffection with the feminine role. The psychic life of woman moves in much the same rules, as that of any human beings who find themselves the possessors of a strong feeling of inferiority because of their situation in the scheme of things.[114]

When this 'psychic life of the woman' is over-stretched, the spirit of resistance emerges, a spirit that is unfamiliar to men.

The spirit and militancy of the Aba women's riot was a turning point in the way men viewed women and it inspired more research about women. It is worth noting that women see themselves too as powerful. Looking at the activities of the *umuada* political group mentioned in chapter 1 of this book, they are aware of their inherent power to change any narrative. With the Aba women's riot, this power in them came to full glare. With it, the "British administration began to encourage research about Igbo women, especially after the Aba Women's riot in 1929."[115] The riot remains a land mark in the history of Igbo women, in particular, and

---

113. Downey, *Understanding Christian Spirituality*, 14.
114. Adler, *Understanding Human Nature*, 133.
115. Ibewuike, *African Women*, 23.

Nigerian women in general, as the incident made its way into history books. The riot depicted how women can change their status quo:

> As far back as 1929 there was a spectacular demonstration of women's resentment against oppression (or what they regarded as such). This incident, popularly referred to as the Aba Women's War, was initiated by Igbo women who interpreted a headcount of women as a first step towards forcing them to pay tax. Although they were mistaken, one could not blame them, for a previous headcount for men had, in fact, resulted in the payment of tax by men, even though no one had been told that the count was for that purpose. The demonstration which began in Aba and Owerri spread rapidly over much of the then Eastern Provinces, including Calabar and Opobo . . .
>
> Although a few women carried machetes, most were unarmed. They relied entirely on their bodies for protection. Many of them were said to have been half-naked and to have walked and danced in an obscene manner. Some men were said to have taken fright and have to have fled at the sight of the marching women. The women were right in their forecast that their naked bodies and brazen behavior would scare their menfolk. It was an unnerving demonstration of their uncanny insight into men's psychology. Pressing their luck, the women sacked court buildings and physically assaulted warrant chiefs, whom they accused of oppression and corruption—and quite highly.[116]

This act yielded much in the way of dividends at that time, and if the spirit had been sustained, Igbo women's liberation—especially those suffering from the effects of infertility—would have been in another phase. Consider the words of Ifi Amadiume, an Igbo female anthropologist, on the spirit of the Aba women's riot:

> After both peaceful and violent mass demonstrations, riots, and finally open war with British colonial government in 1929 . . . Igbo women were universally recognized as the most militant women. It is therefore not surprising that data on Igbo women have been cited or included in most important contributions to feminist anthropology.[117]

Not only were Igbo men taken aback, scampering for safety from the rioting women, the British colonial masters saw the steel Igbo

---

116. Amadi, *Ethics in Nigerian Culture*, 73–74.
117. Amadiume, *Male Daughters, Female Husbands*, 13.

women were made of. Amadiume writes, "[t]he women were rebellious and rioting all over the place, with militancy unfamiliar to White men."[118] Uchem, too, provides an understanding about the British when she notes that, "[t]he British had underestimated the Nigerian women. They shockingly realized their false assumptions about Igbo women, which they had projected from their own Victorian concepts of women as feeble and subservient."[119] Igbo women should thus take their destiny into their hands, knowing fully well they have the inherent power to initiate their own liberation. While we argue that a social change from the outside is necessary, we should equally argue for a social change and a change of mind set from within. The force from within will most likely be formidable. It is true that the patriarchal fist is heavy and hard but a revolution of mind from women can effect a change. The timeless quote of a Ghanaian self-help activist is effective here. Lailah Gifty Akita writes "your liberty will not be freely given to you. You must be bold to liberate yourself."[120] Sure a major change can come from women themselves as they look inwardly and try to liberate themselves and in the process liberate the oppressors too. In all, the event at Aba shows that when pushed to the wall, Igbo women are capable of achieving far-reaching results.

UNCOVERING THE PSYCHOLOGY OF MEN'S FEAR OF WOMEN

Elechi Amadi underscores the fact that some men are aware of the limitations of their power, and so they may try to control women, knowing that women have a lot of powers.

> If men are so sure of their powers, why do they go to such lengths to discriminate against women, who are their life-long and inseparable companions? There are two possible reasons: either men hate women or they fear them. The possibility of hatred must be ruled out in view of the strong emotional bond between the sexes. It must be, then, that men fear women. Why? Fear is generated only by the realization that the feared object has more power than one can cope with. It is suggested here that men discriminate against women because they believe women have a power which they cannot match or control. This power is

---

118. Amadiume, *Male Daughters, Female Husbands*, 13.
119. Uchem, *Overcoming Women's Subordination*, 50.
120. Akita, "Your liberty . . ."

obviously sexual power. Every woman has it, and every normal man is susceptible to it. The power is awesome because women cannot be deprived of it. Moreover, it operates all the time.[121]

Igbo women must know that men control them including their sexuality, because men fear them. Women can use the inherent power in them to liberate themselves from the fear of men and cultural subjugation. Because of this fear, men will want to put women in a box; they will want to confine them to only specific professions. But all this is because of men's insecurity which accounts for why Amadi would argue thus: "Although men argue, sometimes with justification, that women are unfit for certain jobs, they do not hesitate to grab even those jobs which ideally should be done by women. The field of gynaecology (sic), for instance, is flooded with men. Again, men say that a woman's place is in the kitchen, but the world's great chefs are men."[122] Since men do this, then Igbo women can explore this fear which men have for women, and liberate themselves by 'standing their ground.' It is true that the Lord Jesus has liberated all believers, but we are still in the world with all the evils therein. Therefore, while in the world, we can work toward liberating ourselves from the forces of evil. In this way, women can liberate themselves from the evil of oppression. Surely a major change can come from women themselves, by responding with the kind of spirit they used during the Aba riot as they try to free their minds, too, from cultural slavery.

With the experience of the Aba women's riot, Igbo culture 'knows' that when the weak threaten to do something sinister, they are not to be taken for granted. An Igbo proverb says, "*o buru na onyeisi asiba gin a ya ga-atuwa gi isi, I mara na o nwere okwute o zodoro ukwu*" which literally means, "if a blind man threatens to break your head with a stone, then, know that he is already hiding one under his foot."[123] If women brace up tomorrow as they did during the Aba riot, then a change will surely be imminent. This change will introduce the new life we are arguing for, a new life for all couples who suffer infertility.

---

121. Amadi, *Ethics in Nigerian Culture*, 78–79.
122. Amadi, *Ethics in Nigerian Culture*, 78.
123. Onwudufor, *Mmanu E ji Eri Okwu*, 112.

CULTURAL RENAISSANCE—A WORK IN PROGRESS

With the interactions of Christian tradition and colonialism, Igbo culture metamorphosed. Despite these changes, to a great extent, Igbo culture has been sustained by the principle of *onye aghala nwanne ya*. It is true that in every culture "the technical aspects of the way of life can become easily changed while the deeper aspects of life dealing with institutional norms and belief systems which should accompany them are very slow to undergo change."[124] In this case, one can argue that *onye aghala nwanne ya* has remained one of the "deeper aspects of life" that has remained almost unchanged, though not fully applied. Therefore it remains a work in progress.

In dealing with issues that concern African culture in general and Igbo culture in particular, we must take into consideration that many things are intertwined within the cultural package, some good and some bad. Sometimes it appears like the biblical image of allowing "both to grow together until the harvest" (Matthew 13:30) might work, but in some cases an outright uprooting of evil is necessary. Despite her crusade for African women's liberation, Oduyoye recognizes the intricacies of most African cultures, wrapped with religious beliefs. She observes that it can be difficult to make clear distinctions between religious beliefs and culture:

> We also need to note at the outset that we are dealing with a religious-based culture. Africans live in a spiritual universe. Whatever has an outward appearance also has an inner essence and we have to stay in touch with God from whom we came to inhabit this dimension of reality. The traditional way of life is closely bound up with religion and religious beliefs in such a way that there is a mutual interdependence of religion and culture. We note in the second place that African Religion provides a holistic view of life. It enables persons to understand and accept their status and identity and passes on beliefs that explain prevailing conditions. African Religion teaches its adherents how to survive and thrive in the world in which they have been placed. This religion undergirds the shaping of the moral, social and the political, and even, at times, the economic. Hence, the moral obligations that weigh so heavily on African women are firmly hooked on to beliefs.[125]

---

124. Onyeneke, *African Traditional Institutions*, 68.
125. Oduyoye, *Introducing African Women's Theology*, 25.

This cultural patriotism makes the women's case more difficult to handle, per cultural anthropologist Ina Corrine Brown:

> no culture, belief, or behavior can be understood out of its social or cultural context. That is, any item of behavior, any tradition or pattern, can be evaluated correctly only in the light of its meaning to the people who practice it, its relationship to other elements of the culture, and the part it plays in the adaptation of the people to their environment or to one another, no custom is "odd" to the people who practice it.[126]

However, when cultures interact with other cultures, there is always a tendency to comparatively see clearly some behaviors or traditions in one's culture that are inherently bad. As such, the 'bad' ones can either be modified or done away with. One can concur with the idea that "there is a definite conservatism in all cultures and in order to maintain cultural continuity people are enculturated early in life to believe that their culture is the 'right one' (ethnocentricism)."[127]

Though everyone may believe that their cultural paradigm is the best, no culture lives in absolute isolation, and in that regard change takes place one way or another. Most socio-cultural changes take place by accident, but so too some take place with deliberate efforts. Despite any religious ties, aspects of culture that denounce some of her members for no fault of their own must be renounced. That is why the crux of this book is the ultimate goal of transformation of Igbo society into one where Igbo women and men can participate and enjoy the institution of marriage without fear of the consequences of infertility.

CONCLUSION

Despite this call for action and social change, one should not lose sight that some achievements have been recorded in terms of protecting and liberating the most vulnerable, especially women, from the shackles of some aspects of Igbo culture. Many years back, when childhood betrothal was rife, little girls were married off at a young age of about five, though they lived in their parents' house until maturity. In those days, when a parent was indebted to another man and he was incapable of paying his debt, he may give out his daughter to the creditor or to the creditor's male

126. Brown, *Understanding Other Cultures*, 3.
127. Akukwe, *Towards a New Society*, 11.

child to marry. In this case, the female had no choice in the deal. The man could have been old enough to be the girl's father, but she just had to go.

This scenario is captured well by Buchi Emecheta in her novel *The Joys of Motherhood* where she asks a rhetorical question: "How can a woman hate a husband chosen for her by her people?"[128] Referring to Akan-Asante folktales, Oduyoye shares the same view, "[a] favored theme in many folktales is that girls should not be strong-willed in matters of the choice of a spouse or marriage."[129] Hausa people's idiom puts this kind of scenario well: "If you let girls please themselves, they will bring home a man-eating pumpkin."[130] This thinking finds expression in many African folktales, where "parents are portrayed as the best judges of who would be a suitable spouse and several stories tell of fathers testing prospective husbands."[131] Things have changed to some extent in this respect. Nowadays, family members and parents can give suggestions and recommendations of who a girl could marry, but the girl has the final say of who to marry. This is a great improvement. As the Nupe people of Northern Nigeria say: "*Nini nini bici ewaju cya bo*" meaning "one by one legs are taken out of a boat."[132] Which means, we shall get there taking it one after another in re-shaping some of the cultural practices in Igbo land, especially the ones that are oppressive to Igbo couples suffering from infertility.

---

128. Emecheta, *The Joys of Motherhood*, 71.
129. Rattray, *Akan-Ashante Folktales*, as cited in Oduyoye, *Daughters of Anowa*, 43.
130. Rattray, *Hausa Folk-Lore*, 300–308.
131. Oduyoye, *Daughters of Anowa*, 44.
132. Rattray, *Hausa Folk-Lore*, 300–308.

6

Conclusion

THOUGH IT WAS PROPOUNDED before him, the Athenian moral philosopher Socrates elucidated the Greek aphorism, "Man, know thyself."[1] He had reinvented the aphorism to encourage self-examination. Later, he would say that an unexamined life is not worth living. The need for a community to have self-knowledge, and the examination of its life, necessitated an analysis of the socio-cultural context of Igbo culture. In describing the Igbo cultural and religious milieu, we were able to lay bare the Igbo world so that we can fully appreciate the Igbo moral magisterium, and the religious and cultural space where their vital force is drawn.

In doing this, this study reviewed and examined the history of the Igbo people, with attention to their origin, how patriarchy is sustained, and the course of their development. It identified their communication tools, with proverbs and names given to new born babies as a source of their moral compass to communicate their experiences and eternal truths. Having explored the Igbo terrain, attention was paid to infertility. Some comparative analyses were made, especially in the blaming of women that is prevalent in Igbo land. Solutions to infertility in traditional Igbo culture, and in the technologically-advanced Western culture were examined. At the end, consideration of the marriage procedure in Awo-Omamma unveiled what constitutes a marriage, and the ultimate goal of marriage among Igbo people.

---

1. Eyo and Ogar, "Socratic 'Man Know Thyself,'" 69–73.

Thereafter, this work focused on selected African theologians and ethicists. A review of their theology of liberation was made; noting strengths and weaknesses with a view of making a proposal that the indigenous ethic of *onye aghala nwanne ya* has what it takes to help liberate Igbo couples suffering from infertility. Having identified the paradox of this ethical principle with regard to the beautiful Igbo culture on one hand, and the discrimination of one or more of its own on the other hand in the sad case of infertility, constructive alternatives were proposed that would affect positive changes. Such change can initiate a new dispensation, resuscitating a true Igbo renascent spirit and culture. The spirit can awake the Igbo moral imperative to include the care of all, especially childless couples. These points were considered with recourse to the institution of the Roman Catholic Church, the Bible and events from the Igbo historical experience.

There are many sources of African ethics. African theologians and ethicists have identified three basic sources: the Bible, ATR, and the Christian tradition. Toward understanding and fully applying the ethical principle of *onye aghala nwanne ya*, we copiously drew from these sources to make our suggestion attractive and comprehensible to varied audiences, thus making our work both African and Christian.

With globalization, emigration and immigration, the past can no longer be fully re-captured; a healthy blend will be the best way forward. The healthy mixture of ATR, Christianity, and to some degree Western civilization itself will re-establish the Igbo culture with a new firmament of cultural expression, but without losing the core values of her civilization. In this new cultural expression, everyone in the community can discover that all can be new agents for further growth. With much scholarly work done so far by Igbo scholars on the Igbo world, gone are those days when Africans and their scholars kept blaming the white missionaries and colonial masters for their spiritual confusions. They can begin now to retrace their steps and embrace the lofty goals of *onye aghala nwanne ya*. They have to be conscious that Igbo people love to search for 'higher values' in ATR, where they are fully at home. Unfolding the values of the Igbo culture immersed in ATR especially the connection with veneration of *Ani* the earth goddess, and the *chi* phenomenon will remain a sound way to respond to a complex issue like infertility in marriage in Igbo land.

This debate for the liberation of infertile couples is open-ended. This book is not the final word, because even the solutions offered will subsequently raise new problems. Full liberation for infertile Igbo couples might entail embracing all that Oduyoye, Uchem and Bujo have advanced. It might mean incorporating only some of what they advocated for. While *onye aghala nwanne ya* can be a strong stimulus for the liberation of Igbo couples suffering from infertility, it is worth noting that this book does not claim to be an exhaustive work on *onye aghala nwanne ya*. It does not equally pretend to propose all the solutions to unravel the existential problems wrapped in a patriarchal package affecting infertile Igbo couples. However, it has strongly challenged the Igbo patriarchal structure, laying bare its inherent contradictions. Future studies and research could be carried out toward implementing what has been diagnosed and suggested in this book.

This area of research could unveil the experiences of those who have felt the cruel brunt of childlessness, and those who have engaged with those who have suffered from this social malaise. Further research could include individual and group interviews, with open-ended questions to capture the wide range of beliefs, attitudes and behaviors amongst the Igbo people in their understanding and perception of infertility in marriage. In this way, the 'why' and the 'how' of the phenomenon could be elucidated, which could help influence the Igbo people in their common understanding of the place of men and woman in Igbo culture, marriage and infertility.

Since shaming, ego and infertility among Igbo people are common problems, a resolution will require patience, continuous engagement, workshops, and seminars among women and men's groups. Results can be used toward trying new styles of total emancipation of Igbo couples from the shame of infertility in marriage. A patient approach can be slow, but it can be profitable and progressive too. Patience is necessary because 'speed' is a common phenomenon in Igbo culture—people drive at break-neck speed, and the result is all too often a fatal accident. In the same way, a renaissance at lightning-speed would create new problems. Patience and continuous engagement can lead to desirable results.

Appendix 1[1]

Umuokpara Family Marriage List
Umuifa—Ubachima Awo-Omamma

1. Taking of list (for the first visit of prospective in-laws)

    1 crate of Star beer
    1 crate of Maltina
    1 bottle of hot drink
    1 pot of palm wine

    cash of N400.00.

2. The Umunnadi (marriage items for kinsmen)

Ego ikpuhe akwukwo	N1, 000.00
Ego itutuihe	N500.00
Ego itummanya	N400.00
Ego ndi Nze	N500.00
Ego ode akwukwo	N500.00
Ego ndi isi oche	N600.00
Ego okpokiri umunnadi	N10, 000.00
2 cartons of Star beer	
2 crates of Maltina	
2 heads of tobacco	

---

1. The list was made available to me by the secretary Mr. Callistus Okoro, of the Umuokpara kindred family meeting of Umuifa, Awo-Omamma, received January 29, 2017.

2 lumps of potash
2 packets of cigarettes
2 bottles of snuff
2 bottles of hot drink
2 pots of palm wine

3. For the Parents

    5 bottles of snuff
    2 cartons of Star beer
    6 lumps of potash
    2 cartons of maltina
    5 packets of cigarettes
    2 bottles of hot (St Remy)
    8 gallons of palm wine
    2 bottles of wine
    2 bottles of hot drink
    2 heads of tobacco
    2 cartons of small stout
    2 bottles of snuff
    2 lumps of potash

4. Ihe iyi Agba

    8 packets of cigarettes
    2 cartons of Star beer
    10 gallons of palm wine
    2 crates of Maltina
    4 bottles of hot drink
    2 heads of tobacco
    4 cartons of stout
    2 packets of cigarettes
    2 lumps of potash

5. Ida Abali Ano

    1 carton of stout
    6 cartons of star beer
    2 pots of palm wine
    cash of N2,000.00
    2 bottles of hot drink
    2 cartons of small stout

Umuokpara Family Marriage List

6. Ida Abali Asato

    2 packets of cigarettes
    8 cartons of Star beer
    2 pots of palm wine
    8 cartons of Maltina
    1 crate of small stout,
    1 crate of malt 8 heads of tobacco
    chieftaincy wear/regalia, cap, walking stick.
    8 bottles of snuff
    8 lumps of potash

7. Ihe Umuada (for daughters of the family or bride's kinswomen)

    2 bottles of snuff
    2 crates of Maltina

8. Ihe Umuokorobia (for youths)

    2 cartons of Star beer
    2 crates of mineral water
    2 gallons of palm wine
    2 packets of cigarettes
    cash of N2,000.00

Appendix 2

Umuokpara Family Women Marriage List

1. Taking of List

  Njija uzo   N1,000.00
  Meeting the parents   N1,00.00
  Mother's items
   2 big stock fish
   2 cartons of soap
   2 wrappers (George)
   2 big fish.
   2 cartons of canned malt drink
   2 gallons of kerosene
   2 pairs of hair ties
   2 pairs of black shoes
   2 big basins (white)
   1 bag of rice
   2 big goats
   1 bag of cassava
   2 gallons of red oil
   cash of N100.000.00

Bibliography

Abanuka, Bartholomew. *A New Essay on African Philosophy*. Nsukka, Nigeria: Spiritan, 1994.

———. *Myth and the African Universe*. Nsukka, Nigeria: Spiritan, 1999.

Achebe, Chinua. *Things Fall Apart*. New York: Anchor, 1994.

Achebe, Chinwe. "The Ogbanje Phenomenon: An Interpretation." In *Healing and Exorcism: The Nigerian Experience (Proceedings, Lectures, Discussions and Conclusions of the First Missiology Symposium on Healing and Exorcism—the Nigerian Experience, Organised by the Spiritan International School of Theology (SIST), Attakwu, Enugu, from May 18–20, 1989)*, edited by Luke Nnamdi Mbefo and E. Elochukwu Uzukwu, 22–42. Enugu, Nigeria: Snaap, 1989.

Acholonu, Catherine, et al. *They Lived Before Adam*. Abuja, Nigeria: CARC, 2009.

Adichie, Chimamanda Ngozi. *Dear Ijeawele, or a Feminist Manifesto in Fifteen Suggestions*. London: Fourth Estate, 2017.

Adler, Alfred. *Understanding Human Nature*. Eastford, Connecticut: Martino, 2010.

Agbasiere, Joseph Therese. *Women in Igbo Life and Thought*. London: New York: Routledge, 2000.

Akah, Josephine. "The Resilience of Igbo Culture amidst Christianity and Westernization in Orlu Local Government Area of Imo State in Nigeria." *International Journal of Theology and Reformed Tradition* 8 (2016).

Akita, Lailah Gifty. "Your liberty . . ." www.jarofquotes.com/view.php?id=your-liberty-will-not-be-freely-given-to-youyou-must-be-bold-to-liberate-yourself-lailah-gifty-akita.

Akukwe, Francis Nnalue. *Towards a New Society: Introduction to Social Development*. Onitsha, Nigeria: Directorate of Social Services, Archdiocese of Onitsha, 1988.

Amadi, Elechi. *The Concubine*. London: Heinemann, 1975.

———. *Ethics in Nigerian Culture*. Ibadan, Nigeria: Heinemann, 1982.

Amadi-Azuogu, Chinedu Adolphus. *Biblical Exegesis and Inculturation in Africa in the Third Millennium*. Enugu, Nigeria: Snaap, 2000.

Amadiume, Ifi. *Male Daughters, Female Husbands: Gender and Sex in an African Society.* Atlantic Highlands, NJ: Zed, 1987.

Amaechi, Ngozi. *Religion in the Political Culture of Ngwa Society.* https://manlyacademia.wordpress.com/2013/05/07/religion-in-the-political-culture-of-ngwa-society.

Amoah, Elizabeth. "Preface." In *African Women, Religion and Health: Essays in Honor of Mercy Amba Ewudziwa Oduyoye*, edited by Isabel Apawo Phiri and Sarojini Nadar, xvii–xxii. Eugene, OR: Wipf & Stock, 2012.

Amoah, Elizabeth, and Mercy Amba Oduyoye. "The Christ for African Women." In *With Passion and Compassion: Third World Women Doing Theology*, edited by Virginia Fabella and Mercy Amba Oduyoye, 35–46. Maryknoll, NY: Orbis, 1988.

Appiah, Kwame Anthony. *Cosmopolitanism: Ethics in a World of Strangers.* New York: Norton, 2007.

Appiah, Simon Koffi. "The Challenge of a Theologically Fruitful Method for Studying African Christian Ethics: The Role of the Human Sciences." *Exchange: Journal of Contemporary Christianities in Context* 41.3 (2012).

Aquinas, Thomas. *Summa theologica.*

Arinze, Francis A. *Sacrifice in Ibo Religion.* Ibadan, Nigeria: Ibadan University Press, 1970.

Arrupe, Pedro. "Letter to the Whole Society on Inculturation." *Studies in the International Apostolate of Jesuits* 7.1 (June 1978) 1–9.

Arthur, Leonard G. *Lower Niger and its Tribes.* London: Macmillan, 1906.

Atado, J. C. *African Marriage Customs and Church Law.* Kano, Nigeria: Modern, 1988.

Audu, Idrisa. "Infertility." In *Comprehensive Gynaecology in the Tropics*, edited by E. Y. Kwawukume and E. E. Emuveyan, 333–45. Accra Graphics Packaging, 2005.

Awolalu, J. Omosade. *West African Traditional Religion.* Ibadan: Nigeria: Onibonoje, 1979.

Azubike, Aliche, and Stella Nwokeji. *The Culture Wars Within: An Examination of Marriage in the Context of Culture Conflict.* Milville, NJ: Power Education Foundation, 2012.

Badejo, Emmanuel Adetoyese. *Catholic Men and Social Transformation: Challenge with Great Prospects.* www.csnigeria.org/docs/g38.pdf.

Basden, George Thomas. *Among the Ibos of Nigeria.* CreateSpace, 2017.

Battle, Michael. *Ubuntu: I in You and You in Me.* New York: Seasbury, 2009.

Bediako, Kwame. *Jesus and the Gospel in Africa: History and Experience.* New York: Orbis, 2004.

Benedict XVI, Pope. *Caritas in Veritate.* http://w2.vatican.va/content/benedict-xvi/en/encyclicals/documents/hf_ben-xvi_enc_20090629_caritas-in-veritate.html.

Best, Megan. *Fearfully and Wonderfully Made Ethics and the Beginning of Human Life.* Kingsford: N.S.W.: Matthias Media, 2012.

Bleeker, Sonia. *The Ibos of Biafra.* New York: William Morrow, 1969.

British Council. "Introduction." In *Gender in Nigeria Report 2012.* www.britishcouncil.org/partner/track-record/gender-nigeria-report-2012.

Brown, Ina Corrine. *Understanding Other Cultures.* Englewood Cliffs, NJ: Prentice-Hall, 1963.

Browne, R. et al.: "Embryo Donation at an Australian University In-vitro Fertilization Clinic: Issues and Outcomes," *Medical Journal of Australia* 178.3 (February 2003).

Bujo, Bénézet. *African Theology in Its Social Context.* Maryknoll, NY: Orbis, 1992.

———. "Distinctives of African Ethics." In *African Theology on the Way: Current Conversations*, edited by Diane B. Stinton, 79–89. London: SPCK, 2010.

———. *The Ethical Dimension of Community: The African Model and the Dialogue between North and South*. Nairobi, Kenya: Paulines Africa, 1998.

———. *Foundations of an African Ethic: Beyond the Universal Claims of Western Morality*. New York: Crossroad, 2001.

———. "Solidarity and Freedom: Christian Ethic in Africa." *Theology Digest* 44.1 (1997).

Byron, John. *Infertility and the Bible 2: The Defective Wife*. http://thebiblicalworld.blogspot.com/2011/01/childlessness-and-bible-2-defective.html.

Carr, Ann. *Transforming Grace: Christian Tradition and Women's Experience*. San Francisco: Harper, 1988.

Catechism of the Catholic Church. New York: USCCB, 1995.

Catholic Women's Organization Magazine. May, 1994.

Chadwick, Ian. *The Municipal Machiavelli: Machiavelli's The Prince Rewritten for Municipal Politicians*. www.ianchadwick.com/machiavelli/chapters-8–14/chapter-8-does-the-end-justify-the-means/.

Changing Minds, *Hall's cultural factors*. www.changingminds.org/explanations/culture/hall_culture.htm.

Childress, James F., and John Macquarrie, eds. *A New Dictionary of Christian Ethics*. London: SCM, 1986.

Chuku, G., ed. *The Igbo Intellectual Tradition: Creative Conflict in African and African Diasporic Thought*. New York: Palgrave Macmillan, 2013.

Congregation for the Doctrine of the Faith. *Donum Vitae*. www.vatican.va/roman_curia/congregations/cfaith/documents/rc_con_cfaith_doc_19870222_respect-for-human-life_en.html.

Curran, Charles E. *Issues in Sexual and Medical Ethics*. Notre Dame, IN: University of Notre Dame Press, 1978.

Dike, Victor. *The Osu Caste Discrimination in Igboland: Impact on Igbo Culture and Civilization*. iUniverse, 2007.

Dorcas, Olubanke Akintunde. "Women as Healers: The Nigerian (Yoruba) Example." In *African Women, Religion, and Health: Essays in Honor of Mercy Amba Ewudziwa Oduyoye*, edited by Isabel Apawo Phiri and Sarojini Nadar, 157–72. Eugene, OR: Wipf & Stock, 2012.

Downey, Michael. *Understanding Christian Spirituality*. New York: Paulist, 1996.

Ebelebe, Charles. *Africa and the New Face of Mission : A Critical Assessment of the Legacy of the Irish Spiritans Among the Igbo of Southeastern Nigeria*. Lanham, MD: University Press of America, 2009.

Edeh, Emmanuel M. P. *Towards an Igbo Metaphysics*. Chicago: Loyola University Press, 1985.

Ebelebe, Charles. *Africa and the New Face of Mission: A Critical Assessment of the Legacy of the Irish Spiritans among the Igbo of Southeastern Nigeria*. Lanham, MD: UPA, 2009.

Ehusani, George Omaku. *An Afro-Christian Vision: Ozovehe? Toward a More Humanized World*. Lanham, MD: University Press of America, 1991.

Ekeocha, Obianuju. *Target Africa: Ideological Neocolonialism in the Twenty-first Century*. San Francisco: Ignatius, 2018.

Ekwere, P. D., et al. "Infertility among Nigerian Couples as Seen in Calabar." *Port Harcourt Medical Journal* 2.1 (November 2007).

Ekwunife, Anthony N. O. *Consecration in Igbo Traditional Religion*. Onitsha, Nigeria: Jet, 1990.

Ekwuru, Emeka George. *The pangs of an African culture in travail: ụwa ndị Igbo yaghara ayagha: the Igbo world in disarray*. Abuja, Nigeria: Totan, 1999.

Ela, Jean-Marc. *African Cry*. Translated by Robert R. Barr. Maryknoll, NY: Orbis, 1980.

Elmer, Duane. *Cross-Cultural Connections : Stepping Out and Fitting In Around the World*. Downers Grove, IL: Intervarsity, 2002.

Emecheta, Buchi. *The Joys of Motherhood*. New York: George Braziller, 2013.

Eyo, E. J., and J. N. Ogar. "The Socratic 'Man Know Thyself' and the Problem of Personal Identity." *Sophia: An African Journal of Philosophy* 15.1 (January 2014).

Fabella, Virginia, and Mercy Amba Oduyoye. "Introduction." In *With Passion and Compassion: Third World Women Doing Theology*, edited by Virginia Fabella and Mercy Amba Oduyoye, ix–xv. Maryknoll, NY: Orbis, 1988.

Falola, Toyin, and Raphael Chijioke Njoku, eds. *Igbo in the Atlantic World: African Origins and Diasporic Destinations*. Bloomington: Indiana University Press, 2016.

Farley, Margaret. *Just Love: A Framework for Christian Sexual Ethics*. London: Bloomsbury Academic, 2008.

Ferm, Deane William. *Third World Liberation Theologies: An Introductory Survey*. Maryknoll, NY: Orbis, 1986.

Fletcher, Joseph. "Ethical Aspects of Genetic Controls." *The New England Journal of Medicine* 285.14 (August 1971).

Gbadegesin, Segun. "The Moral Weight of Culture in Ethics." In *African American Bioethics: Culture: Race, and Identity*, edited by Lawrence J. Prograis and Edmund D. Pellegrino, 25–46. Washington, DC: Georgetown University Press, 2007.

Gibellini, Rosino, ed. *Paths of African Theology*. Maryknoll, NY: Orbis, 1994.

Glave, Dianne D. *Rooted in the Earth: Reclaiming the African American Environmental Heritage*. Chicago: Chicago Review, 2010.

Gutierrez, Gustavo. *A Theology of Liberation: History, Politics, and Salvation*. 15th anniversary ed. Maryknoll, NY: Orbis, 2014.

Hall, Edward T. *Beyond Culture*. New York: Anchor, 1976.

Haring, Bernard. "The Curran Case: Conflict Between Rome and a Moral Theologian." In *Readings in Moral Theology, No. 6: Dissent in the Church*, edited by Charles E. Curran and Richard A. McCormick, 370–86. New York: Paulist, 1988.

Harrison, Keri Day. "Forging Community and Communitas—Toward a De-Masculinization of Christology in Black Churches." In *Walk Together Children: Black and Womanist Theologies: Church and Theological Education*, edited by Dwight N. Hopkins and Linda E. Thomas, 137–47. Eugene, OR: Wipf & Stock, 2010.

Hiatt, Kim Piper. *Role of Women in "Things Fall Apart."* www.scribd.com/document/246743932/Things-Fall-Apart-Role-of-Woman.

Hobbes, Thomas. *Leviathan: Clarendon Edition of the Works of Thomas Hobbes*. New York: Oxford University Press, 2012.

Hood, Robert E. *Must God Remain Greek? Afro Cultures and God-Talk*. Minneapolis, MN: Fortress, 1990.

Horton, W. R. G. "God, man and the Land in a Northern Igbo Village Group." *Africa: Journal of the International African Institute* 26.1 (January 1956).

Bibliography

Ibeabuchi, Apollos Oziogu. "Amadioha, the Igbo Traditional God of Thunder." *Vanguard News*. September 20, 2012. www.vanguardngr.com/2012/09/amadioha-the-igbo-traditional-god-of-thunder/.

Ibewuike, Victoria Oluomachukwu. *African Women and Religious Change a Study of the Western Igbo of Nigeria: With a Special Focus on Asaba Town*. Uppsala, Sweden: 2006.

Idowu, Bolaji. *African Traditional Religion: A Definition*. Maryknoll, NY: Orbis, 1973.

Ifemesia, Chieka. *Traditional Humane Living among the Igbo: An Historical Perspective*. Enugu, Nigeria: Fourth Dimension, 1979.

Ifesieh, Emmanuel Ifemegbunam. *Prayer in Igbo Traditional Religion: Some Traditional Models. A Case Study*. In *Religion and African Culture: Inculturation: A Nigerian Perspective*, edited by E. Elochukwu Uzukwu. Enugu, Nigeria: Spiritan, 1988.

Igbo Contact Forum e.V. "Igbo Idiom of the Week: Year 2011." www.i-c-f.net/main_idiom.html.

Ikechebelu, J. I., et al. "High Prevalence of Male infertility in Southeastern Nigeria." *Journal of Obstetrics and Gynaecology* 23.6 (2003).

Ikenga, Ozigbo. *Roman Catholicism in South eastern Nigeria 1885–1931*. Onitsha, Nigeria: Etukokwu, 1988.

Ikuenobe, Polycarp. *Philosophical Perspectives on Communalism and Morality in African Traditions*. Lanham, MD: Lexington, 2006.

Ilesanmi, Simeon. "Inculturation and Liberation: Christian Social Ethics and the African Theology Project." *The Annual of the Society of Christian Ethics* 15 (1995).

Ilogu, Edmund. *Christianity and Ibo Culture*. Leiden, Netherlands: Brill, 1974.

Isichei, Elizabeth. *A History of the Igbo People*. London: Palgrave Macmillan, 1975.

Isichei, Elizabeth, ed. *Igbo Worlds: An Anthology of Oral Histories and Historical Descriptions*. Philadelphia: Institute for the Study of Human Issues, 1978.

Jaide, Don. *Ani the Mother of the Igbos: The Many Manifestations of Ishtar*. www.africaresource.com/rasta/sesostris-the-great-the-egyptian-hercules/ani-the-mother-of-the-igbos-the-many-manifestations-of-ishtar/.

John Paul II, Pope. "Address of October 29, 1983, to the 35th General Assembly of the World Medical Association." *Acta Apostolicae Sedis* 76 (1984).

———. *A Fresh Approach to Evangelizing People and Cultures*. www.vatican.va/roman_curia/pontifical_councils/cultr/documents/rc_pc_cultr_doc_20000126_jp-ii_addresses-pccultr_en.html.

Jones, G. I., and H. Mulhall. "An Examination of the Physical Type of Certain Peoples of South Eastern Nigeria." *The Journal of the Royal Anthropological Institute of Great Britain and Ireland* 79.1–2 (August 1949).

Kalu, Ogbu U. *The Embattled Gods: Chrisitianization of Igboland, 1841–1991*. Trenton, NJ: Africa World, 2004.

King, Martin Luther, Jr. "Injustice anywhere . . ." www.brainyquote.com/quotes/martin_luther_king_jr_122559.

Kunhiyop, Samuel Waje. *African Christian Ethics*. Grand Rapids, MI: Zondervan, 2008.

Kwesi, Bimwenyi. "Religions Africanes et Christianisme." *Colloque International de Kinshasha* 11 (1978).

Lightfoot-Klein, Hanny, et al. *Prisoners of Ritual: An Odyssey into Female Genital Circumcision in Africa*. New York: Routledge, 1989.

Linden, Ian. *Global Catholicism: Diversity and Change since Vatican II*. New York: Columbia University Press, 2009.

Lueberin, J. E. "Emil Ludwig: German Writer." www.britannica.com/biography/Emil-Ludwig.

Lysaught, M. Therese. "Assisted Reproductive Technologies." In *On Moral Medicine: Theological Perspectives on Medical Ethics*, edited by M. Therese Lysaught et al. 3rd ed. 846–49. Grand Rapids, MI: Eerdmans, 2012.

MacIntyre, A. *After Virtue: A Study in Moral Theory*. 2nd ed. Notre Dame, IN: 1981.

Maina, Wilson Muoha. *The Making of an African Christian Ethics: Bénézet Bujo and the Roman Catholic Moral Tradition*. Eugene, OR: Pickwick, 2016.

Mashai, Tema Elia. "Pastoral Counseling Encounter with African Traditional Values and the Acculturation Process." Master of Theology diss., University of South Africa, 1979.

Mbaegbu, Celestine Chuwkuemeka. "A Philosophical Investigation of the Nature of God in Igbo Ontology." *Open Journal of Philosophy* 5.2 (2015). http://file.scirp.org/Html/2-1650506_54394.htm.

Mbiti, John S. *African Religions and Philosophy*. Garden City, NY: Doubleday, 1970.

———. *African Religions and Philosophy*. 2nd ed. Portsmouth, NH: Heinemann, 1990.

MedlinePlus. "Primary Infertility." www.medlineplus.gov/ency/imagepages/17074.htm.

Medscape. "Peritonitis and Abdominal Sepsis: Background, Anatomy, Pathophysiology." https://emedicine.medscape.com/article/180234-overview.

Meek, C. K. *Law and authority in a Nigerian tribe; a study in indirect rule*. London: Oxford University Press, 1937.

Metuh, Emefie Ikenga. *African Religions in Western Conceptual Schemes: The problem of interpretation*. 2nd ed. Onitsha, Nigeria: Imico, 1991.

———. *Comparative Studies of African Traditional Religions*. Onitsha, Nigeria: Imico, 1987.

Mott, Stephen Charles. *Biblical Ethics and Social Change*. New York: Oxford University Press, 1982.

Murchison, William. *The Cost of Liberty: The Life of John Dickinson*. Wilmington, DE: Intercollegiate Studies Institute, 2013.

National Assembly of Nigeria. "Same-Sex Marriage (Prohibition) Act, 2013." www.refworld.org/docid/52f4d9cc4.html.

———. "Chapter 21 Offences against Morality." In *Laws of the Federal Republic of Nigeria: Criminal Code Act*. www.nigeria-law.org/Criminal%20Code%20Act-PartIII-IV.htm.

Ndiokwere, Nathaniel I. *Search for Security: Freedom from Sinister Forces that Threaten Life in African Society*. Benin City, Nigeria: Ambik, 1990.

Nelson, Leonard J. III. *Diagnosis Critical: The Urgent Threats Confronting Catholic Healthcare*. Huntington, IN: Our Sunday Visitor, 2009.

Neuliep, James W. *Intercultural Communication: A Contextual Approach*. 5th ed. Thousand Oaks, CA: Sage, 2011.

New World Encyclopedia. "Igbo People." www.newworldencyclopedia.org/entry/Igbo_People.

Nisa Hospital. "First IVF Baby in Nigeria." https://nisa.com.ng/tag/first-ivf-baby-in-nigeria/.

Nnamani, Amuche Greg. "Gender Equality in the Church and in the Society: Our Obligation Towards Change." In *Gender Equality from a Christian Perspective*, edited by Rose Uchem, 24–43. Enugu Nigeria: Snaap, 2005.

Nnoromele, Salome C. *The Way People Live—Life Among the Ibo Women of Nigeria*. San Diego, CA: Lucent, 1998.

Ntloedibe-Kuswani, Gomang Seratwa. "Translating the Divine: The Case of Modimo in the Setswana Bible." In *Other Ways of Reading: African Women and the Bible*, edited by Musa W. Dube Shomanah, 78–100. Atlanta, GA: Society of Biblical Literature, 2001.

Nwabuisi, Elobuike M. "Socialization and the Nigerian Child: A Case Study of Ebe Child-Rearing." In *Inculturation—A Nigerian Perspective*, edited by Elochukwu Uzukwu, 10–21. Enugu, Nigeria: Spiritan, 1988.

Nwafor, Polycarp. "Jewish/Igbo Relationship: Jewish Scientists Storm Nnewi to Conduct DNA Test." Vanguard News. February 8, 2017. www.vanguardngr.com/2017/02/jewishigbo-relationship-jewish-scientists-storm-nnewi-conduct-dna-test/.

Nwala, Uzodinma T. *Igbo Philosophy*. Abuja, Nigeria: Niger, 2010.

Nwaoga, Chinyere. "Socio-Religious Implications of Child Adoption in Igboland South Eastern Nigeria." *Mediterranean Journal of Social Sciences* 4.13 (November 2013).

Nwapa, Flora. *Efuru*. Reissue edition. Long Grove, IL: Waveland, 2013.

Nwonwu, Francis. *Philosophy of Proverbs in Igbo Culture: The Chicken Metaphor*. Bloomington, IN: AuthorHouse, 2014.

Nzewuba, Ugwug. *The Sights and Sounds of the Igbo Nation*. Owerri, Nigeria: Imico, 2012.

Obergefell v. Hodges. 135 S. Ct. 2584, 2015. www.supremecourt.gov/opinions/14pdf/14-556_3204.pdf.

Obiego, Cosmas Okechukwu. *African Image of the Ultimate Reality: An Analysis of Igbo Ideas of Life and Death in Relation to Chukwu-God*. Frankfurt am Main: Peter Lang, 1984.

Obilor, John I. *The Doctrine of the Resurrection of the Dead and the Igbo Belief in the 'Reincarnation': A Systematico-Theological Study*. Frankfurt am Main: Peter Lang, 1994.

Oduah, Chika. "Nigeria's Igbo Jews: 'Lost Tribe' of Israel?" CNN. February 1, 2013. www.cnn.com/2013/02/01/world/africa/nigeria-jews-igbo/index.html.

Oduyoye, Mercy Amba. *Beads and Strands: Reflections of an African Woman on Christianity in Africa*. Maryknoll, NY: Orbis, 2004.

———. *Daughters of Anowa: African Women and Patriarchy*. Maryknoll, NY: Orbis, 2005.

———. *Hearing and Knowing: Theological Reflections on Christianity in Africa*. Maryknoll, NY: Orbis, 1986.

———. *Introducing African Women's Theology*. Cleveland, OH: Pilgrim, 2001.

———. "The Meaning of Solidarity." In *A Reader in Feminist Theology*, edited by Prasanna Kumari, 115–31. Gurukul Madras: Gurukul Lutheran Theological College and Research Institute, 1993.

Oduyoye, Modupe. "Man's Self and Its Spiritual Double." In *Traditional Religion in West Africa*, edited by E. A. Adegbola, 273–88. Ibadan, Nigeria: Daystar, 1983.

Ogbaa, Kalu. *Igbo*. New York: Rosen, 1995.

Okafor, Ikenna U., and Kurt Appel. *Toward an African Theology of Fraternal Solidarity: UBE NWANNE*. Eugene, OR: Pickwick, 2014.

Okafor, Nneka I., et al. "Perceptions of Infertility and In Vitro Fertilization Treatment among Married Couples in Anambra State, Nigeria." *African Journal of Reproductive Health* 21.4 (December 2017). www.ajol.info/index.php/ajrh/article/view/166544/155977.

Okere, Theophilus, et al. "All Knowledge is First of all Local Knowledge." In *The Postcolonial Turn: Re-Imagining Anthropology and Africa*, edited by René Devisch and Francis B. Nyamnjoh, 275–90. Bamenda, Cameroon: African Books Collective, 2011. https://books.google.com/books?id=6Ljao_1bLH4C&printsec=frontcover&dq=isbn:9956726656&hl=en&sa=X&ved=0ahUKEwjTlfee14jfAhWFn4MKHZK.

Okonkwo, Emmanuel. *Marriage in the Christian and the Igbo Traditional Context: Towards an Inculturation*. Frankfurt am Main: Peter Lang, 2003.

Okorie, Joseph B. *Oji Igbo, The Igbo Kola Nut: Presenting and Blessing of Kola Nut in Igbo Land*. Milpitas, CA: St. Elizabeth Church, 1995.

Okoro, Damasus. "Christian Marriage and Divorce: A Challenge to the Nigerian Church." Bachelor's diss., University of Nigeria Nsukka, 2000.

———. "The concept of Ogbanje in Elechi Amadi's The Concubine." Diploma diss., Spiritan School of Philosophy Nsukka Nigeria, 1996.

Okorocha, Cyril C. *The Meaning of Religious Conversion in Africa: The Case of the Igbo of Nigeria*. Aldershot England: Gower Pub Co, 1987.

Okwu, Augustine S. O. *Igbo Culture and the Christian Missions 1857–1957: Conversion in Theory and Practice*. Lanham: UPA, 2009.

Okwuosa, Lawrence N., et al. "The Disappearing Mammy Water Myth and the Crisis of Values in Oguta, South Eastern Nigeria." *HTS Teologiese Studies/Theological Studies* 73.3 (September 2017).

Online Etymology Dictionary. "Origin and Meaning of Palaver." www.etymonline.com/word/palaver.

Onwudufor, Fidelis. *Mmanu E ji Eri Okwu*. Nimo: Nigeria: Rex Charles and Patrick, 2015.

Onwuka, Azuka. "How Stigmatisation [sic] Promotes Bay Factories in Igboland." www.scannewsnigeria.com/opinion/how-stigmatisation-promotes-baby-factories-in-igboland/.

Onwurah, P. E. C. "Marriage: Christian and Traditional: A Social and Theological Study of the Interaction of Ethical Values in the Igbo Society of Nigeria." PhD diss., Columbia University Teachers College, 1982.

Onyeneke, Augustine O. *African Traditional Institutions and the Christian Church: A Sociological Prologue to Christian Inculturation*. Nsukka, Nigeria: Spiritan, 1993.

Oxford Dictionaries, "Definition of Palaver in US English." https://en.oxforddictionaries.com/definition/us/palaver.

Pace, Edward. "Dulia." In *The Catholic Encyclopedia*, 1–3. New York: Robert Appleton, 1909. www.newadvent.org/cathen/05188b.htm.

Pachocinsk, Ryszard. *Proverbs of Africa*. St. Paul, MN: Paragon House, 1998.

Panicola, Michael R., et al. *Health Care Ethics: Theological Foundations, Contemporary Issues, and Controversial Cases*. 2nd ed. Winona, MN: Anselm Academic, 2007.

Panti, Abubakar, and Sununu Yusuf. "The Profile of Infertility in a Teaching Hospital in North West Nigeria." *Sahel Medical Journal* 17 (2014). www.smjonline.org/text.asp?2014/17/1/7/129145.

Paris, Peter J. *The Spirituality of African Peoples*. Minneapolis, MN: Fortress, 1994.

Paul VI, Pope. *Humanae Vitae*. http://w2.vatican.va/content/paul-vi/en/encyclicals/documents/hf_p-vi_enc_25071968_humanae-vitae.html.

———. *Gaudium et Spes, Pastoral Constitution on the Church in the Modern World.* www.vatican.va/archive/hist_councils/ii_vatican_council/documents/vat-ii_const_19651207_gaudium-et-spes_en.html.

———. *Populorium Progressio.* http://w2.vatican.va/content/paul-vi/en/encyclicals/documents/hf_p-vi_enc_26031967_populorum.html.

Paul, Richard, and Linda Elder. *Miniature Guide to Understanding the Foundations of Ethical Reasoning.* 5th ed. Tomales, CA: Foundation for Critical Thinking, 1994.

Pence, Gregory. *Medical Ethics: Accounts of Ground-Breaking Cases.* 6th ed. New York: McGraw-Hill Education, 2010.

Phiri, Isabel Apawo, and Saojini Nadar. "Introduction: Treading Softly But Firmly." In *African Women, Religion, and Health: Essays in Honor of Mercy Amba Ewudziwa Oduyoye*, edited by Isabel Apawo Phiri and Sarojini Nadar, 1–18. Eugene, OR: Wipf & Stock, 2012.

Pontifical Council for Justice and Peace. *Compendium of the Social Doctrine of the Church.* www.vatican.va/roman_curia/pontifical_councils/justpeace/documents/rc_pc_justpeace_doc_20060526_compendio-dott-soc_en.html.

Rae, Scott B. *Outside the Womb: Moral Guidance for Assisted Reproduction.* Chicago: Moody, 2011.

Ramsay, Paul. *Basic Christian Ethics.* Louisville: Westminster John Knox, 1950.

Rattray, Robert Sutherland. *Akan-Ashante Folktales, Collected and Translated.* New York: AMS, 1983.

———. *Hausa folk lore: customs, proverbs, etc.* Oxford: Clarendon. 1913.

Rawls, John. *A theory of Justice.* Cambridge: Harvard University Press, 1971.

Rebera, Ranjini. "Challenging Patriarchy." In *Feminist Theology from the Third World: A Reader*, edited by Ursula King, 105–12. Maryknoll, NY: Orbis, 1994.

Rousseau, Jean-Jacques. *The Social Contract.* Lexington: CreateSpace, 2013.

Russell, Bertrand. *Human Society in Ethics and Politics.* London: Unwin Hyman, 1954.

Russell, Letty M. "Mercy Amba Ewudziwa Oduyoye: Wise Woman Bearing Gifts." In *African Women, Religion and Health: Essays in Honor of Mercy Amba Ewudziwa Oduyoye*, edited by Isabel Apawo Phiri and Sarojini Nadar, 43–58. Maryknoll, NY: Orbis, 2006.

Saideman, Stephen M. "Explaining the International Relations of Secessionist Conflicts: Vulnerability versus Ethnic Ties." *International Organization* 51.4 (1997).

Schineller, Peter. *A Handbook on Inculturation.* Paulist, 1990.

Schover, Leslie R., and Anthony J. Thomas. *Overcoming Male Infertility: Understanding its Causes and Treatments.* New York: Wiley, 1999.

Schreiter, Robert J. *Constructing Local Theologies.* Maryknoll, NY: Orbis, 1985.

Shorter, Aylward. *African Christian Theology.* London: Geoffrey Chapman, 1979.

———. *African Culture, an Overview: Socio-Cultural Anthropology.* Nairobi, Kenya: Paulines Africa, 1998.

Shuman, Joel, and Brian M. D. Volck. *Reclaiming the Body: Christians and the Faithful Use of Modern Medicine.* Grand Rapids, MI: Brazos, 2006.

Smith, Daniel Jordan. "Promiscuous Girls. Good Wives: and Cheating Husbands: Gender Inequality, Transitions to Marriage and Infidelity in Southeastern Nigeria." *Anthropol Q.* 83.1 (2010). www.ncbi.nlm.nih.gov/pmc/articles/PMC3831578/pdf/nihms513234.pdf.

Spitzer, A. *Marriage.* NCE IX.

Stith, Richard. "Toward Freedom from Value." In *On Moral Medicine: Theological Perspectives on Medical Ethics*, edited by M. Therese Lysaught et al., 734–47. 3rd ed. Grand Rapids, MI: Eerdmans, 2012.

Suglia, Elena. "Receptive yet Grounded: Igbo Continuity and Change in Chinua Achebe's Novels." https://esuglia.wordpress.com/2016/05/17/receptive-yet-grounded-igbo-continuity-and-change-in-chinua-achebes-novels/.

Sunday Missal: The New Translation of the Order of Mass for Sundays. London: HarperCollins, 2011.

"Supplement to the London Gazette," 1 January, 1934. www.thegazette.co.uk/London/issue/34010/supplement/13.

Talbot, P. A. *Tribes of the Niger Delta*. New York: Barnes & Noble, 1967.

Tappa, Louise. "The Christ-Event from the Viewpoint of African Women: A Protestant Prospective." In *With Passion and Compassion: Third World Women Doing Theology*, edited by Virginia Fabella and Mercy Amba Oduyoye, 30–34. Maryknoll, NY: Orbis, 1988.

Thomas, Owen C., ed. *Attitudes Toward Other Religions*. London: SCM, 1969.

Tutu, Desmond. "If you are neutral . . ." www.brainyquote.com/quotes/desmond_tutu_106145.

———. *No Future Without Forgiveness*. New York: Image, 2000.

Uadia, Patrick Ojeifo, and Abiodun Mathias Emokpae. "Male infertility in Nigeria: A Neglected Reproductive Health Issue Requiring Attention." *Journal of Basic and Clinical Reproductive Sciences* 4.2 (July–December 2015). www.jbcrs.org/articles/male-infertility-in-nigeria-a-neglected-reproductive-health-issue-requiring-attention.pdf.

Ubah, C. N. "Religious Change among the Igbos During the Colonial Period." *Journal of Religion in Africa* 18.1 (1988). www.deepdyve.com/lp/brill/religious-change-among-the-igbo-during-the-colonial-period-4ymXW2ccZX.

Uchem, Rose. "Becoming All Things to All Persons: Gender, Human Identity and Language, Towards Healing and Reconciliation as Mission." *Transformation: An International Journal of Holistic Mission Studies* 31.2 (April 2014).

———. "Eradicating Women Trafficking: A Religious Educational Perspective." *Research on Humanities and Social Sciences* 4.3 (May 2014).

———. "Gender Equality in Africa: Religious Educational Perspectives." In *Layers of Inequality: Reflections from Africa*, edited by B. Maphosa and N. Morgan, 1–13. Cape Town, South Africa: HSRC, 2017.

———. "Gender Inequality as an Enduring Obstacle to Mission." *Sedos Bulletin* 38.9–10 (September 2006).

———. "The National Christian Religious Studies Curriculum and the Imperative for Change in an Era of Globalization." *Asian Academic Research Journal of Multidisciplinary Studies* 16.1 (June 2013).

———. "Overcoming Women's Subordination in the Igbo African Culture and in the Catholic Church: Envisioning an Inclusive Theology with Reference to Women." PhD diss., Graduate Theological Foundation, Donaldson, Indiana, 2001.

———. "Rose Uchem, Senior Lecturer at University of Nigeria, Nsukka." https://la.linkedin.com/in/rose-uchem-98b4a647.

———. "University of Nigeria Staff Profile: Sister (Dr) Rose Uchem." www.unn.edu.ng/internals/staff/viewProfile/ODEy.

Bibliography

Uchem, Rose, ed. *Gender Equality from a Christian Perspective*. Enugu, Nigeria: Snaap, 2005.
Uchendu, Victor Chikezie. *The Igbo of Southeast Nigeria*. Fort Worth, TX: Harcourt Brace Jovanovich, 1965.
Udeani, Chibueze C. *Inculturation as Dialogue: Igbo Culture and the Message of Christ*. Amsterdam: Rodopi, 2007.
Ugwu-Oju, Dympna. *What Will My Mother Say?* Chicago: Taylor, 2004.
Umeora, Odidika, and I. Obu. "Cultural Misconceptions and Emotional Burden of Infertility in South East Nigeria." *The Internet Journal of Gynecology and Obstetrics* 10.2 (December 2008). www.ispub.com/IJGO/10/2/3277.
———. "Dr. Odidika Ugochukwu Joannes Umeora." www.omicsonline.org/editor-profile/Odidika_Ugochukwu_Joannes_Umeora/.
Umoren, Anthony Iffen. "Theological Basis of Gender Equality." In *Gender Equality from a Christian Perspective*, edited by Rose Uchem, 57–87. Enugu, Nigeria: Snaap, 2005.
UNICEF. "Girls for Sale." In *Equality. Development and Peace*. www.unicef.org/publications/files/pub_equality_en.pdf.
United States Conference Of Catholic Bishops. *Ethical and Religious Directives for Catholic Health Care Services*. Washington, DC: USCCB, 2009.
US Catholic. "Father Bénézet Bujo." www.uscatholic.org/authors/father-b%C3%A9n%C3%A9zet-bujo.
Uzukwu, Elochukwu. "The Birth and Development of a Local Church: Difficulties and Signs of Hope." In *The African Synod: Documents, Reflections, Perspectives*, edited by Maura Browne, 3–8. Maryknoll, NY: Orbis, 1996.
———. *God, Spirit and Human Wholeness: Appropriating Faith and Culture in West African Style*. Eugene, OR: Wipf & Stock, 2012.
———. "Sacramentology." Class lecture, Spiritan International School of Theology, Enugu Nigeria, October 2, 1997.
Van der Poel, Cornelius. *Ethical Principles in Medical Care*. Onitsha, Nigeria: Spiritan, 2001.
VanDrunen, David. *Bioethics and the Christian Life: A Guide to Making Difficult Decisions*. Wheaton, IL: Crossway, 2009.
Warren, Max. "Approaching another people, another culture, another religion." www.uua.org/worship/words/quote/approaching-another-people-another-culture-another-religion.
Waters, Brent. *From Human to Posthuman: Christian Theology and Technology in a Postmodern World*. Aldershot, Hants, UK: Burlington, 2006.
World Council of Churches. "What is the World Council of Churches?" www.oikoumene.org/en/about-us.
World Health Organization. "Infertility Definitions and Terminology." www.who.int/reproductivehealth/topics/infertility/definitions/en/.
———. *WHO laboratory manual for the Examination and processing of human semen*. 5th ed. Geneva: WHO, 2010. https://apps.who.int/iris/handle/10665/44261.

www.ingramcontent.com/pod-product-compliance
Lightning Source LLC
Chambersburg PA
CBHW060608230426
43670CB00011B/2022